SHIRLEY TEMPLE AND THE PERFORMANCE OF GIRLHOOD

SHIRLEY TEMPLE AND THE PERFORMANCE OF GIRLHOOD

KRISTEN HATCH

RUTGERS UNIVERSITY PRESS
NEW BRUNSWICK, NEW JERSEY, AND LONDON

Library of Congress Cataloging-in-Publication Data
Hatch, Kristen.

Shirley Temple and the performance of girlhood / Kristen Hatch.

pages cm.

Includes bibliographical references and index.

ISBN 978–0–8135–6326–8 (hardcover : alk. paper) — ISBN 978–0–8135–6325–1 (pbk. : alk. paper) — ISBN 978–0–8135–6327–5 (e-book)

1. Girls in motion pictures. 2. Temple, Shirley, 1928–2014—Criticism and interpretation. 3. Child actors—United States. I. Title.

PN1995.9.G57H34 2014

791.43'652352—dc23

2014014282

A British Cataloging-in-Publication record for this book is available from the British Library.

Visit our website: http://rutgerspress.rutgers.edu

Manufactured in the United States of America

CONTENTS

ACKNOWLEDGMENTS

It is a pleasure to thank the many people who have given their friendship, advice, and support during the writing of this book. At UCLA, Chon Noriega and Vivian Sobchack were early mentors who offered invaluable guidance. There I also received research funding from the Center for the Study of Women.

At UC Irvine, I have had the tremendous good fortune to have Victoria Johnson as a friend, mentor, and department chair. Lucas Hilderbrand has helped to keep me on task, which is no easy feat considering my cat brain. Fatimah Rony has been a good friend and occasional carpooler. And I've enjoyed the friendship and good spirits of Bliss Lim, Bridget Cooks, and Allison Perlman. There I have also learned from students in the Department of Film and Media Studies and the Visual Studies Program, particularly Diana Anselmo, Stacey Birk, Mary Trent, and Jenna Weinman.

I've enjoyed tea and conversation with Allison McCracken, whose insights into early twentieth-century popular culture have helped shape the book. Paige Harding provided valuable research assistance. And I owe a huge debt to Murray Pomerance, who patiently talked me through Photoshop.

At Rutgers University Press, Leslie Mitchner has been the ideal editor. She patiently saw this project to its end, and her editorial suggestions have vastly improved the introduction. And Lisa Boyajian has met every delay on my part with patience and grace.

The book has benefitted greatly from the insights of the press's readers. Mary Desjardins's suggestions helped me to turn this from a proposal into a book. And Pamela Robertson Wojcik helped guide it to its current form, for which I am extremely grateful.

My family has always provided love and support. Thanks to Deanna, David, Catherine, Andy, Luke, Julia, Elvin, and Sue. My father, Elvin Hatch, has offered perceptive critiques of the manuscript and an idyllic writing retreat. Thanks go especially to Jason Myers, who built me a room of my own in which to write, and a reason to come out from behind the computer.

I am tremendously saddened that two women will not be here to help me celebrate the publication of this book. My grandmother, Cathryn Fries, inspired and entertained me with stories of her life, which spanned nearly 100 years. And Carole Myers generously welcomed me into her family and introduced me to the joys of Forked Lake.

SHIRLEY TEMPLE AND THE PERFORMANCE OF GIRLHOOD

INTRODUCTION

SEX AND SHIRLEY TEMPLE

For four years during the Depression, from 1935 through 1938, Shirley Temple was celebrated as Hollywood's most profitable star. According to *Time* magazine, at the height of her fame she sold more sheet music than Bing Crosby and was more photographed than President Franklin D. Roosevelt.[1] Congress reportedly declared her "the most beloved individual in the world," and Roosevelt is said to have celebrated her as a universal antidote to the nation's malaise: "When the spirit of the people is lower than at any other time during this Depression, it is a splendid thing that for just 15 cents, an American can go to a movie and look at the smiling face of a baby and forget his troubles."[2] Her popularity wasn't limited to the United States. When Soviet premier Nikita Khrushchev made his historic visit to the United States in 1960, he revealed that he, too, had been a fan of the young star during his childhood. She was a mascot to the Chilean Navy; she was interviewed by Thomas Mann and H. G. Wells; and she received fan mail from every continent. In the 1930s, during a period of national and international crisis, when capitalism was on the brink of failure, the entire world seemed to take comfort in the mass-produced image of a little girl.

On the face of it, Temple appears to have been an anomaly. She is the only child to reach the No. 1 spot on Quigley's list of top box-office stars since the poll began in 1932, and the only female star other than Doris Day to reach that position with such frequency.[3] Certainly she remains one of the most recognizable child stars in the history of Hollywood, and one of the best remembered stars of the 1930s. However, when we take a broader view, considering Temple in relation to silent-era film and even late nineteenth-century theater, it becomes clear that her stardom came at the end of a long period in which little girls held a central place in both theater and film. Prior to Temple, Hollywood's most popular female star had been a child impersonator, Mary Pickford, and one of the most well-known characters on the American stage was Little Eva, the angelic child who befriends Uncle Tom in *Uncle Tom's Cabin.* Indeed, young girls appear to have played a quite prominent role in early twentieth-century film.

This is not a biography of Shirley Temple or an analysis of her film career as a whole. Rather, Temple functions here as a touchstone for understanding the centrality of girlhood to the first decades of Hollywood film. I am less interested in identifying what was unique about Temple's star persona than I am in understanding how her stardom was shaped, in part, by traditions that developed on the nineteenth-century stage and were adapted by Hollywood. Temple thus serves as a familiar landmark in the unexplored terrain of early child stardom.

Contemporary histories have a tendency to describe Shirley Temple as a beginning. In his examination of what he terms the "culture of child molesting," for example, James Kincaid traces Hollywood's eroticization of childhood back to Shirley Temple.[4] This book argues for a change in perspective. I argue that Temple signals not a beginning but the end of a long period in which girls held a central place in American popular theater and film. Whereas Kincaid attributes our culture's uneasy fascination with eroticized children to the strange legacy of eroticized innocence bequeathed by the Victorians, I argue that the Victorian fascination with childhood appears perverse because we read innocence through a paradigm that was only beginning to emerge in the 1930s. Indeed, Temple's career marked the end of the child-star era, which I define as ranging from roughly the 1880s through the 1930s. Temple was certainly a product of a specific moment in American history, a period overshadowed by a disastrous economic depression. However, her stardom was also shaped by conventions that emerged out of the theater and were developed in Hollywood during the silent era. In many ways, Temple was an heir to Elsie Leslie, the theatrical star who entranced New York audiences in the late 1880s and counted Mark Twain and Oliver Wendell Holmes, Sr. among her ardent admirers.

A number of things about Shirley Temple's stardom seem perverse to contemporary audiences. Temple made her screen debut playing harlots and vamps in a series of short films called the Baby Burlesks; during a decade scarred by racial violence, she was consistently paired, both on screen and off, with a black man; many of her films were marketed as love stories between the child and her adult male costars; and adult men played a visible role in her stardom. None of this has gone unnoticed by recent observers, a number of whom have identified Temple's popularity as a sign of national pedophilia.[5]

For the most part, however, Depression-era audiences did not find these aspects of Temple's career to be troubling or even unusual. In fact, during the late nineteenth and early twentieth centuries, it was not uncommon for child performers to engage in sexualized mimicry or for adult men to publicly proclaim their love for very young girls. These practices functioned to assert the child's innocence, the impossibility of her experiencing or arousing sexual desire.

They emerged on the nineteenth-century stage and were adapted by Hollywood during the silent era. In the 1930s, when a handful of audience members began to complain about girls' impersonations of sexualized women, their objections were met with bafflement and outrage by the film studios, the censors, and the courts, as I discuss in chapter 4.

Clearly, the popular understanding of Temple's appeal has undergone a significant transformation. These very different interpretations of Temple's career—that her popularity rested on the inviolability of her innocence, or that it was built around her pedophilic appeal—point to a significant shift in the definition of childhood innocence that occurred in the mid-twentieth century. According to the *Oxford English Dictionary*, the term *pedophilia*, referring to "sexual desire directed toward children," didn't enter the English medical vernacular until 1906 with the publication of Havelock Ellis's *Study of the Psychology of Sex*, volume 5. The term *pedophile*, referring to a class of person, entered usage much later, in 1941, the year after Temple "retired" from Twentieth Century-Fox, bringing her career as a child star to an end (though she would soon return to the screen in adolescent roles).

To understand the discrepancy between Depression-era responses to Shirley Temple and those published from the late twentieth century onward, we must not unquestioningly accept current interpretations that Temple's popularity rested on her veiled eroticism or reductively assume we are more enlightened than prior, supposedly naïve audiences who failed to recognize the erotic invitation embedded in her performance. Rather than focus on the ways in which Temple's stardom seems to confirm the perception that popular culture caters to pedophilic desire, I hope to destabilize contemporary notions of childhood innocence and demonstrate that they arise out of a Freudian understanding of sexuality that was only beginning to be popularized during Temple's heyday.

Certainly, the unwillingness to acknowledge white men's capacity to sexually abuse children was dangerous, contributing to children's victimization. In her history of medical and legal investigations into father–daughter incest during the Progressive Era, for example, Lynn Sacco demonstrates that doctors and the courts refused to recognize that white, upper- and middle-class girls were subject to abuse by their fathers. During this period, criminal behavior was widely attributed to heredity. Therefore, when middle-class children contracted sexually transmitted diseases, doctors and social workers were often unwilling to trace their infection to molestation by men who were presumed to be of good breeding. Instead, they attributed genital infection to contact with the working classes, going so far as to warn that girls risked becoming infected with gonorrhea from using toilet seats in public restrooms rather than acknowledge that upstanding members of society were capable of raping their daughters.[6]

However, the perception that children are in constant danger from men's unchecked desires is also harmful. Most violence against children, sexual or otherwise, occurs within families. Yet moral panics over child sexual abuse invariably focus on "stranger danger." The imperative to protect children from the sexual advances of strangers has been the driving force behind a range of laws that work to limit sexual expression and curtail the rights of adults, particularly gay men. The figure of the child imperiled by ungovernable male desire has been effectively deployed by anti-gay rights campaigns, ranging from Anita Bryant's calls to "Save Our Children" in the mid-1970s to early twenty-first-century ad campaigns in California, which invoked fears about the precariousness of childhood innocence to help pass Proposition 8 and ban same-sex marriage. And fears about pedophilia have been used to justify Megan's Laws, which require all sex offenders to be registered in a publicly available database for the remainder of their lives, regardless of the severity of their crimes, which might range from public urination to violent rape.[7] Indeed, the numerous parallels in the development of legal and scientific discourses about homosexuality and pedophilia throughout the twentieth century should make us deeply suspicious of the idea of pedophilia that dominates political and popular discourse today.

The endangered child is at the center of what Lee Edelman polemically decries as the tyranny of reproductive futurity, whereby adult freedoms are sacrificed in the name of protecting the child's presumed heterosexuality.[8] Edelman argues for a refusal of what he terms "reproductive futurity," an ideology that demands that adults repress their desires for the sake of protecting the child's future capacity to reconstitute the family. Resting on the psychoanalytic theories of Sigmund Freud and Jacques Lacan, he argues instead for the embrace of the death drive.

> Queers must respond to the violent force [of anti-queer rhetoric and policies] not only by insisting on our equal rights to the social order's prerogatives, not only by avowing our capacity to promote that order's coherence and integrity, but also by saying explicitly what Law and the Pope and the whole of the Symbolic order for which they stand hear anyway in each and every expression or manifestation of queer sexuality: Fuck the social order and the Child in whose name we're collectively terrorized; fuck Annie; fuck the waif from *Les Mis*; fuck the poor, innocent kid on the Net; . . . fuck the whole network of Symbolic relations and the future that serves as its prop.[9]

Edelman calls for the overturning of our culture's preoccupation with the needs of the child that are so clearly designed to enforce a very narrow vision of sexuality and citizenship. Indeed, reproductive futurism does no more good for children than it does for adults. The figure of the sexually endangered child on which this ideology rests forecloses the child's own subjectivity, particularly with regard to sexuality, and it distracts us from the pressing problems of poverty and violence that mar children's lives. It is, therefore, important to denaturalize the figure of the imperiled, innocent child in order to drain it of its iconic power.

One means of denaturalizing this understanding of childhood innocence is to historicize it, to demonstrate that the pedophile and the sexually imperiled child emerged out of a very specific paradigm and do not represent the timeless truth that adults' fascination with children is governed by unacknowledged sexual desire. Indeed, at the height of Shirley Temple's stardom, child loving was understood to have a beneficial effect on society.

Duck/Rabbit

Contemporary viewers are likely to find the image of Shirley Temple riding Jack Haley perverse. Haley is on his hands and knees, straddled by the child, who swishes a riding crop against his backside and loosely holds a leather strap around his neck. Temple's famous dimples and curls frame a face that seems too knowing for such a young girl. Her half-closed eyes look down slyly at the man, while her lips turn up into a disconcerting grin. How could we not see in this a pedophilic fantasy of domination and submission? And yet it is impossible to believe that Twentieth Century-Fox would deliberately stage its highest-grossing star in such a disturbing photograph.

For Depression-era audiences, the photograph is likely to have produced an entirely different set of meanings. Today, we tend to understand children to be imperiled by adult male sexuality. By contrast, during Shirley Temple's reign as Hollywood's top box-office star from 1935 through 1938, childhood innocence seemed inviolable. Although it is difficult for us to see anything but pedophilia in the photograph of Temple and Haley, it would have been difficult for early twentieth-century audiences to see the same image as anything but benign. The man in the photo is white, well-dressed, and apparently middle class, with clean white cuffs held together neatly by cufflinks, his curly hair tamed by a generous helping of pomade. He wears a suit, the uniform of the office rather than the home, and the two are posed as though caught in the act of playing horsey, a game in which the man submits his powerful body to the demands of the tiny child. It is a game that Temple played with adult male costars in several films, and it signified the man's capitulation to the child's charms. The photograph was designed to represent child loving rather than pedophilia.[10] And while audiences might have seen submission in the image, this would not have conjured sexualized images of domination but rather it would have signaled the man's self-control.

The photograph of Temple riding Haley produces two entirely different sets of meanings because our culture has undergone a paradigm shift regarding childhood innocence. In *The Structure of Scientific Revolutions*, Thomas S. Kuhn draws upon Ludwig Wittgenstein's discussion of the gestalt shift produced by a

1. Jack Haley and Shirley Temple in a production still for *Poor Little Rich Girl*, 1936. One's interpretation of the image rests on a specific paradigm of innocence. Author's collection.

duck-rabbit—an image that appears as a duck or a rabbit depending on where one's focus falls—to describe the effects of a paradigm shift in scientific thinking.

> Practicing in different worlds, [the proponents of competing paradigms] see different things when they look from the same point in the same direction. Again, that is not to say that they can see anything they please. Both are looking at the world, and what they look at has not changed. But in some areas they see different things, and they see them in different relations to the other.[11]

2. Duck/Rabbit.

Like the duck-rabbit, the image of Temple and Haley appears as one thing—pedophilic exploitation—when perceived through the lens of one paradigm, and something else altogether—benevolent child loving—when viewed through another. Each interpretation is equally true because our paradigms are the frameworks through which we evaluate the veracity of a claim. For the same reason, it can be difficult to see the truths produced within paradigms we do not share or to see beyond the truths produced by our own paradigms.

Shirley Temple's film career stood at the juncture of two very different paradigms of childhood. It was built upon the fairly stable conception of the white child's innocence as transformative, capable not only of deflecting adult sexuality but of transforming adults for the better.[12] However, it risked being undone by an emergent discourse of pedophilia that framed men's interest in child stars as sexual, a discourse that gained traction with the ascendance of Freud's theories of sexuality and the unconscious in the postwar period.

In the 1930s, Graham Greene was the rare critic who called attention to what he perceived to be the perversity of Shirley Temple's performances, identifying her appeal as dangerous rather than transformative. In 1936, he published a now notorious review of *Captain January*, describing the film as "sentimental, a little depraved, with an appeal interestingly decadent."[13] A year later, Greene found Temple's performance in *Wee Willie Winkie* to be even more perverse. In his review of the film, he described the child's appeal as erotic and identified her interactions with men as implicitly sexual: "In *Captain January* . . . her neat and well-developed rump twisted in the tap-dance; her eyes had a sidelong, searching coquetry. Now, in *Wee Willie Winkie*, wearing short kilts, she is a complete totsy. . . . [W]atch the way she measures a man with agile studio eyes, with dimpled depravity."[14] Unlike reviewers who celebrated the transformative effect of girl stars, Greene found Temple to be "depraved" and "decadent."

Greene's reviews of Temple's films draw on a Freudian paradigm to explain that Temple's adult male admirers "respond to her dubious coquetry, to the sight of her well-shaped and desirable little body, packed with enormous vitality, only because the safety curtain of story and dialogue drops between their intelligence and their desire."[15] Greene relies on the idea of the unconscious—Freud's revolutionary conception of the human psyche—when he imagines an audience of men who do not recognize that the source of their pleasure in the child is sexual. His "safety curtain" functions as a Freudian screen that permits men in the audience to disavow an unconscious desire. What had once signified manly self-control now seemed to signal repressed desire, and within this new paradigm repressed desire has a tendency to erupt into violence.

Freud's ideas were already widely disseminated in the United States prior to Temple's film debut in 1932, a year after the founding of the New York Psychoanalytic Institute. Freud had visited the United States in 1909, and his ideas were embraced by the American intelligentsia in the teens and 1920s. F. Scott Fitzgerald's 1934 novel, *Tender is the Night*, illustrates the degree to which Freudian ideas had entered the mainstream of American thought. In the novel Dick Diver is a psychoanalyst who marries a patient whose neuroses arise from her having been raped by her father. The novel implicitly links this incestuous relationship to a culture infatuated with children through the character of Rosemary, a teenaged film star celebrated for her role in the film *Daddy's Girl*. Through Rosemary, Fitzgerald mocks the countless films of the period in which men are transformed by innocent girls. In *Daddy's Girl*, "before [Rosemary's] tiny fist the forces of lust and corruption rolled away."[16]

However, Freud did not provide the dominant paradigm for interpreting Temple's career during her heyday, and Greene's review did not inspire like-minded critics to publicly identify Temple's performances as perverse. When a London news agent refused to sell issues of the magazine in which the review appeared, *Night and Day* elected to exploit the agent's outrage and advertised the issue with placards promising "Sex and Shirley Temple." Unfortunately, their advertising proved a bit too successful, and Twentieth Century-Fox learned of Greene's review. The studio successfully sued Greene and the magazine for what the courts deemed a "gross outrage" against the child, driving the magazine out of business and Greene out of the country.[17] It is more than likely that the suit effectively silenced other, like-minded reviewers, though in the United States news of the suit was limited to cryptic announcements that Greene and *Night and Day* had been sued for publishing an article that criticized the child's acting.

Greene's reviews anticipate the current perception that there is something perverse about Temple's popularity. However, in the 1930s, his was a minority view, and one easily quashed by the studio. It would not be until the mid-twentieth century that our current understanding that children's sexual innocence is vulnerable to adult interference would come to underwrite children's film roles and shape the discourse about child performers.

Scholarship on the cultural import of the child in Western culture tends to stress continuities from the eighteenth-century discursive invention of childhood innocence to present-day images of childhood. With the publication of *Child Loving: The Erotic Child and Victorian Culture* in 1994, James Kincaid helped to reinvigorate the field of childhood studies by arguing that Victorian culture produced an ideal of the child that was inherently erotic and that the pedophile functions as a means of disavowing our erotic investment in the child even as we indulge it. Kincaid followed up that examination of Victorian culture with analyses of more recent phenomena—the popularity of Shirley Temple and Macaulay Culkin as well as Michael Jackson's trial for child molestation—that emphasize what he perceives as continuities between the Victorian culture of child loving and twentieth-century panics over child molestation.[18] However, it wasn't until the late 1930s that the pedophile began to emerge as a national scapegoat.[19] Prior to then, other scapegoats helped to preserve the ideology of childhood innocence, as I discuss in chapter 5.

Contrary to Kincaid, I argue that the meaning of innocence underwent a significant change in the early twentieth century. White children's innocence once seemed invulnerable to adult interference—it was thought to be so powerful, in fact, that it was capable of transforming even the most reprobate of adults for the better, provided that the adult in question was capable of recognizing the child's cuteness. Today, children's innocence appears just the opposite, for it seems to be imperiled by adult desire and in danger of being corrupted through contact with the world of adults. Where Kincaid focuses on continuities between Victorian and contemporary childhoods, I argue that innocence was radically redefined in the twentieth century. It is important to acknowledge this shift in order to understand that contemporary fears about children's vulnerability to male desire are the product of a specific ideology and to recognize that contradictory meanings and practices continue to shape contemporary images of children. Shirley Temple's career provides a fascinating window into this shift because her star persona exemplified the previous understanding of childhood innocence at the very moment that it was being redefined.

In *The Queen of America Goes to Washington City*, Lauren Berlant demonstrates how the innocent child functions as the symbolic linchpin of contemporary political discourse. Invocations of childhood innocence produce an ideal of what Berlant terms "infantile citizenship," in which political rights and protections are apportioned in direct relation to the subject's perceived innocence. Sentimental fictions, Berlant argues, help to shape political debate, and within these fictions, the child is figured as the blameless victim whose needs and desires must be protected at all costs. Berlant traces a direct line from Harriet Beecher Stowe's Little Eva in *Uncle Tom's Cabin* to Lisa Simpson of Fox's long-running animated television show *The Simpsons.*[20] However, when we recognize that the meaning of childhood innocence changed in the early twentieth century, it becomes clear that Eva's political effectiveness rested on one definition of innocence, characterized by what Robin Bernstein describes as "a state of deflection: a constantly replenishing obliviousness [to sexuality, race, etc.] that causes sexual matters to slide by without sticking," whereas contemporary children are understood to be absorptive rather than deflective, their fragile innocence in need of adult protection.[21]

Looking at Temple's career in light of the history of child stardom in the United States, it becomes apparent that Temple's star persona was built on a set of conventions that had been in practice for at least fifty years and that were interpreted in light of a paradigm that understood the white child's innocence to be transformative. In this sense, I build on Gaylyn Studlar's project of understanding how youth, like gender, was constructed within studio-era Hollywood. In *Precocious Charms*, Gaylyn Studlar examines six stars—Mary Pickford, Shirley Temple, Deanna Durbin, Elizabeth Taylor, Jennifer Jones, and Audrey Hepburn—to understand how each produced what she terms "juvenated" femininity. Studlar is particularly interested in exploring the ways in which these stars negotiated the border between adult and child, between innocence and sexuality. She argues that "all of these stars showed the powerful appeal of juvenation linked to feminization and to eroticization, whether this appeal is thought of as speaking to anxieties, generating utopian fantasies about the nature of ideal girlhood, or constructing pleasures dependent on some element of contradiction."[22]

Studlar stresses the continuity between the six stars she examines, whereas I would argue that the process of juvenation she describes underwent a profound change in the 1940s when Freudian theories of sexuality and the unconscious began to dominate popular discourse. Practices that had been in place for half a century were marginalized in the 1950s. It was no longer common for adult women to impersonate young girls, as Mary Pickford did in the 1910s and 1920s. And men's adoration was no longer central to young girls' stardom, as it had been for Shirley Temple.

Studlar draws on a tradition of feminist psychoanalytic film scholarship to theorize audiences' engagement with on-screen images of juvenated femininity. I am more interested in historicizing the ways in which discourse about Temple and her films announced normative gendered responses to girl stars, responses that are often unimaginable to twenty-first-century audiences. In this way, I hope to demonstrate how Hollywood worked to produce an understanding of what a normative response to the child would be.

A History of Innocence

Thomas Kuhn describes a paradigm shift as occurring rapidly; one framework for understanding the world is immediately displaced by a new one. However, he is discussing what he terms "scientific revolutions," in which revolutionary insights overturn schools of scientific thought. By contrast, as new frameworks disseminate within popular thinking, one paradigm is seldom completely overturned in favor of another. Rather, competing logics may coexist indefinitely. Such is the case with our understanding of childhood, which has long been shaped by competing conceptions of innocence.

Karin Calvert has examined the material culture of colonial America to demonstrate that, until the eighteenth century, childrearing was predicated on a Calvinist model of childhood. Believing that the child was inherently sinful, born into depravity, Christian parents sought to usher their children as rapidly as possible into adulthood and salvation, encouraging them to walk upright rather than crawling, for example.[23] In the eighteenth century, however, John Locke and Jean-Jacques Rousseau helped to redefine childhood as a period of innocence. Rather than characterizing the child in terms of "infant depravity," these Enlightenment thinkers conceived the child as a "tabula rasa," a blank slate to be protected from adult influence and the corruption of human society.

Out of this Lockean conception of childhood innocence, the Romantics developed a vision of divine childhood that permeated nineteenth-century art and literature. William Wordsworth's "Ode: Intimations of Immortality from Recollections of Early Childhood" (1807) captures this Romantic vision of childhood as a divine state:

> Trailing clouds of glory do we come
> From God, who is our home:
> Heaven lies about us in our infancy![24]

The innocent child, come directly from God, offered those around her a nostalgic glimpse into a premodern, pre-industrial past, and a feeling of proximity to the divine.

This view of the sacred child became central to the burgeoning sentimental literature and melodrama in the late nineteenth century. Novels and plays were structured around the Romantic notion of childhood innocence as redemptive and transformative. In melodrama and sentimental fiction, the innocent child played the ideal victim, utterly innocent and utterly deserving of help. And, innocent of evil, the child was understood to have a natural understanding of right and wrong, untainted by human prejudices or social hierarchies. Due to the child's innocence—signaled by his or her immature body—the child was able to differentiate between good and evil and share this wisdom with her elders.

As the child became increasingly marginal to economic life—removed from the labor force and into the school room—she assumed a more prominent role in the popular imagination. The child functioned as an antidote to the ravages brought by modern life and as a repository of all that was lost with the turn toward rationalism and industrial capitalism. As industrial capitalism infiltrated more and more aspects of European life, the pure, middle-class child was relegated to the home and protected from the corrupt capitalist marketplace through prohibitions on child labor. While industrial labor demanded self-control and restraint from its workers, the impish child remained the repository of fun. And as the concept of "culture" developed in opposition to that of "nature," the child came to be associated with the latter, imagined to exist in a blissful period of innocence untainted by the artificiality of adult society. Through association with the innocent child, it was imagined that adults could reconnect with wonder and nature and return temporarily to a pure, protected sphere beyond the pervasive grasp of the capitalist marketplace. The Enlightenment, with its focus on reason and rationality, had marginalized wonder and the marvelous. According to Gary Cross, "This quality of wonder was largely lost when the natural world became an object of control, predictability, and systematic reason to adults. Subtly, across the late 18th and 19th centuries, the look and feeling of wonder shifted to the child. . . . The magic of wonder, sacrificed to rationality, could be renewed in the 'smile' of the child as she or he encountered nature."[25]

The child provided both a means of regress—a temporary respite from modernity—and a metaphor to describe those who have not benefitted from industrial capitalism. Indeed, the myth of progress that defines modernity is built on the metaphor of childhood. The idea of modernity rests on a teleological understanding of history, a belief that societies develop out of primitivism and toward a civilized state, implying that a society that is not modern is not advanced or mature. Failure to flourish within the capitalist system is ascribed not to the exploitative relations that lie at the heart of capitalist and colonial relations but to a belief that some individuals and societies remain in their infancy and need the guiding hand of the "adult" industrialized nations. So strong was the association of "civilization" with adulthood and the "primitive" with childhood that psychologists reversed the metaphor, asserting that children reenacted the development of the species in their individual development; according to recapitulation theory, the child was a throwback to his primitive ancestors, becoming barbaric in youth, and, given the right breeding, developing into civilized adulthood in adolescence.[26]

Viviana Zelizer has traced economic indicators of this radical redefinition of childhood innocence between the 1870s and 1930s; as children assumed increased sentimental importance, they were no longer expected to contribute to the family economy. In Zelizer's terms, as the child became "sacralized," she was redefined as "economically useless"—removed from the labor force—and "emotionally priceless," as indicated by the amounts paid to parents in wrongful death suits and paid by parents for funerals and adoption. The first decades of the twentieth century witnessed the relocation of children from the workforce into the schoolroom with the introduction of mandatory schooling laws and minimum age requirements for wage labor. At the same time, parents were pressured to express their love for their children through consumer purchases, and a booming industry in goods for children was born.[27]

Childhood became even more contradictory in the early twentieth century with the proliferation of images of childhood in commercial culture. The ideal of childhood wonder described by Gary Cross was adeptly harnessed by advertisers in order to sell all manner of things. Ironically, the child whose image seemed to offer an escape from the modern, capitalist marketplace became an effective means of enticing consumers to buy new products. Cross demonstrates that the advertising industry and childrearing manuals of the early twentieth century produced two distinct, often contradictory visions of childhood. While childrearing manuals exhorted parents to exert discipline on the child, advertisers advocated indulgence.

When Shirley Temple reigned as one of Hollywood's leading stars, these contradictory ideologies of childhood coexisted; one understanding of childhood dominated in advertising, another in childrearing manuals, another in pedagogical theory, another in the newly emerging field of psychoanalysis. During a period when a Freudian understanding of sublimation and childhood sexuality were disseminated within other discourses, Hollywood clung to an understanding of childhood that had developed in relation to nineteenth-century stage melodrama. Central to children's performances was the notion that the innocent child was not only immune to sexual desire, but she was even able to re-instill innocence in adults. As I discuss in chapter 1, this sentimental child was adapted to address an emerging, modern taste culture. Nonetheless, Hollywood's children remained relatively untouched by the Freudian ideas of childhood sexuality that began to be popularized in the United States during the 1920s, though Freud's ideas would ultimately undermine the concept of innocence that was so central to Shirley Temple's star image.

Maiden Tribute

Several scholars have suggested that the ideal of childhood innocence was seriously undermined in the late nineteenth century in the wake of a sensational exposé of child prostitution in London. In 1885, the British reformer and journalist William T. Stead published a series of incendiary articles in London's *Pall Mall Gazette* in which he reported that the impoverished girls of London's East End were being systematically lured into prostitution in order to meet the seemingly unquenchable thirst for virgins among the city's upper-class men. Stead's "Maiden Tribute of Modern Babylon" told of girls between the ages of thirteen and sixteen who had been sold by drunken and indifferent parents, befriended and seduced by procuresses, and driven by ignorance and poverty to part with "what a woman ought to value more than life."[28] Historians have questioned the veracity of Stead's account, and his methods—he abducted a thirteen-year-old girl in the process of his investigation—landed him in jail.

Regardless of whether his exposé accurately describes the extent to which girls were employed as prostitutes or their reasons for entering the profession, "The Maiden Tribute of Modern Babylon" caused a furor in both Britain and the United States. The articles prompted British Parliament to pass the Criminal Law Amendment Act, which raised the age of consent for girls from thirteen to sixteen. (The same amendment also proscribed consensual sex between adult men and increased restrictions on prostitution.) And in the United States, Stead's articles contributed to developing concerns about white slavery that prompted many states to raise the age of consent, which ranged from seven to twelve years of age in the late nineteenth century, to between fourteen and eighteen in the 1920s.

Catherine Robson suggests that Stead's articles marked the beginning of the end of the ideal of childhood. Robson examines "girl loving" among the British upper class, arguing that men's preoccupations with girls was born of an association of girlhood with the men's own lost youth. Stead's articles, according to Robson, forced Victorian society to reassess its fascination with young girls: "'The Maiden Tribute of Modern Babylon' emits the last gasp of the myth of ideal girlhood, a myth that had contained the power to solace and delight the Victorian imagination."[29] Carolyn Steedman, too, argues that Stead's articles helped to change the popular perception of the Victorian cult of the child. More specifically, according to Steedman, "some commentators of the 1880s were utterly certain of the correlation between sexual desire for the child and its public display."[30] She cites one *Pall Mall Gazette* reader who blamed the traffic in children on the proliferation of public amusements in late nineteenth-century London:

> The peculiar evil which the *Pall Mall Gazette* has been warning was unknown at the West End of London when I began life. It came in with the roller skating at Prince's [where] for the first time, the great body of men about town were brought into daily contact with beautiful children, not members of their own family. The little things, in their nescience, were only too prodigal of smiles and glances. A passion sprang up for little children. The ruin of the children themselves was out of the question, but the procuresses found little east-enders to bear the curse vicariously.[31]

Another reader pointed to children's employment in the theater as producing both a supply and demand for child prostitutes:

> When the London season is over, and the theatres closed, certain money-making agents have instituted companies of small children, selected for their good looks, girls mostly, who dressed in boys' costumes, are taken down to the various racecourses to sell programmes, ices, and other light refreshment. While thus engaged they are called upon to perform feats of agility, dancing, tumbling, etc.... Petted and spoilt, these children are introduced to the worst phases of fast life [and hired out] to pose for the nude in classical groups and subjects.[32]

It would appear, then, that Stead's articles prompted new fears on the part of London readers that child performers would invite the unwelcome, licentious gaze of their male audience.

However, Stead's articles do not seem to have inspired similar concerns that children's presence in public spaces had contributed to their becoming objects of an erotic male gaze on this side of the Atlantic. Indeed, *Little Lord Fauntleroy* debuted on the New York stage only three years after the publication of Stead's articles, helping to launch the child-star craze in the United States.[33] And men's transformational love for children remained central to Hollywood's child stars through the 1930s. Nonetheless, Stead's rhetoric did have an effect on US reformers. Elbridge Gerry, the founding head of the New York Society for the Prevention of Cruelty to Children (known as the Gerry Society), echoed the language of Stead's exposé in his efforts to regulate children's performances. However, to his mind the display of young thespians did not produce a demand for young girls but rather its supply. In 1892, seven years after the publication of Stead's articles, a bill was introduced in the New York state legislature that would have severely limited Gerry's jurisdiction over child performers by allowing children to perform provided they had the permission of their parents and a medical examiner. In his successful fight to defeat the bill, Gerry wrote an angry letter to *The New York Times*. In a dire warning that echoes Stead's claim that he was able to purchase a young girl for £5, Gerry warned, "In my personal experience I have known a parent to bargain and sell his child for $30 to be used for immoral purposes."[34] And he predicts that the theater will produce a ready supply of adolescent prostitutes if children are permitted to perform without the approval of the Gerry Society:

> The story is too old of young girls from twelve to sixteen years of age enticed into occupations which lead to their complete destruction. The demand for young girls in such places is as inexhaustible as the supply, which will pour in if the law permits.... This bill permits [children] to be employed by night in performing and getting a tuition in vice, and by day in rehearsing for the night.... The brokers who deal in 'supplies' for every wrong demand are responsible, with the drunken and criminal parents, for the continual outcry [against Gerry's regulation of child labor].[35]

Unlike the London reader whose letter was published in the *Pall Mall Gazette*, Gerry is not concerned that children's presence in public places will produce desire in the men of the upper classes. Rather, he believed young girls would be corrupted by their association with the theater. According to Gerry, child performers "are constantly brought into contact with persons about whose morality or virtue the less said the better. Constantly exhibiting in such troupes, the girls soon lose all modesty and become bold, forward, and impudent. When they arrive at the limit of the age of the law, they have usually entered on the downward path and end in low dance-houses, concert saloons, and the early grave which is the inevitable conclusion of a life of debauchery."[36] Clearly, Gerry was not concerned that girls' presence on the stage might incite desire in an adult, male audience but that girls' association with the theater did not offer a proper moral foundation. Indeed, when he complains that "a child of tender years is forced to sing and dance at night, half clad in scanty theatrical costume," he is not concerned for her modesty but for her health; she performs in a theater "where the draughts are incessant and where the exertion of the performance constantly overheats the system so as to render the exposure still more dangerous."[37]

The ideal of inviolable innocence remained firmly in place even after the publication of Stead's incendiary descriptions of child prostitution in London. In the United States at least "Maiden Tribute of Modern Babylon" does not appear to have inspired even critics of children's theatrical labor to perceive audiences' pleasure in children's performances as anything but benign. This may be because Stead was primarily concerned with raising the age of consent in Britain, which was thirteen at the time; he did not ask readers to recognize children's vulnerability to adult desire but rather to broaden their definition of childhood to include adolescent girls. In fact, he claims that there was very little market for children below the age of thirteen.

Although the moment of Romantic literature may have passed, the Romantic child persisted in sentimental fiction, where the child continued to influence those around her by virtue of her transformative innocence. And, contrary to Robson's and Steedman's argument that the articles spelled the end of the cult of the child, the furor over Stead's articles does not appear to have tempered audiences' pleasure in child loving.

The Performing Child

During the child star era, from the 1880s through the 1930s, theatrical agents and Hollywood studios developed a set of formulae for producing child stars that played a significant role in shaping Temple's career.[38] The emergence of child actors on stage corresponds with the shift of the popular theater from a masculine sphere to a feminine one. At the beginning of the nineteenth century, according to Richard Butsch, the theater was an almost exclusively masculine realm. In the 1820s, beer was sold in theater lobbies and prostitutes plied their trade in the gallery boxes. However, when ticket sales flagged in the wake of the economic downturn in the 1870s, Butsch argues, some managers began to develop tactics for attracting reputable women to their theaters. The newly opened department stores had only recently begun to invite women into the public sphere, contributing to the development of a new visual culture that catered to the female gaze. In an effort to attract this new, female audience, such disreputable pleasures as beer and sex were banned from the theater, rowdy audiences were compelled to be orderly, and matinees were added to the bill. What had been a strictly masculine realm became, by the end of the nineteenth century, a feminine one.[39]

The feminization of the popular theater had effects that went beyond the elimination of beer and prostitutes and the introduction of matinees. New types of performers began to be favored. Rather than the virile men of the early nineteenth-century stage, Butsch argues, the late nineteenth-century stage was peopled by gentler men and stronger heroines. While Butsch focuses on the shift in adult male roles and performers that resulted from the growing importance of women in the audience, the increased visibility of children on the stage was also clearly a product of this redefinition of the audience from a masculine one to a feminine one. Not coincidentally, the vogue for young children on the American stage reached a peak in the 1880s with the production of *Little Lord Fauntleroy.* In the decades that followed, children proliferated on vaudeville, Broadway, and in regional performances of such popular melodramas as *Uncle Tom's Cabin, The Little Red Schoolhouse* and *Mrs. Wiggs of the Cabbage Patch.*

During this same period, advertisers, likewise vying for the attention of female consumers, began to rely on images of children to sell their products.[40] In fact, there was a good deal of overlap between the children who performed on stage and screen and those who appeared in advertisements. In a widely distributed ad campaign, young Madge Evans appeared nude, transformed into a fairy, over the caption, "Have you a little fairy in your home?"[41] The campaign was successful enough that the child was recruited to star in Hollywood films in 1914. Conversely, advertisers used established young stars to endorse their products. Jackie Coogan and Baby Peggy dolls were marketed throughout the United States, Evans had a line of hats, and Shirley Temple endorsed a number of products, from Quaker Oats to Dodge cars, despite the fact that she was far too young to drive.

From the emergence of the Hollywood studio system in the late teens through the 1930s, children held a prominent place in Hollywood. During the teens, no film studio was complete without its resident child star; Helen Badgley was the "Thanhouser Kid," Matty Roubert the "Universal Boy," and Little Mary Sunshine (Baby Marie Osborne) was with Balboa. Fox even went so far as to develop an entire troupe of children, the Fox Kiddies (including Francis Carpenter, Virginia Lee Corbin, Carmen DeRue, and Violet Radcliffe, a little girl who was typecast as the male "heavy") and featured them in lavish, feature-length films. Jackie

Coogan, who began his film career starring with Charlie Chaplin in *The Kid* (Charles Chaplin, 1921), became the best known of the silent-era child stars, but he was far from alone. Zoe Rae, Madge Evans, Bobby Connelly, Jane and Katherine Lee, Baby Peggy, Wesley Barry, Ben Alexander, and Mary McAlister are but a handful of the children who achieved stardom during this period. Hal Roach's popular series of two-reel comedies, "Our Gang," began production in 1922 and continued through the 1930s. "Our Gang" helped to inspire a number of producers to develop film shorts that featured children, including "Snookums" starring "Sunny" Jim McKeen; "Big Boy" with Malcolm Sebastian; "Buster Brown" with Arthur Trimble; the "Mickey McGuire" series, starring a very young Mickey Rooney; and the "Baby Burlesks," which introduced Shirley Temple to the screen.

Sound technology brought a new influx of child stars. Al Jolson sang to Little Davy Lee in *The Singing Fool* (Lloyd Bacon, 1928) and *Say It With Songs* (Lloyd Bacon, 1929), nine-year-old "Baby" Rose Marie brought her sultry voice from radio to a handful of short Vitagraph films, and eight-year-old Mitzi Green signed a long-term contract with Paramount. In the early 1930s, Jackie Cooper graduated from Our Gang to star in feature films, as did Dickie Moore and Spanky McFarland, and Baby LeRoy and Cora Sue Collins made their film debuts. In 1934 Shirley Temple became an international phenomenon, her success inspiring a new cycle of child stars that included Jane Withers, Edith Fellows, Sybil Jason, and Freddie Bartholomew. Sol Lesser, who had produced films for Jackie Coogan, brought singing sensation Bobby Breen from radio to film, and Fox signed the famous Dionne quintuplets and starred five-year-old ice skater Irene Dare in a handful of films. Hollywood continued to promote child stars in the 1940s, MGM's Margaret O'Brien among the most prominent of them, but the nature of child stardom changed during the postwar era, when family audiences and child performers gradually migrated to television.

Shirley Temple's Stardom

Hollywood drew on the ideal of innocence associated with the sentimental or sacrilized child in its production of the child star. This ideal—so strongly associated with the nineteenth century and seemingly so thoroughly overturned by Freud—persisted well into the twentieth century and helped to shape Shirley Temple's star persona in ways that were quite productive for Depression-era audiences.

It is important to consider Temple in relation to a larger history of child performers not only so that we can differentiate the idiosyncratic from the conventional aspects of her career but also so that we can understand how these conventions functioned and why the child star had such prominence during this period. As Richard Dyer notes, the star's biography, written and disseminated by the studio publicity department and reproduced in magazine and newspaper articles, establishes the star as both ordinary—a person with a similar background, values, and desires as the presumed reader—and extraordinary, particularly in her effect on audiences.[42]

Temple was an unparalleled international phenomenon, but her career and publicity—her star persona—were somewhat formulaic. Several things are consistent in the biographies of child stars. Unlike her ambitious adult counterparts, the child is emptied of desire, other than the desire to play and to please, and her labor is made to disappear. The story of the star's "discovery" generally omits the grueling work of auditions and instead describes a director or producer spotting the child and recognizing her natural brilliance. Temple's publicity often repeated the story that she was discovered hiding under a piano at the Meglin Dance Studio when Jack Hays came looking for children to appear in his Baby Burlesks. A Fox producer then spotted Temple in one of the Frolics of Youth films and knew he had found the perfect child for *Stand Up and Cheer.* By contrast, in her autobiography, Shirley Temple Black describes her mother driving her across Los Angeles for auditions at various studios and training her to approach strangers, introduce herself, and describe her performance abilities, suggesting that her career was built as much on perseverance and hard work as it was on her charm.

Financial motivations are generally eliminated from the biographies that the studios constructed for their child stars. Temple was unusual in that she lived with both her parents and her father had steady employment as a white-collar worker. A large proportion of child stars were either the offspring of vaudevillians (Mitzi Green, Jackie Coogan) or they were raised by single women who had few alternatives than to hire out their children for pay (Mary Pickford, Margaret O'Brien). Indeed, Gertrude Temple appears to have initially sought work for Shirley in order to supplement her husband's small income.

Shirley Temple was born in 1928, though in 1934 Fox shaved a year off her age in all her publicity in order for her to seem more precocious and precious, so that both she and her audience believed her birth date to be in 1929. Her early childhood offers a glimpse into the world of subsidiary businesses that mushroomed around Hollywood to exploit the parents who hoped to see their children in film. As a toddler, Temple was enrolled in the Meglin Dance Studio, whose students—the Meglin Kiddies—were often recruited to appear in a number of feature-length and short films. (Judy Garland was also a member of the Meglin Kiddies in the 1930s.) In 1932, Temple was signed to a two-year contract by Jack Hays, who was developing a troupe of child actors to appear in a series of short films, the Baby Burlesks. While under contract with Hays, Temple was loaned out to the studios for walk-on parts—or, rather, what she describes in her autobiography as "carry-on" parts, since she was usually held in the arms of an actor. Hays's role as a producer seems to have functioned as a feeder for his acting school, the Hays Baby Stars Training School; for a fee, he promised parents that their children would appear on film. However, when it became apparent that the children were no more than extras, parents started to complain and Hays was investigated by the Labor Commission and the Child Welfare Bureau. He filed for bankruptcy in 1933, and Shirley's father, George Temple, bought her contract for $25.

In late 1933, Temple was signed to appear in a Fox film, *Stand Up and Cheer* (originally titled *Fox Follies*), one of three musicals being filmed on the Fox lot in January of 1934. (The most elaborate of the three, *George White's Scandals*, featured the Meglin Kiddies in two dance numbers and would play a significant role in the development of child stardom, as I discuss in chapter 4.) In *Stand Up and Cheer*, Temple plays the daughter of a vaudevillian (James Dunn). Their performance of "Baby, Take a Bow" would prove to be one of the most popular sequences of an otherwise forgettable film. Though the role was small, it was enough to gain the attention of Winfield Sheehan, head of production at Fox, who signed Temple to a one-year contract with an option for an additional seven years.

In 1934, Temple became one of Fox's leading stars. That year, she was loaned to Paramount to star in *Little Miss Marker*, an adaptation of a Damon Runyon short story about a New York bookie (Adolph Menjou) who takes a young girl as a marker on a bet. Temple was widely praised for her role in the film, and this success, combined with her celebrated performance in *Stand Up and Cheer*, prompted Fox to reconceive a crime drama that the studio had in development as a vehicle for Temple and James Dunn. The film was retitled *Baby Take a Bow* in order to capitalize on their popular number together in *Stand Up and Cheer*. Next, Temple was loaned out to Paramount for *Now and Forever*, which starred Gary Cooper and Carole Lombard as a pair of con artists, but this was the last time Fox would part with Temple until she withdrew from her contract in 1940. Temple and Dunn were paired together a third time in *Bright Eyes*, in which Temple sang what would become her signature tune, "On the Good Ship Lollipop." The film was a tremendous success, and in 1935 Temple displaced Will Rogers as number 1 in Quigley's poll of top-grossing stars. That year, too, Temple made her first appearance beside legendary tap dancer Bill Robinson in *The Little Colonel* and danced alongside him again in *The Littlest Rebel*, and she appeared in the first of her adaptations of Mary Pickford films, *Curly Top*, which was loosely based on *Daddy Long Legs*.

Twentieth Century-Fox developed nineteen films featuring Shirley Temple between 1934 and 1940, and only two of them—*The Blue Bird* and *Young People*—were outright flops.[43] Nonetheless, as she neared puberty Temple's popularity waned, and the studio dropped her contract in 1940 when she was twelve years old (though she and the public imagined she was only eleven). Temple continued making films in the 1940s, working with MGM, Universal, and producer David O. Selznick, but she was never able to establish herself as an adolescent or adult star. When she appeared on television in the 1950s, as the narrator for

ABC's *Shirley Temple's Storybook* (1958–1961), the show capitalized on her status as a former child star.

Overview

This book examines how children's performances of innocence functioned to neutralize the dangers that seemed to arise from the rapid social and cultural changes of the early twentieth century. I chart the uses of the innocent child in contexts that contemporary audiences have retrospectively read as pedophilic: white women's performances of girlhood; white men's adoration of young child stars; the pairing of white children with black men; children's impersonations of sexualized adults. Childhood innocence meant something different in the early twentieth century from what it does today, for while we understand the child to be endangered by adult sexuality, in the early twentieth century, the white child's innocence was not perceived to be endangered, but rather an impenetrable shell that deflected adult sexuality and was, in turn, capable of transforming for the better the adults who came into her orbit.

Shirley Temple's ascendance to stardom came close on the heels of Mary Pickford's retirement from the screen. Chapter 1, "America's Sweethearts," identifies the ways in which both Pickford and Temple addressed a deep division in early twentieth-century American culture, that between traditional, WASP values and modern mores. As a growing proportion of the country relocated from rural to urban areas and as machine technology assumed a greater role in Americans' lives, a new aesthetic emerged that spoke to the new experience of modern life. Andres Huyssen examines nineteenth-century literature to argue that mass culture was being defined and denigrated as feminine during this period. Modernism, which Huyssen identifies as a reaction against the perceived femininity of mass culture, began its ascent in high art. And what Gilbert Seldes described as the "lively arts"—popular music, film, vaudeville, and other commercial amusements—were bent on producing sensation and thrills through laughter or sex appeal. Sentimentalism—once the dominant strain of American culture—became the stuff of middle-brow culture and, by the time Temple became the country's No. 1 box-office draw, the child's sentimental appeal was understood to be old-fashioned. Pickford and Temple—in appearance so like the young, female heroines of nineteenth-century sentimental literature—helped to negotiate this shift by integrating the two aesthetics. At the same time, they both worked to reconcile other ideological tensions associated with the conflict between Victorian and modern culture. However, whereas Pickford offered audiences the possibility of regress, Temple helped audiences to find familiar comforts in modern life.

In chapter 2, "A Terrible Amour," I explore Temple's appeal to adult men. Men, both on screen and in the audience, were besotted with Temple and represented a significant share of her audience. Indeed, when box-office receipts for her films began to wane in 1939, exhibitors attributed the drop in attendance not to the quality of her films (*The Little Princess* remains one of the most enduringly popular of her films) or to her advancing age (her public believed she was ten), but to the fact that adults, particularly men, could no longer be lured to her films. Temple represents one of the last in a long line of children who were celebrated for their ability to capture the hearts of men. California miners had showered gold upon five-year-old Lotta Crabtree, while Mark Twain and Oliver Wendell Holmes, Sr. were among the countless men who publicly proclaimed their love for twelve-year-old Elsie Leslie in the 1880s. Early child screen stars helped to recruit young men to enlist in the army during wartime, and they were celebrated as an antidote to the risqué charms of adult women. Men were applauded for befriending the young girls of the stage or even adopting them. For, rather than suggesting pedophilic desire, these accounts of "child-loving bachelors" celebrated men's readiness to pursue innocent pleasures rather than the more bawdy ones on offer in the mass media. Thus men's preference for Shirley Temple over Mae West, for instance, was taken as a sign of their willingness to keep their sexual appetites in check.

Chapter 3, "Immaculate Amalgamation," explores another aspect of Temple's career that has puzzled contemporary audiences: her pairing with black performers, particularly Bill "Bojangles" Robinson. The legendary tap dancer was featured in four of Shirley Temple's films and played a significant behind-the-scenes role as her choreographer and dance instructor in a fifth. This chapter considers how the pairing of the black man with the white girl helped to carve out a place for black performers in the national media while also working to reinstate the ideology of racial difference that seemed to have been undone by the ubiquity of jazz music and dance in the United States and abroad. Through her pairing with Bill Robinson, Temple helped to narrate the emergence of jazz as an unthreatening fusion of black and white cultures, working to dispel fears about the "mongrelization" of American modernity.

Shirley Temple began her career playing showgirls and prostitutes in a series of short films called the "Baby Burlesks." Though it may be hard to believe now, these performances appear not to have seemed perverse to Depression-era audiences. Chapter 4, "Baby Burlesks and Kiddie Kabarets," considers how these performances functioned to help early twentieth-century audiences negotiate rapidly changing gender roles. In the early twentieth century, it was not uncommon for children to engage in erotic impersonations that audiences today find pedophilic. In *Aladdin and His Wonderful Lamp* (1917), for example, three-year-old Virginia Lee Corbin appears naked in her bath in a scene inspired by Theda Bara's shocking performance as Cleopatra earlier that year. Baby Peggy, one of the most popular child performers of the 1920s, entertained audiences with an impersonation of Salomé's dance of the seven veils in *Sweetie* (1923), while in *George White's Scandals of 1934*, a young girl of roughly four or five reproduces Sally Rand's risqué fan dance, singing: "Oh! You nasty man!/I know you're hoping I'll drop my fan." These, along with Temple's performances in the Burlesks, for which she was billed as a "devastating 36-month-old siren," helped to announce the impossibility of a child's arousing adult desire. Watching a child impersonate Cleopatra at her bath or Marlene Dietrich's "Hot Voodoo" number in *Blonde Venus*, audiences collectively laughed at the images of female sexuality that seemed so threatening in other contexts, thereby undermining the erotic power of Hollywood's controversial female stars.

Even as Temple's career relied on and helped to promote the ideal of innocence, this ideal was undone by her stardom. Childhood innocence was founded on the child's supposed immunity from the effects of both capitalism and sexuality, but she undermined both aspects of innocence through her status as a laborer and commercialized image. In chapter 5, "Economic Innocence," I consider the demise of the ideology of innocence upon which Temple's stardom rested. I demonstrate that Depression-era audiences were far more concerned about threats to Temple's economic innocence than they were about the possibility of her being sexualized.

Ultimately, identifying Temple's appeal as primarily pedophilic is more indicative of our own cultural moment than it is of Temple's. More importantly, it distracts us from exploring the reasons behind the centrality of child stars to the popular imagination in the 1930s. By examining what Temple meant to audiences who did not identify their interest in the star as sexual, it is possible to demonstrate the centrality of Shirley Temple to Hollywood and the American imagination not as an object of desire but as a means of addressing a range of problems associated with the burgeoning of American mass culture. At the same time, I hope to destabilize the iconic power of the innocent white child.

CHAPTER 1

AMERICA'S SWEETHEARTS

MARY PICKFORD, SHIRLEY TEMPLE, AND THE "DECLINE OF SENTIMENT"

Before Shirley Temple became a star in 1934, the most popular icon of American girlhood was not a girl at all but an adult woman, Mary Pickford. Pickford was one of the first stars to emerge out of the fledgling film industry, having made her screen debut in 1909 at the age of seventeen. Throughout the teens and 1920s, Pickford was consistently identified as the most popular performer in the world, her name synonymous with movie stardom. She did not play children exclusively; indeed she enacted adult roles in the majority of her films. However, following the First World War, she began playing children with increased regularity, and publicity photographs often showed her in the guise of young girls. Indeed, her screen persona was so strongly associated with youth that she was imagined to be the very personification of childhood: "The spirit of spring imprisoned in a woman's body; the first child in the world."[1] Although her popularity had waned considerably by the end of the 1920s, as late as 1933 Pickford was in discussions with Walt Disney to play Alice in *Alice in Wonderland*.[2]

Shirley Temple's ascendance to stardom in 1934 prompted journalists to recall Pickford's heyday, and Twentieth Century-Fox nurtured such comparisons by starring Temple in remakes of several of Pickford's most popular films: *Daddy Long Legs* (released as *Curly Top*), *Poor Little Rich Girl, Rebecca of Sunnybrook Farm*, and *A Little Princess*.[3] More than Temple's reprisal of roles associated with Pickford, however, Pickford and Temple were linked by virtue of their tremendous popularity. Several journalists noted that Temple had displaced Pickford as "America's Sweetheart," claiming that "Shirley's only feminine rival as a box-office draw in the whole history of films is Mary Pickford."[4] And both were icons of girlhood whose images reached far beyond the movie theater, entering into the popular vernacular. Thus, girlhood held a prominent place in the iconography of Hollywood during the industry's formative years. Scholars have often attributed the prominence of girlish stars in the silent era to the pleasures associated with what Gaylyn Studlar terms a "pedophilic gaze."[5] However, when we consider Temple's career as an outgrowth of Pickford's, it becomes clear that their performances of girlhood played an important role in negotiating the twentieth century's first culture war by evoking what might be better termed a "juvenated" gaze.

In his seminal study of film stardom, Richard Dyer argues that the elusive quality that helps to transform performers into stars—the quality of "charisma"—arises out of the star's ability to embody ideological tensions. Marilyn Monroe, for example, "has to be situated in the flux of ideas about morality and sexuality that characterized '50s America. . . . [Her] combination of sexuality and innocence is part of that flux, but one can also see her 'charisma' as being the apparent condensation of all that within her. Thus, she seemed to 'be' the very tensions that ran through the ideological life of fifties America."[6] Pickford, Temple, and other performers of girlhood likewise embodied a cluster of tensions within American society, tensions that might best be understood in relation to what Lea Jacobs describes as the "decline of sentiment" in American culture, the overturning of a traditional aesthetic of Truth and Beauty in favor of fun and and what was popularly termed "realism."

Mary Pickford's screen career reached its apex in the wake of World War I, when the United States began to assume its central position in the world's industrial economy and the conditions of a distinctly American modernity began to develop. As the economy boomed, Americans incorporated emerging technologies—automobiles, streetcars, movies—into their lives, and the texture of everyday life underwent profound change. At the same time, the United States was shifting from a largely rural nation to a predominantly urban one. Following the war, workers flocked to American cities—New York, Chicago, Detroit, Los Angeles—to labor in these new centers of machine-age production. Black sharecroppers migrated from the South, white farm workers moved from small towns and rural areas, and immigrants relocated from Asia and southern and eastern Europe to these metropolitan centers. By 1920, for the first time in its history, the majority of Americans lived in cities.[7] Inhabitants of these urban environments found themselves surrounded by people whom they didn't consider to be of their own kind, while they remembered an idealized past of homogeneous, small-town life that was intelligible and orderly, in memory at least. Further, workers experienced a diminution in their autonomy as labor in the new, industrial economy was governed by the time-clock, the boss, and the machine. At the same time, the social controls governing private life were relatively scarce given the potential for anonymity within the city.

This shift from an agrarian to an industrial economy, from a nation of small towns to one of large cities, gave rise to a host of other changes, not least of which was the proliferation of commercial amusements—including the cinema—that catered to a mass audience of wage earners. In the 1920s, the center of American cultural production had relocated from Protestant New England to polyglot

3. Child impersonator Mary Pickford. Author's collection.

New York. Whereas the WASP stronghold of New England had once been the nation's literary center, the publishing industry was now located in the borough of Manhattan, which was also the site of Tin Pan Alley, Broadway, and the Harlem Renaissance, all of which helped to bring black and Jewish artists and musicians to the center of American cultural production. As a consequence, the WASP tastes and values that had defined nineteenth-century culture began to be derided as old-fashioned in some quarters. Hollywood, overseen by Jewish movie moguls, peopled by immigrant actors and directors, and transforming working-class men and women into influential stars, was perceived as a threat to middle-class, Protestant hegemony.

During a period in which the United States became the exemplar of modernity, Pickford and Temple embodied the tensions that accompanied the nation's rapid urbanization and helped Hollywood to navigate this culture war. Both Pickford and Temple were strongly associated with their blonde hair, Pickford's falling down her back in a voluptuous cascade of curls, Temple's carefully corralled into precisely fifty-six ringlets. Their curls helped to link them to a tradition of sentimental literature that featured innocent, blonde girls modeled after Harriet Beecher Stowe's Little Eva from *Uncle Tom's Cabin.* And their curls signaled their status as innocent, an innocence bound to their whiteness and youth. In many ways, it was precisely this image of innocence that seemed most under threat in the early twentieth century: white hegemony threatened by migration and immigration, and children potentially corrupted by the burgeoning mass culture. Pickford's and Temple's indelible innocence worked to proclaim the stability of these categories in a modern setting, thereby appearing to reconcile the tensions between Victorian and modern aesthetics and values, suggesting that the treasured elements of America's past need not be lost to modern life.

Sweetness and Light

In a letter written to Alice Stuart-Wortley in 1917, the British composer Edward Elgar captured the feelings of loss and nostalgia provoked by industrialization and the mechanized killing of World War I: "Everything good & nice & clean & fresh & sweet is far away—never to return."[8] His was a sentiment shared by many who understood the changes that attended rapid industrialization in terms of loss rather than progress. American film, which developed in tandem with this destruction, was experienced as both a catalyst and an antidote to this sense of loss. It was a catalyst insofar as it was representative of modernity: a nineteenth-century invention turned commercial amusement for the entertainment of audiences who labored in the industrial economy. And it was an antidote to the extent that it offered a respite from the hurly burly of modern life.

Elgar's mourning the loss of what was "good & nice & clean & fresh & sweet" might be understood to refer not only to the imagined simplicity of pre-industrial life but also to a public sphere that was characterized by decorum and restraint. Mary Pickford and Shirley Temple both offered the promise of reconciling old values with emerging mores, of recapturing these lost qualities and transplanting them to modern entertainments. However, more than simply appealing to conservative tastes, these stars worked, in Richard Dyer's formulation of stardom, to embody the tensions between old-fashioned values and a new, modern aesthetic.

Girlhood had been a staple of sentimental melodrama throughout the nineteenth century, associated with virtue and pathos in the multitude of stage plays that featured children: *Bootle's Baby, Editha's Burglar,* and especially *Uncle Tom's Cabin*, which was performed continuously from 1852 until the 1930s. However, American culture at the turn of the twentieth century had begun to reject sentimentality in favor of laughter and what Ann Douglas terms "terrible honesty," which was popularly termed "realism." This shift in taste is reflected in attitudes toward Little Eva, one of the central characters in the countless stage adaptations of *Uncle Tom's Cabin.* Previously, Little Eva had been one of the most beloved characters in American culture. In the late 1870s and early 1880s, the death of little Eva was regarded as the high point of the Tom show. When one production eliminated Eva's deathbed scene in 1878, reviewers found the change "inexcusable."[9] And when the scene was interrupted by a heckler during a Boston production in 1880, "he was promptly and almost fiercely hissed into silence."[10]

However, at the turn of the century the angelic child had begun to be reviled as a manifestation of old-fashioned, sentimental culture. Eva came to be regarded as "a sickly, puling little prig,"[11] and her scenes with Uncle Tom "the most transcendent piece of claptrap known to the stage."[12] Rather than eliciting tears, Eva's preoccupation with her own death now seemed absurd: "[Eva] has become ridiculous. A child whose only subject of conversation is speculative interest in heaven and whose only yearning is to die is not now an engaging creature."[13]

This rejection of Little Eva is one manifestation of a much broader shift in American taste culture, one that saw the overturning of the ideals of Truth and Beauty that had once shaped American literature. Andreas Huyssen attributes this shift, in part, to a rejection of mass culture. He traces the development of an association of the popular arts (particularly novels) with women to the late nineteenth century, arguing that Modernism developed as a reaction formation against the perceived femininity of mass culture.[14] According to Huyssen, the rejection of idealism that began to take hold in European art and literature in the nineteenth century was also a rejection of a mass culture that had come to be defined as feminine. Similarly, Ann Douglas identifies a "matricidal" impulse in both high art and popular culture during the 1920s, an impulse that was often expressed in terms of a rejection of the "feminizing" effects of sentimental culture. Under the influence of Freud, Marx, and Nietzsche, artists and writers favored brutal truths over uplift and decorum. Innocent young girls had been a staple of nineteenth-century sentimental art and literature, and they were anathema to modernism.[15]

Hollywood was not untouched by the sea change in popular and high-art aesthetics. Lea Jacobs demonstrates that, during the 1920s, Hollywood filmmakers and film reviewers, too, rejected sentiment in favor of naturalist aesthetics. Tracing what she describes as the "history of the decline of sentiment," Jacobs demonstrates that during the 1920s trade reviewers evaluated films in accordance with an aesthetic that rejected the sentimentalism that had dominated American tastes just a decade earlier.

Hollywood's celebration of girlhood would therefore seem to be at odds with the general trend in American mass culture. Even before Pickford adapted such classic novels as *Daddy Long Legs, Rebecca of Sunnybrook Farm,* or *Pollyanna* to the screen in the late teens, these stories were considered old-fashioned. They came in for as much invective as they did praise, maligned as saccharine and overly sentimental. Writing of Ruth Chatterton's performance as Judy in the Broadway production of *Daddy Long Legs*, one reviewer described the play as "sentimentalism sentimentally interpreted, [a] turnip smothered in sugar, offered as an apple of life." Audiences' craving for the empty calories of sugary sentiment is attributed to the drab monotony of modern life: "living lives emotionally impoverished, performing dull chores or engaged in routine jobs, they sink back in blissfulness at this version of a dream come true. . . . [I]n monotonous lives there is a great craving for sweetness, and so, since the disguise is plausible, the general public is glad to be cheated to indulge in this perversion of life."[16] The review captures the emerging terms by which popular performances were understood. No longer associated with uplift, sentiment was now viewed with suspicion, understood to be a means of manipulation rather than inspiration, a drug to dull the senses rather than a stimulant to moral feeling.

And yet the emergent taste culture was far from universally celebrated. For every reviewer who bemoaned the treacly sentiment of *Rebecca of Sunnybrook Farm* or *Pollyanna*, there were others who railed against the vulgarity of modern literary and popular culture. For example, Edward Wagenknecht describes Lillian Gish's pale, "Dresden doll" complexion as "immensely precious: doubly so because she lives in an age when . . . everything must be frank and open, everything ruthlessly displayed, no matter how ugly it may be."[17] Indeed, Lea Jacobs understands the debates over the censorship of the movies, debates that were a key element of both Pickford's and Temple's stardom, to be a manifestation of the controversies that emerged alongside the new taste culture. "In my view," writes Jacobs, "the problem censorship posed for the industry was not simply one of enforcing a particular moral agenda but also, and more importantly, of negotiating very different sets of assumptions about the subject matter deemed fit for inclusion in a film and the manner in which it could be represented: it was an issue of decorum as much of morality."[18]

Pickford and Temple walked a fine line between these two taste cultures. On the one hand, they tapped into what Raymond Williams would term the "structures of feeling" associated with Victorian values, which were threatened by modern life.[19] One reason their films were so successful was that they appealed to the Victorian tastes that had come to be rejected by much of American popular culture. At the same time, though, they also signified American modernity. By updating a stock figure of sentimental fiction, Pickford and Temple suggested that the nation still held to traditional values, that girlhood innocence could thrive even in the soil of modern America.

Just a Grown-Up Child

Despite their shared ability to bridge the divide between Victorian and modern culture and values, Pickford and Temple emerged out of two distinct cultural moments and theatrical traditions. Whereas Temple was often promoted as a prodigy—celebrated for her precocious ability to sing, dance, and act—Pickford was a child impersonator, exhibiting a remarkable ability to transform herself from a woman into a little girl and back again. This difference points to an essential contrast in their appeal. Whereas Temple helped audiences to embrace the changes brought by modernity, Pickford invited audiences to indulge in fantasies of regression and to rebel against modern life, even as she was celebrated as a sign of the United States' emergence as a dominant force in the modern world.

Pickford was not the first woman to build a career by playing child parts. Theater critics generally identify the French actress Pauline Virginie Dejazet (1798–1875) as the progenitor of the tradition. Dejazet played child roles on stage until she retired at the age of seventy, having founded her own theater and helped to establish the career of playwright Victorien Sardou. She was so strongly associated with the practice of impersonating young boys and girls that for nearly a century, any woman who impersonated children was identified as a "dejazet." Lotta Crabtree (1847–1924), known as Miss Lotta to her public, was the premier child impersonator on the American stage of the late nineteenth century. Like Dejazet, she was equally adept at playing young boys and girls. When she was twenty-nine, one critic described her as "so youthful in appearance, and her voice . . . so childlike and sweet, that one can never think of her as a woman."[20] Also like Dejazet, Lotta continued playing juvenile roles on stage until her retirement in 1888, at the age of forty-one, by which time she had earned enough money to be declared one of the wealthiest women in the United States. The practice of child impersonation continued into the twentieth century. For example, Maude Adams was thirty-three years old and a well-established Broadway actress when she introduced Peter Pan to the American stage in 1905, the first of many women to play the role of the boy who never grew up.[21]

Pickford's stardom was one iteration of a general fascination with girlhood that Christine Gledhill links to the nation's position on the cusp of change in the early twentieth century. "If psychologically the 'threshold' implies a state of transition, the Girl is its archetypal representative: her culturally assigned femininity open to empathic feelings; her youth to mutability; her body and psychology to physical and emotional change; her cultural position veering between the carefree irresponsibility of childhood and idealism of the young adult."[22] And, just as the mutable adolescent will inevitably grow to a stable adulthood, so the nation, too, could be assured of surviving its growing pains.

In the early twentieth century, the New York stage was overrun with plays about girls' growing into womanhood, and these plays depended on ingénues who could be equally convincing as young girls and adult women. In 1913, nineteen-year-old Edith Taliaferro starred in the stage production of *Rebecca of Sunnybrook Farm*, based on the 1903 novel by Kate Douglas Wiggin. The play chronicled Rebecca's development from an imaginative young child to a young woman. Ruth Chatterton was twenty-two when she starred in *Daddy Long Legs*, adapted from Jean Webster's popular 1912 novel. Over the course of the play, her character, Judy Abbott, develops from a young orphan child into an adult woman who marries her adoptive father. Helen Hayes was seventeen years old when she played the eponymous Pollyanna, "the Glad Girl," in the 1917 stage adaptation of Eleanor H. Porter's novel *Pollyanna*, which likewise depicted the girl's transformation from childhood into young womanhood. And Mary Pickford starred in popular screen adaptations of each of these "Growing-Girl" narratives.[23]

Director D. W. Griffith translated this fascination with young girls' blossoming into womanhood to the early Hollywood screen. He was known for grooming his leading ladies to "look more innocent than anybody . . . could possibly be."[24] Pickford played her earliest film roles under his direction, and he helped her to develop the persona of "Little Mary" who was to become so beloved to screen fans. Pickford was not the only Griffith ingénue associated with child roles. Mae Marsh was twenty-one when she played fifteen-year-old "Little Sister" in Griffith's *The Birth of the Nation* (1915) and Lillian Gish was twenty-six when she appeared as the twelve-year-old waif in *Broken Blossoms* (1919), though unlike the Growing Girls of the stage, neither of these characters survives into adulthood.

Not surprisingly, Pickford's tremendous popularity led a number of production companies to develop stars who, they hoped, would rival Pickford's ability to portray both children and adults. June Caprice, the "Sunshine Girl," was Fox's answer to Pickford, while Adolf Zukor lured thirty-one-year-old Marguerite Clark from the stage to play children in such films as *The Prince and the Pauper* (Hugh Ford and Edwin S. Porter, 1915), with Clark as both prince and pauper, and *Uncle Tom's Cabin* (J. Searle Dawley, 1918), in which she played both Topsy and Eva. Lila Lee, who had begun her career as a child on the stage, where she was billed as "Cute Cuddles," made the transition to movies when she was a teenager and played the role of the child Mary in *The Secret Garden* (Gustav von Seyffertitz, 1919). Mabel Normand, Mary Miles Minter, Bessie Love, and Ella Hall were also adept at playing child roles.

The child, imbricated in the idea of modernity, provided a fantasy of escape from modern life. Even an adult in child's clothing, like Mary Pickford, could function as an antidote to modernity, "an ambassadress of sunshine to a war worn, weary world."[25] One celebration of Pickford portrayed her as an angel of sorts, come to comfort audiences worn down by the stress of modern life: "[Her] smiles beam lovingly as if in benediction upon the shabby, tired shop girl and the worn man of the listless gaze."[26] A poem submitted by one of Pickford's fans to *Motion Picture* magazine imagines Cupid crying to his mother, Venus, that the world has been turned "cold" by modern capitalism, and "hearts are being bought with gold" so that he cannot make people fall in love. Venus offers Cupid a "helpmate" in the form of "Little Mary," whose smile will restore "love and sympathy" to cold-hearted audiences.[27] And a journalist imagines audiences across the continent dipping in to the theater to enjoy a respite from the hardships of modern life: "As Cinderella, [Pickford] delights a New York broker, and for a few hours he is able to forget troubled Wall Street. In Pittsburgh at the same moment perhaps as Tess, she is temporarily divorcing an overworked millionaire manufacturer from his business cares and worries. . . . Her antics bring a chuckle from a grouchy, dyspeptic invalid at Hot Springs as readily as from some tired business man in South Bend. . . . In Denver, likely, many a busy shopper deserts enticing bargain counters to see her little favorite in the latest release."[28]

In a society that was increasingly subject to dictates of rationalized time—to time clocks and train schedules—Pickford and her imitators offered a fantasy of interrupting this forward flow and reversing time's progress. Commentators celebrated Pickford's ability to be simultaneously young and old, adult and child. Indeed, she appeared to become younger with each passing year. While photography and film often invite us to dwell on feelings of loss and nostalgia, particularly when we note the temporal gap between the child whose youth continues unabated on film while she rapidly matures off screen, Pickford and other child impersonators seemed to hold time at abeyance. "Viewing Miss Pickford [in *Little Annie Rooney*] is like turning the clock back," wrote one reviewer in 1925. "[T]his charming actress has not changed perceptibly since the early days of pictures."[29]

Pickford and other child impersonators of the silent era thus seemed to offer a relief from the inexorable forward drive of modernity while simultaneously representing modern progress. Pickford was, after all, among the first stars to emerge out of the motion picture industry, the first mass-produced sweetheart. The tension between her simplicity and naturalness and her status as a product of mechanical reproduction is captured in another poem written by a fan: "Mary Pickford blooms today/Blooms a thousand times an hour."[30] Her success was grounds for celebrating a new era of American imperialism. Revising the famous celebration of the extent of the British empire, several commentators observed that "the sun never sets on the face of Mary Pickford."[31] And her international appeal followed the path of American influence throughout the world: "The world has made her its sweetheart . . . her beautiful eyes are as familiar to the Chinese, the Filipinos, the Indians, and the South Americans as they are to Americans. . . . People of all races write to her from every part of the world."[32]

The Juvenated Gaze

Feminist film theory has taught us to consider film spectatorship in gendered terms, to understand how films speak to us as gendered subjects. In her examination of what she aptly terms Mary Pickford's "juvenated" star persona, Gaylyn Studlar attributes Pickford's popularity to female identification and male desire, arguing that Pickford offered a spectacle of freedom and power to female audiences and appealed to the "pedophilic gaze" of male admirers. "I do not wish to argue that Pickford appealed to male admirers who were actual pedophiles. What I do wish to suggest is that Pickford appealed to and through a kind of cultural pedophilia that looked to the innocent child-woman to personify nostalgic ideals of femininity."[33]

Rather than rest on the diagnosis of cultural pedophilia to explain Pickford's appeal, it is worth considering how early twentieth-century audiences interpreted their own love of Mary Pickford. Studlar and others suggest that early twentieth-century performances of childhood depend on the audience members' disavowal of their sexual desire for the performers on screen. In the early twentieth century, however, audiences understood their pleasure to rest on the disavowal of the performer's status as an adult ("I know she is a woman, but . . ."). As one reviewer exclaimed, Pickford was "so marvelously a child that the truth that she is not a child seems a monstrous fiction."[34]

So complete was audiences' disavowal of the womanliness of child impersonators that audiences did not perceive the possibility of sexual contact between a black man and a white woman when a mature actress assumed the role of Little Eva in stage performances of *Uncle Tom's Cabin*. Indeed, in at least one instance the actors playing Tom and Eva were married to one another, yet their off-stage relationship doesn't appear to have disrupted audiences' pleasure in the image of the couple on stage.[35] A review of a 1907 production of the play describes the hilarity produced when Tom held not a child but a grown woman in his arms:

> But Little Eva! . . . when she was once on the stage, the audience saw nothing else and thought of nothing else. Baby Beland, the programme gave her name, but Baby emerged from the cradle several years ago, and has never been back there since. . . . [T]he possibility of Uncle Tom's lifting her in his arms to carry her from the stage, as Uncle Toms are wont to do, made one

> fairly tremble at the possibilities. Happily, he tried nothing of the sort and Little Eva's only ride was on a pony cart.[36]

Likewise, one tommer reminisced in 1928 about a traveling Tom show that found itself without an Eva:

> But we found a girl working in a cigar store who had played Little Eva ten years before. She was at this period about 18 years old, and had the development and appearance of a woman of 35, but she was the only thing in the way of Eva that we could find, so she got the part. When she sat in my lap and asked Uncle Tom to tell her about the new Jerusalem, poor old Uncle Tom was nearly covered by her comparative immensity, but the production was a huge success.[37]

One would imagine that such performances of Little Eva by adult women would suggest the possibility of cross-racial sexual contact. However, the tradition of disavowal—in this case of the woman's adulthood— was powerful enough that these performances were greeted not with outrage but with laughter due to the fact that Eva was understood to be not sexually mature, but merely oversized.

Studlar's concept of the "pedophilic gaze" suggests that the audience shaped the meaning of a given performance and that performances of childhood became sexualized when perceived through the eyes of an adult. Early twentieth-century audiences had a very different conception of the relationship between performer and audience. Their disavowal of the child impersonator's status as a woman permitted them to be transformed from knowing adults into innocent children for the duration of a performance. For this reason, it would be more accurate to say that the child impersonators invited a juvenated rather than a pedophilic gaze; rather than being transformed into sexual objects, child impersonators were capable of transforming their spectators into innocent subjects.

Pickford's appeal may have rested on identification and desire, but at the time these were not understood to conform to a strictly gendered design. Pickford's status as a child impersonator permitted male and female audiences alike to engage in fantasies of escaping the reach of modernity even as they indulged in one of the signature amusements of modern life by going to the movies. Men and women alike were understood to identify with Pickford and other girlish stars and thereby have their youth restored, if only for the length of the movie. Indulging in Pickford's screen antics, an audience member could have "Youth brought back for an hour."[38] Ann Pennington's performance in *The Antics of Ann* was "age reducing," and Lila Lee was celebrated for her ability to "bring back memories."[39] "What man or woman hasn't a memory of his [*sic*] first love? Oh, the exquisite joy and the equally potent anguish of those affairs of tender years when we stood on the brink of the stream beyond which lay man or womanhood!"[40] And in desiring these women, audiences were understood to be indulging in a youthful, innocent eroticism. Bessie Love, for example, reminded audiences of "the little girl next door for whom you had your first desperate 'case.' Come to think of it, that's probably the reason the fans always call again after they have seen her once up on the screen."[41]

Certainly, men were romantically drawn to Pickford. Prior to her well-publicized marriage to Douglas Fairbanks in 1920, fan magazines reported that she received numerous marriage proposals from male fans who were disappointed to discover that she was already married to Owen Moore. However, women, too, were smitten by Pickford. *Photoplay*, for example, describes a female fan who was overcome by "one of those 'boarding-school crushes' which are the inevitable result of [Pickford's] popularity."[42] The perceived "inevitability" of such a crush suggests that erotic attachment on the part of female fans was not understood to be unusual, while its association with "boarding school" announces that such desire is, by definition, immature, the stuff of girlhood and therefore not particularly dangerous or disruptive.

Further, fans' adoration of Pickford and other child impersonators was understood to be built not on base desire but on an admiration for the stars' purity, an admiration that was akin to religious devotion. "Why do the people love Mary?" asked Vachel Lindsay,

> Because of a certain aspect of her face in her highest mood. Botticelli painted her portrait many centuries ago. . . . The people are hungry for this fine and spiritual thing that Botticelli painted in the faces of his muses and heavenly creatures. Because the mob catch the very glimpse of it in Mary's face, they follow her night after night in the films. They are never quite satisfied with the plays, because the managers are not artists enough to know they should sometimes put her into sacred pictures and not have her always the village hoyden. . . . But perhaps in this argument I have but betrayed myself as Mary's infatuated partisan."[43]

For Lindsay, the motion picture industry, churning out cheap melodrama, was not up to the task of providing appropriate vehicles for the sacred charms of Pickford and her contemporary, Marguerite Clark. Yet audiences returned to the movie theater in hopes of catching a glimpse of "this fine and spiritual thing" that was as impervious to modernity as a Botticelli painting. Writing nearly twenty-five years after Pickford's retirement from the screen, Edward Wagenknecht explains: "I should have felt it blasphemous" to think of her sexually.[44] Pickford's appeal was linked to her ability to convey sexual innocence and thereby invite audiences to mirror her regression. "[H]er greatest charm lies in the sublimation of her sex. . . . [T]hough adorably lovable, she is as sexless as a young Greek goddess."[45] Indeed, in offering a respite from the demands of modernity and sexuality alike,

Pickford and other child impersonators invited audiences to regress to a childlike pleasure untroubled by licentiousness.

The Heart of a Woman, the Head of a Man, the Body of a Child

Pickford's girlishness also helped audiences to make sense of modern gender roles in the years following World War I. The late teens and 1920s saw women's growing presence in the public sphere and their rejection of the ideal of sexual purity. Together, Pickford and her imitators helped to define women's new behaviors in terms of immaturity rather than rebellion.

Not least of the changes that were disrupting American life in the early twentieth century was the redefinition of womanhood. American women were, after all, given the vote in 1920, when Pickford was at the height of her popularity. The term "New Woman" was coined during the Progressive Era to describe the women who forged identities outside the home. But the meaning of the term shifted in the early twentieth century as a new generation of women enjoyed an unprecedented degree of independence. Nancy Cott has identified the 1910s as a turning point in women's political activism, characterizing this period as providing the "grounding of modern feminism." During this period, a new generation of women—more diverse and more radical than the feminists of previous generations—began to rally for women's suffrage and sexual freedom, rejecting the ideal of the "angel in the house" that defined middle-class femininity in terms of sexual purity and self-sacrifice and which had undergirded the rhetoric of nineteenth-century abolitionists and suffragettes.[46] Alongside the New Woman emerged a new class of women often identified as "women adrift," working-class women who were unbound to fathers or husbands and who enjoyed a degree of economic independence by virtue of their wage labor.[47]

Not only were these New Women and "women adrift" more visible than previous generations of women had been, they also subscribed to new sexual norms. Paula Fass has shown that during the late teens and throughout the 1920s young high school and college students as well as working-class girls were helping to redefine sexual mores, contributing to a "generation gap" and "sexual revolution" decades before these became household terms in the 1960s. The burgeoning consumer culture catered to American youth who embraced new fads in fashion, music, and dance. Young women adopted behaviors that were once the reserve of prostitutes—smoking, spending time unchaperoned in the company of men, wearing hemlines above the ankle, and bobbing their hair—and their elders often interpreted these, along with the new ideal of female sexual fulfillment, as signs of young women's sexual promiscuity and therefore a threat to the traditional family.[48] While Mary Pickford was at the peak of her stardom, the flapper emerged as a stock character of American cinema. Several of the child impersonators who had hoped to rival Pickford began to embrace these flapper roles. Bessie Love, for example, was introduced to film audiences as an innocent child-woman with long, blonde curls, but by the mid-1920s she had bobbed her hair and was dancing the Charleston on screen.

The tension between old and new ideals of femininity was played out in the relationship between Pickford's on- and off-screen personae. An examination of the discourse about Pickford suggests that her appeal to men and women alike was related to her ability to be both child and woman, both old-fashioned and modern. Studlar suggests that Pickford's impersonations of childhood helped to render the more transgressive elements of her career—her role as a powerful figure in the film industry and her somewhat scandalous marriage to Douglas Fairbanks—acceptable to audiences who might otherwise have rejected these signs of New Womanhood. I propose that it was not Pickford's childishness alone that was responsible for her immense popularity. Rather, this very tension—between childhood innocence and adult knowledge—was the source of her widespread appeal. Published responses to Pickford and other juvenated stars' performances, both on and off screen, suggest that it was their ability to traverse the boundary between adult and child that was the source of their popularity.

Contradiction is at the heart of Hollywood stardom. In his history of the development of the star system in American film, Richard deCordova points to the distinction between what he identifies as "picture personalities" and "stars."[49] As production companies developed relatively stable troupes of actors during the nickelodeon era, a recognizable performer—Little Mary, for example—was known to audiences entirely through her film performances. Around 1913, however, newspapers and magazines began to carry stories about the off-screen lives of film actors. According to deCordova, the discourse of stardom developed out of the production of knowledge about the on-screen and off-screen lives of the stars. Initially, the stars' off-screen lives carefully mirrored their on-screen personae; girlish stars were imagined to be as girlish off-screen as they were on. However, by the end of the teens, print journalism was offering readers insights into their favorite stars that could not be gleaned from their film appearances alone, producing what Richard Dyer identifies as the public/private dialectic that characterizes film stardom.[50] Mary Pickford's fans were well aware that, while she might skillfully play the helpless waif on screen, off screen she was a savvy businesswoman who earned a good deal more than did her husband, Owen Moore. (The joke was that, since their marriage in 1911, he was "owin' no more."[51]) Thus, one element of fans' pleasure in stars lies in recognizing this contradiction between the star's on- and off-screen personae, in knowing that Little Mary Pickford was "really" one of Hollywood's most powerful producers and stars; or that while Shirley Temple might play with dolls on screen, off screen she "really" went by the nickname "Butch," and her most treasured plaything was a toy machine gun.

For Pickford, this contrast between on- and off-screen personae was one means by which she embodied the tensions between traditional and modern norms of femininity. As a successful businesswoman and a divorcee, Mary Pickford was the embodiment of New Womanhood. Far from downplaying Pickford's business acumen, the press celebrated her off-screen accomplishments. Her fans were well aware that, while she might play the waif on screen, she was a powerful woman in her own right; upon her marriage to Douglas Fairbanks, the *Boston Post* described the bride as a "moving picture actress, scenario writer, business woman, authoress, and multimillionaress . . . [whose] income was twice that of Fairbanks.'"[52]

Throughout her career, journalists noted the contradiction inherent in the fact that this exemplar of modern womanhood was also the embodiment of girlhood. "She has the manner and simplicity of a child. Yet she speaks with the philosophical directness of a woman of 40. In fact she is but 20 years old."[53] Publicity reveled in her contradictions: "Though married, she is just a grown-up child. . . . A frail, tiny child of unutterable sweetness, with her halo of golden hair, her mystic hazel eyes, and her quizzical smile, sometimes mirthful, sometimes melancholy—she had a habit of talking as if she were an old woman and her mother an infant."[54]

The delicacy of her appearance and her lovable demeanor helped to mitigate any threat that might be associated with her status as a powerful businesswoman and thereby produce a new interpretation of women's increased presence in the public sphere. Rather than suggesting a break with traditional ideals of femininity, Pickford's status as a film producer was imagined to be an outgrowth of her childlike charm. When she began to produce her own films in 1918, the *Los Angeles Times* reported that "Mary is doing all the casting her very own self, and neither Wellington Wales, her manager, nor Marshall Neilan, her director, can do anything about it when Mary sets her tiny foot down. . . . Oh, yes, and she helped Agnes Johnston write the screen version of *Daddy Long Legs.*"[55] The invocations of baby talk ("her very own self") and temper tantrums (setting "her tiny foot down") evoke the image of Pickford as the neglected little girl Gwen in *The Poor Little Rich Girl* more than they do a suffragette or New Woman.

Further, Pickford's films associate female rebellion with childhood, assuring audiences that the New Woman isn't new at all but merely an overgrown tomboy. Just as Pickford seemed to simultaneously embody adult and child, so she also blended masculine and feminine qualities in a manner that, due to her ability to signify girlishness, was comforting rather than threatening. She had "the heart of a woman, the head of a man, and the body of a child."[56]

Pickford and other girl impersonators helped to define adolescence at the very moment when the category was being invented. The concept of adolescence was only beginning to develop during the early twentieth century, largely through the writings of G. Stanley Hall, who helped to define adolescence with the publication of his book *Adolescence: Its Psychology and Its Relations to Physiology, Anthropology, Sociology, Sex, Crime, and Religion* in 1904 and who introduced Sigmund Freud to American audiences when Freud accepted his invitation to speak at Clark University in 1909.

In "Femininity and Adolescence," Barbara Hudson argues that girls are caught between two competing discourses: the discourse of adolescence, which she identifies as a masculine construct, and that of femininity, which demands that girls be passive and dependent, tender and emotional, not competitive, adventurous, aggressive, or ambitious. According to Hudson, girls' behavior is evaluated as normative or aberrant depending upon the framework being used to describe it, such that "so often if [girls] are fulfilling the expectations of femininity they will be disappointing those of adolescence, and vice versa."[57] Whereas girls might be admonished for being unfeminine when they engage in behaviors associated with masculinity, their feminine behaviors are equally at risk of being considered prematurely sexual.

Though Hudson mentions that adolescence emerged as a category "at the same time as the steam engine," she draws primarily from mid-twentieth-century discourses in her characterization of adolescence as masculine.[58] However, in the early twentieth century, the category was not so clearly gendered. Childhood had long been associated with femininity. In her examination of nineteenth-century authors' and artists' preoccupation with girlhood, *Men in Wonderland*, Catherine Robson argues that men's fascination with little girls arose, in part, from the nineteenth-century association of childhood with femininity; the middle-class nursery, overseen by mothers and nannies, was a feminine realm lost to boys when they were sent away to school. Writing about, painting, and photographing young girls, artists and authors like Lewis Carroll were working to recapture their own "lost" childhoods. Conversely, psychologists and other experts in the newly developed field of child psychology were preoccupied with boyhood, as Kenneth Kidd demonstrates.[59]

Pickford and other child impersonators helped to establish the association of adolescence with masculinity even as they contributed to the prominence of adolescent girlhood in the popular imagination. In their performances, they helped to identify girls' rebelliousness with immature masculinity that would be exchanged for feminine decorum when the girl was awakened to heterosexual desire and made the transition to womanhood. Bessie Love reinforces the idea that adolescence is a period of freedom from the constraints of adult femininity when she explains to *Motion Picture* magazine that her character in *Spring of the Year* "is not at all grown up—I'm just a mischievous, sixteen-year-old girl all the way through."[60] Over and over again in their films, child impersonators engage in all manner of masculine activities only to be transformed into elegant young women when they fall in love. Indeed, Mary Pickford, Mae Marsh, Bessie Love, and Marguerite Clark all played characters who disguise themselves as boys. Marguerite Clark's 1917 film *The Amazons* is a particularly compelling example of the genre. In the film, Clark plays "Lord Tommy," one of three sisters who have been brought up as boys by a mother who had hoped to have sons. On a trip to London, Tommy becomes bored and "dresses herself in nifty chappy's evening clothes to seek excitement in a seedy music hall. There she flirts too much with a girl usher, punches a rowdy, and makes her escape by dashing into a taxicab, alighting into the welcome arms of Bill Hinckley."[61] Initially he mistakes her for a boy, but the two fall in love and her mother, "seeing that girls will be girls, . . . gives them her blessing."[62] The film ends in a triple wedding.

Even when they're not disguising themselves as boys, these child impersonators offered a pleasing fantasy that the ideal of female purity had not been lost to the era's flappers and New Women. By identifying rebelliousness with youth, these stars and their films offered audiences the promise that these behaviors were inherently innocent and that, in any case, girls would soon grow out of them. Publicity for Bessie Love, one of Pickford's numerous imitators, invokes the star's "boyishness" in order to assert her childishness and, implicitly, her sexlessness.

> [O]utside of working hours Bessie does not sew socks for soldiers or string ribbons in her lingerie. She lets naturalness take its course, and the wholesome boyish spirit, her dominant characteristic, bubbles over. Bessie's mother has long since given up trying to persuade her daughter to wear fashionable clothes such as famous screen stars are supposed to effect. . . . [H]eavy, ribbed boy's stockings are not only Bessie's choice for apparel, but are the only garments which do not succumb to the wear and tear of baseball and kindred sports. . . . She excels in tennis, drives her own car, and confesses that her only grief in life is that she is not a boy, so that she can indulge in the "greatest game in the world, baseball." . . . She's a most boyish, girlish, individual is this Bessie Love.[63]

Pickford's characters can be seen indulging in the very practices that scandalized the nation when they were enacted by flappers. In *Daddy Long Legs* she and a young boy become drunk on cider; in *The Hoodlum*, she dances the shimmy with another young boy; and she was habitually costumed in short skirts that revealed her legs. However, within the context of Pickford's films, these activities signaled her status as a child rather than the disruption of gender roles. Much of the humor of her films arises from Pickford's acting out behaviors defined as masculine. In *Rebecca of Sunnybrook Farm*, for example, Rebecca engages in an aggressive rivalry with another girl, Minnie Smellie, while in *The Poor Little Rich Girl* she enjoys a vigorous mud fight with a group of neighborhood boys. For Pickford's girls, competitiveness, aggression, and rule-breaking are all masculine attributes that will be shed with the transition to womanhood.

These daring and adventuresome characters were described as "hoydens," "tomboys," and "gamines," terms whose association with girlhood implied that the stars' flirtation with these behaviors would be brief, that they would one day become more ladylike. When Pickford played the title role in *Little Lord Fauntleroy*, critics observed that she was "hoydenish rather than boyish."[64] Pickford predicted that "when I grow too old for hoyden parts I will be relegated to the discard," which indeed she was.[65] After she cut off her hair in 1928, Mary Pickford's career effectively came to an end. Without the blonde curls that had signified her innocence for nearly two decades, she lost much of her appeal.

The Age of Rebecca Is Gone

Shirley Temple emerged as Pickford's heir in 1934, in part, because women's impersonations of childhood no longer worked to capture the tensions between Victorian and modern values. Rather, they highlighted these tensions and made them appear more irreconcilable than ever. The difficulty juvenated stars had in negotiating the line between sweetness and sophistication points to how essential this was to Pickford's ongoing popularity.

During the early sound era, a new generation of female stars vied to become America's next "sweetheart." In the early 1930s, Janet Gaynor, one of Hollywood's top-drawing stars, seemed poised to become the successor to Mary Pickford. Before Temple signed a contract with Fox, twenty-six-year-old Janet Gaynor was celebrated as "the curly-haired child of the Fox lot."[66] And, before Temple was announced as the heir to Pickford's title as "America's Sweetheart," Gaynor appeared in remakes of films that Pickford had made famous, *Daddy Long Legs* (Alfred Santell, 1931) and *Tess of the Storm Country* (Alfred Santell, 1932). And, like so many of the childlike women of the silent era, Gaynor played girls who impersonate boys; in *Two Girls Wanted* (Alfred Green, 1927), for example, she dresses as a boy in order to secure a job. Indeed, journalists recognized the affinity between Gaynor and Mary Pickford: "It is possible that under her sweetness, her loveliness, lies something of that same fire and strength so unexpected and so wonderful in Mary Pickford."[67]

However, when Fox cast Gaynor to star in *Rebecca of Sunnybrook Farm*, Gaynor refused the role, considering it "too juvenile."[68] Likewise, when RKO attempted to repeat the success of George Cukor's 1933 adaptation of *Little Women* by casting Katharine Hepburn and Ginger Rogers in *Mother Carey's Chickens*, Hepburn bought out her contract with the studio rather than be typecast in old-fashioned "sweetheart" roles, and Rogers also bowed out. Likewise, Anne Shirley—who took her name from the eponymous character in *Anne of Green Gables*, in which she had starred in 1934—complained in 1936 about being "a bit surfeited with Pollyanna roles."[69]

Apparently, an ambitious ingénue could no longer hope to build a career on "Pollyanna" or "sweetness and light" roles, as they were dismissively called. Indeed, Gaynor, Hepburn, and Rogers enjoyed celebrated careers following these rebellions. However, Anne Shirley remained second-tier, starring in films like *M'Liss* (1936), which Pickford had brought to the screen in 1918; *Mother Carey's Chickens* (1938), based on a novel by Kate Douglas Wiggin, who had also written *Rebecca of Sunnybrook Farm*; and a sequel to *Anne of Green Gables*, *Anne of Windy Poplars* (1940).[70]

Unlike Mary Pickford's films, which had been celebrated for their universal appeal, sound versions of classic Growing-Girl narratives highlighted a rift in American taste culture. Although these films were popular in the small-town and rural areas and in second-run neighborhood theaters that catered to the family trade, they were dismissed by film critics and "sophisticated" audiences who, presumably, objected to their sentimentality. *Anne of Green Gables*, for example, could be expected to "do somewhat better in neighborhood than in the more sophisticated downtown theaters."[71] The film critics, on the other hand, declared, "It is, no doubt, the fault of our narrow, urban existence that we local filmgoers are likely to find that an hour and a half of bucolic charm is just a trifle too much for us."[72] Indeed, the success of *Little Women* was attributed to the film's having "modernists" at its helm, effectively "pepping up" the old-fashioned story. The *Los Angeles Times* predicted that "something vastly wonderful ought to come out of casting Katharine Hepburn in *Little Women* and assigning George Cukor to direct. One step further and it would be Greta Garbo and Ernst Lubitsch."[73] Further, the screenwriters were understood to typify "modernity and sophistication."[74] By contrast, *Rebecca of Sunnybrook Farm*, starring Marian Nixon in the role originally meant for Janet Gaynor, was "done with an odd co-mingling of half modern, half old-time values, with the old-time perhaps most prevailing."[75] The film's dismal box-office returns were attributed to the story's being out of date; *The New York Times* suggested that "the age of *Rebecca* has gone—alas, perhaps, but undoubtedly gone."[76]

In the wake of these failures, and with the emergence of a new age category between childhood and adulthood—the teenager—the child impersonator became obsolete. One measure of the demise of this practice can be seen in the response to Judy Garland's portrayal of Dorothy in *The Wizard of Oz* (Victor Fleming et al., 1939). In Frank Baum's novel, Dorothy is five or six years old. In the first film version of Dorothy's adventures in Oz, *The Wonderful Wizard of Oz* (Otis Turner, 1910), Dorothy was played by nine-year-old Bebe Daniels. When Baum brought Dorothy to the screen in *His Majesty, the Scarecrow of Oz* (L. Frank Baum, 1914), she was played by twenty-nine-year-old Violet MacMillan (in previous Oz films, MacMillan had played a munchkin boy and a king). And in the 1925 *The Wizard of Oz* (Larry Semon), nineteen-year-old Dorothy Dwan enacted the role of Dorothy. Clearly, audiences had little difficulty in accepting either child or adult actresses in the role.

When Samuel Goldwyn bought the rights to the book in 1933 as a vehicle for Eddie Cantor, he considered casting Mary Pickford or Helen Hayes as Dorothy. However, Cantor turned down the role, and Twentieth Century-Fox considered buying the rights as a vehicle for Shirley Temple.[77] But, of course, MGM ultimately bought the rights to the book and, when they couldn't borrow Temple, opted to use the lavish production as a showcase for the talent of one of their own young stars, sixteen-year-old Judy Garland. The studio raised Dorothy's age to twelve and constricted her adolescent body in binding undergarments. Years later, Garland would recall: "They decided my bosom was too big. . . . [S]o at first they tried to tape it down. Then a woman turned up who was called the Cellini of the corset world. She made me a corset of steel and I was laced up in that. I looked like a male Mary Pickford by the time they got through with me!"[78] For the most part, Garland's notices were good, though some reviewers pointed to the discrepancy between her age and that of the character she played. However, the efforts that went into reshaping Garland's body suggest that what had once been one of the distinct pleasures of such impersonations—the woman's ability to be simultaneously adult and child—now threatened to undermine the film's verisimilitude.

Despite the myriad pleasures associated with women's impersonations of childhood, the practice of women playing young girls in anything other than brief comedy sketches began its decline in the 1930s, and by 1948, when Jennifer Jones portrayed the supernaturally growing girl in *Portrait of Jennie* (William Dieterle, 1948), critics complained that she was "not a very convincing little girl, since she looks like nothing so much as a sinister midget."[79] Fanny Brice entertained radio audiences with her portrayal of Baby Snooks from 1938 until her death at the age of sixty in 1951. However, women no longer regularly impersonated young girls on the screen. It was out of this void that Shirley Temple emerged as Hollywood's top-grossing star.

Two Great Women

Like Mary Pickford, Temple appealed to audiences troubled by the new aesthetic that rejected sentiment in favor of "realism." Her films were either celebrated or derided for their sentimentalism. Ads for *Dimples* promoted the film's sentimental appeal: "You'll love [Temple] . . . laugh at [Frank Morgan] . . . and wink away a tear or two when you see these sweethearts nearly parted."[80] And part of Temple's popularity lay not only in her ability to touch the hearts of her audience, but in the image of men crying over her performances as well. In the pressbook for *The Little Colonel*, for instance, Fox included a publicity piece describing the film's director, David Butler, crying over the film's script. The piece deliberately contrasts the director's girth with his capacity for tears, juxtaposing his powerful build with his sentimentality: "Huge director David Butler, who tips the beams at 235 pounds, admits he's a 'pushover' on pathos."[81] It was not only the director who indulged in the sentimental charms of Temple, but the entire film crew as well: "I notice that when something starts my tear ducts flowing, about a dozen hard-boiled carpenters, grips, and electricians are also frisking out handkerchiefs."[82]

While Pickford demonstrated that the modern woman could still embody traditional values, Temple helped to establish that modern culture was not incompatible with girlhood innocence. Pickford stood on one side of the taste divide that she helped Hollywood navigate, Temple on the other. In a 1918 article for *Photoplay*, a journalist favorably contrasts Pickford's screen appearances to those performances that were born of the new "realism": "Once a popular actress in New York, portraying a slavey, desired realism—and in one scene blew her nose. The next day a critic wrote in effect: 'Miss ___ is determined to be natural. Very well, let her have realism if she likes. But please, Miss ___, do not blow your nose!' Mary Pickford, so to speak, never blows her nose."[83] Twenty years later the same magazine approvingly described Shirley Temple's response when her director, Allan Dwan, "accidentally burped on the set [of *Rebecca of Sunnybrook Farm*]. Shirley regarded him sympathetically, saying, 'What's the matter? Your shoes too tight?'"[84]

Gilbert Seldes and Graham Greene, both proponents of the new aesthetic, approvingly identified an unexpected bawdiness in Temple's films in addition to the sentimentality they expected to find there. To Greene, her performance in *Captain January* was "a little depraved, with an appeal interestingly decadent," while Seldes described Shirley Temple's laughter as "positively boisterous, a sort of hoot at the pomposity of the entire grown-up world."[85] What Seldes is surprised to discover in Temple is that she is not merely a cute child—he describes himself as trying his utmost to avoid her films due to his distaste for their presumed sweetness—but that her cuteness is accompanied by a refreshing disregard for propriety and a contempt for what he refers to as "bunk."[86]

Seldes was convinced that Shirley Temple's popularity lay not in her affinity with Mary Pickford but in her similarity to a very different star: Mae West. Temple, wrote Seldes, brought to the screen an air of command, "the certainty that thereafter, you would never look at another woman again, which you find in every movement of Mae West across the screen." For Seldes, these "two great women" were linked not just by virtue of their star presence but also by their "contempt for most of the things we consider important," a contempt "Mae West is always expressing by a look of the eye, or more significant, bodily gestures." Seldes continues:

> I am thoroughly convinced, not only by herself, but by her audience, that the celebrated dimpling and cuteness have very little to do with [Temple's]

> real power, because at her good moments something like a growl of satisfaction arises from the men in the audience. Women may gasp at her charms because it is traditional to care for the sweetness of all children, but I take it that men have plenty of that in their homes, and their roar of approval is not for what is sweet but for what is mocking and hearty and contemptuous.[87]

In his assessment of Temple, Seldes captures an essential aspect of her stardom: her ability to address the rapid changes in popular taste that the Hollywood film industry found itself navigating during the early twentieth century.[88]

However, unlike Janet Gaynor and the other girlish women of the early sound era, this taste divide was redefined in terms not of class or region but of gender, with men appreciating her bucking of authority and women indulging in her sentimental appeal. While Pickford's audience was not explicitly gendered—men and women alike were understood to identify with and desire her—Twentieth Century-Fox actually promoted the understanding that Temple's audience was divided along gendered lines. In "Shirley Temple: Dreams Come True," Kathryn Fuller-Seeley makes the surprising observation that during the four years that Temple was named No. 1 at the box office (1935–1938), she was not a particularly strong draw for the studio-owned theaters. Indeed, Fuller-Seeley reports that Mae West's *Going to Town* (1935) actually beat out Temple's films at the box office, and this in a year that one of Temple's most popular films—*The Little Colonel*—was released.[89] Fuller-Seeley attributes this discrepancy—between the *Motion Picture Herald*'s naming Temple the top box-office star and box-office receipts that suggested the child's films did only middling business—to the fact that these two indicators of popularity were based on reports from two completely different sets of theaters. While the studio-owned and affiliated motion picture palaces supplied information on box-office receipts, it was independent exhibitors who identified Temple as their top box-office draw. Independent exhibitors operated movie houses in rural areas and small towns, and they ran second-run theaters in major cities—what *Variety* referred to as the "sticks" and "nabes" (for neighborhood theaters)—that relied on the "family" audience, whereas the picture palaces catered to more diverse audiences in major cities.

Although Seldes and other critics identified Temple's appeal in gendered terms, her popularity is best understood as regional. She appealed to the "sticks" and the "nabes" more than she did to urban audiences, who were generally identified as "sophisticated." "While no sources quantified the amount of ticket sales her films reaped for those small-town theaters," writes Fuller-Seeley, "as measured by the deliriously happy reactions of independent theater managers it must have been huge."[90] Indeed, in the "What the Picture Did for Me" column of the *Motion Picture Herald*, in which independent exhibitors exchanged information about promotional techniques and audiences' responses to the movies they showed, exhibitors exclaimed exuberantly over Temple. Her films repeatedly sold out and broke house records for independent exhibitors, who described their patrons' driving great distances through bad storms to see her films. According to at least one exhibitor, she drew audiences who did not customarily attend movies.[91] Further, independent exhibitors celebrated her films as an antidote to the risqué material that played well in the cities and that Hollywood produced in great quantities. As one exhibitor exclaimed, "The starved small town people, sick of the introvert junk based on the decadent novels turned out by a generation of fifth-rate writers who have lost the meaning of humanity, turn eagerly to the clever unselfconscious child who says something modern novelists lack genius to say."[92]

It was, in part, the discrepancy between audience tastes at the motion picture palaces and the independent theaters that had given rise to the Production Code in the first place. Hollywood in the 1920s and 1930s was an oligopoly in which a handful of studios were responsible for the bulk of theatrical film production in the United States. As a result, the studios were able to dictate the terms under which independent exhibitors rented their films. During the 1930s, the studios routinely strong-armed exhibitors into engaging in blind bidding and block booking. Under the former practice, exhibitors agreed to rent a studio's films without knowing precisely what those films would be, and the latter meant that they could not select the films that would appeal to their patrons but must book a studio's entire catalog for a given season. As a result, independent exhibitors had little discretion over which films they showed in their theaters beyond choosing to enter into an agreement with one studio over another.

Further, although independent exhibitors represented more than half the ticket sales in the United States, the studios made far more profit off the films shown in their own theaters than they did from film rentals to independent exhibitors. This meant that the studios had much more financial incentive to appeal to large, urban audiences than they did to the more conservative audiences living in small cities and towns or in working-class neighborhoods. Unable to select the films that would appeal to their audiences and less insulated from an irate public than were the studio heads, independent exhibitors joined religious and women's groups in calling on the studios to enforce the Production Code in an effort to pressure the studios to make films that would not offend the sensibilities of small-town and neighborhood audiences.

The division in taste was largely attributed to class; exhibitors identified urban audiences as both more crude and higher class than their middle-brow clientele. In her analysis of the "What the Picture Did for Me" columns that ran in the *Motion Picture Herald* Fuller-Seeley demonstrates that the exhibitors often interpreted their audiences' responses to the studios' films in relation to larger conflicts associated with the growing urban/rural divide. According to Fuller-Seeley, "The small-town exhibitors tended to lump together two divergent groups of films into the 'urban' category. On the one hand, they had argued that 'city' films were too sexually provocative and violent and would appeal mostly to the immigrant working class. On the other hand, 'urban' films could be wordy drawing room farces featuring indolent aristocrats."[93] By contrast, the exhibitors who wrote in to the *Motion Picture Herald* "represented themselves and their rural audiences as a 'wholesome' middle ground that rejected the moral laxity of the city's poorer ethnic thrill seekers and the haughtiness of the city's lascivious rich. . . . [Exhibitors] insisted that city movie audiences were the polar opposite of their village clientele in terms of social class, morality, and cultural taste."[94] Thus, Fuller-Seeley's research suggests that Temple's films appealed to audiences who felt threatened by both the crass sensationalism embraced by the working class and the cosmopolitanism of urban sophisticates.

Temple's popularity with these exhibitors therefore points to an ability to appeal to the tastes of a very specific audience, one that embraced traditional values rather than modern tastes. In the words of *Motion Picture Daily*, Shirley Temple offered "entertainment for any kind of audience, either urban or rural" and was "highly exploitable screen merchandise for any kind of exhibitor."[95] For independent exhibitors who had been hit much harder than the studios by the stock market crash of October 1929 and by the expenses associated with the transition to sound, the emergence of a child star who appealed to conservative family audiences was welcome news indeed.

I'm not suggesting here that Temple appeared in films that would appeal to audiences on both sides of the sentimental/sophisticated divide. Her films were roundly criticized as overly sentimental and cute. Audiences who did not respond to Temple's sentimental appeal were often described as "sophisticated," suggesting that the modern, cynical aesthetic was still associated with the urban elite in the 1930s. Similarly, urban papers were likely to dismiss her films as "skillful hokum."[96] The *New York Times*, for example, described *The Little Colonel* as "shrewdly spiced with humor" and having a "winning quality in the utter shamelessness of its sentimental phases," while *Time* magazine mocked the "embarrassingly sentimental ballad" Temple sings to Frank Morgan in *Dimples*.[97] Nonetheless, Temple's stardom clearly helped conservative audiences and exhibitors engage in the new taste culture without threatening their class values. And, by shifting the discourse about the taste divide from class to gender, Temple's presence made it possible to include "sophisticated" elements in films for an audience that preferred the sentimental mode of filmmaking. In this way, she embodied a tension between urban and small-town values that troubled Depression-era America much as Pickford had embodied both modern and old-fashioned femininity.

Grim Old Maids

While newspaper reviews and exhibitors' reports suggest that the taste divide that Temple helped to negotiate was mapped onto region and social class, with middle-brow audiences in small towns and rural areas embracing Temple while "sophisticated" reviewers in urban areas dismissed her films as "Victorian hokum," Temple's films themselves worked to locate cultural divisions along a gendered axis, much as Seldes had articulated the aesthetic divide between fun and decorum in terms of gender rather than class or region. According to Jacobs, the preference for sentiment had not yet been attributed to women in the 1920s. However, as Seldes's review attests, by the time Shirley Temple emerged as a star, women were already expected to be more responsive to "sweetness" and "traditional" sentimental pleasures than men, who craved "what is mocking and hearty and contemptuous."

Shirley Temple's films entered into debates about film censorship by aligning unmarried women—stand-ins for the religious and women's groups who actively lobbied the film industry to reign in its excesses—with repression and associating the child with fun. An early story outline for *Baby Take a Bow*, written close on the heels of the release of *Stand Up and Cheer*, proposes that the film's central conflict revolve around a reformer's efforts to keep Temple's character, Shirley, off the stage. The film was to take place in 1908 and to pit Shirley and her father against an overzealous agent of the Gerry Society. Although the script was never produced, the treatment introduced a number of elements that would recur throughout Temple's career.

The film was to open with Shirley and her father performing in a small vaudeville theater. In the audience, two women look on disapprovingly. One is Miss Mabel Walters, "a women's club officer—a grim but *not type* old maid—and her best friend, another earnest reformer."[98] Walters is a member of the Society for the Prevention of Cruelty to Children, which was popularly known as the Gerry Society and was dedicated to keeping children off the stage: "Tight-lipped, she is holding forth to her friend, somewhat as follows: 'There! Now do you see what I mean? A little young child like that, forced to prance around the stage at this hour of the night—and why? So that her lummox of a father can roll in money! It's an outrage and it's got to be stopped! . . . He has made her into a little show-off and smart-aleck! What kind of life is that for a child!'"[99] Walters's fears—that the child is being exploited for profit and that she is becoming conscious of her own appeal ("a little show-off")—echo the concerns that shaped discourse about child stars at the time. However, Walters is immediately shown to be wrong. It is Shirley's irrepressible desire to perform that leads her to the stage, not her father's greed. He actively disciplines Shirley when she shows signs of becoming a "stage child," insisting that she forget the stage the moment they leave the theater.

In the story outline, Walters successfully removes Shirley from her father's care only to have the child run away to find him. The outline suggests that the child's welfare is best left to her parent—Shirley's father has his daughter's best interest at heart—rather than the state, in this case in the guise of Miss Walters. And, rather than reflecting a genuine concern for the child's welfare, Walters's objections stem from a general disapproval of the theater, echoing a similar complaint lodged against the Gerry Society.

Although these characters were dropped in favor of a contemporary story in which Shirley's father is an ex-con rather than a vaudevillian, the proposed story for *Baby Take a Bow* does bear a striking resemblance to several other Temple vehicles. In film after film, misguided spinsters stand between Temple and her audience. In *Curly Top* (1935), the sour headmistress of the orphanage where Shirley lives disapproves of the child's past as a circus performer and will not allow her to sing and dance for the other children. In *Dimples* (1936), a wealthy dowager wants to adopt Shirley and end her career as a street performer. In *Rebecca of Sunnybrook Farm* (1938), Shirley's aunt frowns upon the theater, and the child must sneak out of the house at night to make her radio debut. And in *Little Miss Broadway* (1938), a meddlesome landlady threatens to evict Shirley's adopted father and send her back to the orphanage on the grounds that the child's morals are endangered by her association with actors. In each case, the child's desire to perform before an audience prevails over the woman's efforts to restrain her, and the audience's desire to witness her performance is satisfied.

Often in her films the audience is aligned with a man's indulgence in the pleasure of Shirley Temple's image in opposition to a disciplinary gaze. This is played out in *Curly Top* when Edward (John Boles) first spies Elizabeth (Temple) at the orphanage. In the film, Elizabeth sings "Animal Crackers in My Soup" to her fellow orphans, a song that would become one of Temple's biggest hits. The children are swaying in unison to her song when the orphanage's board of trustees enters the dining room and Elizabeth stops in horror and utters her trademark line to the camera, "Oh my goodness!" The film cuts to the crowd of adults who have entered the dining room. At the center of the group stands Edward, a broad smile across his face. He is entranced by the performance. But all other eyes are on the head of the orphanage's board of trustees, Mr. Wycoff, who is outraged at the sight of a child singing in the dining room. In a scene evocative of *Jane Eyre*, in which Mr. Brocklehurst, the director of a charity school, cruelly punishes the angelic Helen for the crime of having a beautiful head of hair, the trustee scolds Elizabeth as a "bad and wicked" child and prescribes a strict course of discipline. Also like Brocklehurst in Charlotte Brontë's novel, Wycoff's interest in the orphanage is motivated by personal greed rather than benevolence; he has made his money from his patented cough mixture and sells the medicine to the orphanage in large quantities. In this sequence, the film suggests that audiences who object to the sort of fun offered by Hollywood movies are no less cruel and narrow-minded than Wycoff.

A similar shift in gaze occurs in *Captain January*. After Star (Temple) and Paul (Buddy Ebsen) perform an exuberant dance, "At the Codfish Ball," a group of sailors gathers around Star to teach her how to spit into the wind. As the sailors watch the child, laughing uproariously, the camera pans to the truant officer

(Sara Haden), who watches disapprovingly. Once again, our pleasure in Temple's image is interrupted by the censorious look of an adult agent of discipline who strives to put an end to the fun. (Ironically, the spitting sequence was added after women's groups protested Temple's performing a hula for the men.)

In this way, Temple's films put audiences on the side of the advocates of fun, against groups that sought to reign in Hollywood's impropriety. Temple's image suggests not only that virtue could be fun, but that perhaps the critics who accused Hollywood of wickedness were out of step with modern life. And in these narratives, Temple is pitted against a dour spinster or widow—representative of oppressive Victorian mores—who is opposed to the innocent fun that Shirley Temple offers.

Streamlined Happiness

The following chapters will suggest the multiple ways in which Temple helped audiences to adapt to modern life, her performances of childhood providing a means of reconciling audiences to changing gender roles and to the incorporation of black culture into mainstream America. As I will explore, she and other child stars helped to demonstrate that so much of what seemed new about modern American life did not necessarily pose a threat to traditional values. More than this, her films suggest a resolution to the seemingly irresolvable conflict over whether the developing national culture should endorse traditional values or embrace the new ethos of fun. Her films pointed to the ways in which media texts might be reimagined to suit the varied tastes of a national audience by marrying the pleasures of sophisticated entertainment with the moral uplift of sentimental fiction.

Temple's films were understood to appeal to audiences who craved sentiment rather than sophistication. However, it was not merely their sentimentality that made her popular with conservative audiences. She was also able to incorporate the new aesthetic without compromising decorum, which was an essential aspect of her appeal. For example, Temple's roles at Paramount reimagined the sorts of crime films that had helped inspire the Code. (Paramount had a lot to make up for, having brought Mae West to the screen.) Consider *Little Miss Marker*, which transformed the gangster film into a child-centered melodrama. Still present is the extravagant street vernacular associated with the gangster film, this time derived from a short story by Damon Runyon. And the tough moral code of the criminals remains central to the narrative. But unlike James Cagney's Tom Powers in *The Public Enemy* (1931), these gangsters are not brutal to the bitter end; they prove to be a bunch of softies when they are brought into the orbit of the adorable child. Similarly, *Now and Forever* featured the sort of charming con artist familiar from films like Ernst Lubitsch's *Trouble in Paradise* (1932), another Paramount film. But whereas Gaston and Lily (Miriam Hopkins and Herbert

Marshall) remain delightfully unrepentant of their crimes in the Lubitsch film, Toni (Carole Lombard) is determined to observe the law the minute a child enters the picture, and Jerry (Gary Cooper) eventually reforms as well.

Nonetheless, Fox and the Production Code Administration began to receive complaints about the number of criminals who populated Temple's films. As the *Los Angeles Times* reported, "The studio is having to stick to the 'straight and narrow' in the Temple films because whenever she is associated with even slightly disreputable characters, there is a terrific protest."[100] As a consequence, Twentieth Century-Fox avoided pairing its most valuable asset with criminals in later films.

Film critics celebrated Temple's ability to smuggle modern entertainment under the guise of old-fashioned sentiment. *Rebecca of Sunnybrook Farm* proved successful for Twentieth Century-Fox, in part because the story had been so radically updated as to be unrecognizable: "I don't ask you to reconcile all this excitement with your recollections of *Rebecca of Sunnybrook Farm*, either as Kate Douglas Wiggins wrote it or Mary Pickford and all those other Rebeccas played it. . . . They were tenderly sentimental works, aimed at the cardiac and lachrymal reflexes. This is a type of product pointed at eye, ear, and in a sense, intellect." Critics noted that "the original *Rebecca* is hardly recognizable and in its place has been substituted a tale of nation-wide radio broadcasts, talent auditions, and commercial advertising. Only as a retreat from the bustle of city life does the farm play a part."[101] And the film's success was attributed to "[r]hythm and its uses, humor unrooted in precocity, and, most of all, [Temple's] sheer professional ability to perform entertainingly."[102]

More than providing a means of updating old-fashioned stories, references to the new medium of radio helped to cement Temple's stardom through the technique of marrying the modern—in this case radio—to the old-fashioned figure of the innocent child. Allison McCracken has shown that during the early 1930s audiences were engaged in heated debates over men's voices on the radio as the nation began to enforce a new style of masculinity during the Depression.[103] In the 1920s and early 1930s, male tenors like Rudy Vallée were the most popular voices on radio. But in 1932, as audiences questioned the suitability for national radio of what many perceived to be effeminate voices, there was an intense backlash against these tenors. According to McCracken, it was not just the pitch of men's voices that caused such controversy. It was also the effect they had on women—wives and mothers—whose erotic desires, it was feared, would be aroused and unsated by such radio shows. Crooners like Rudy Vallée, critics complained, were a narcotic that would lead audiences astray from procreative love. *Poor Little Rich Girl* pokes fun at these fears when Jerry (Alice Faye) sings "When I'm with You" for Peck's radio show. Listening to her sing, the curmudgeonly soap magnate, Peck (Claude Gillingwater), and his assistant, Percival (Arthur Hoyt), are so taken by her romantic rendition of the song that the two men unconsciously begin to hold one another's hands.

Temple's films suggest that radio need not be perceived as a threat to family life. In *Poor Little Rich Girl*, the potentially dangerous media text is literally rewritten by the child. Here Shirley Temple plays Barbara Barry, the daughter of a widowed soap magnate, Richard Barry (Michael Whalen), who is too preoccupied with work to give his daughter the attention she needs. Instead, she is left in the care of a paid nurse, butler, and cook. In a rare moment of intimacy between father and daughter, the two cuddle on the couch and listen to the radio show that Barry's soap company has sponsored. The show's highlight is a song performed by the "Barry Baritone," who croons a romantic tune, "When I'm with You." Listening to the show, Barbara and her father silently mouth the romantic words to one another. During an orchestral interlude, Barbara tells her father she has her own words for the song and begins to croon to him: "I long to hug and kiss you./Marry me and let me be your wife." Today, it is tempting to view this sequence as proof of Temple's pedophilic appeal, to imagine that the sequence provides a thinly veiled eroticization of father–daughter incest.[104] In the 1930s, however, audiences would be more likely to understand Barbara to have adapted the radio broadcast to voice her chaste love for her father. Barbara's rewriting the song to express filial rather than romantic love suggests the child might influence radio's meaning rather than imagining that radio shaped the child's behavior and desires. Long before cultural theorists began to examine the ways in which audiences interpret media texts to suit their own needs and desires, *Poor Little Rich Girl* demonstrates how audiences might turn to popular culture to articulate familial as well as romantic love.

Radio romance is again used to promote an ideal of familial love when Barbara herself sings into a radio microphone. In her audition for radio "Station L*O*V*E," she introduces herself as "Cupid's assistant" and instructs her listeners to cuddle up closer and hold one another's hands. In the background Jimmy (Jack Haley) and Jerry Dolan slide closer to one another and hold hands. In this way, her radio broadcast helps to reconstitute the family rather than threatening it. As Barbara whistles and scats in homage to baritone crooner Bing Crosby, Jimmy and Jerry, who had previously bickered about money and their inability to find work, appear enamored of one another and the child. Conversely, when Barbara does actually sing on the radio, she interrupts her father's romance. Peck's advertising manager, Margaret, has replaced Barbara as Barry's listening companion. Sipping cocktails in her apartment, they listen to Peck's radio hour, Barry oblivious to the fact that his daughter has gone missing. When Barbara sings "When I'm with You," he recognizes his child's voice and rushes to the radio station, where he is reunited with his daughter, Margaret at his side, and a new family is formed. Thus radio serves as a medium not only for commercial entertainments but for forging a family as well. In this way, the film suggests that the new arena of popular, commercial entertainments need not be perceived as a threat to family life. Rather, they might be understood to strengthen familial bonds.

Pickford and Temple both helped Hollywood to negotiate the complicated terrain of changing values as the studios worked to build a national audience. In both cases, their enactments of childhood helped to reconcile an old-fashioned taste for sentiment with the modern pursuit of fun. By negotiating this taste divide, Shirley Temple helped Twentieth Century-Fox to exploit performance practices that audiences might otherwise find objectionable, as I will discuss in the chapters that follow.

CHAPTER 2

"A TERRIBLE AMOUR"

CHILD LOVING IN THE TWENTIETH CENTURY

Contemporary audiences are often struck by what Molly Haskell has described as Shirley Temple's "flirtatiousness with her daddy figures."[1] In *Bright Eyes*, she sings her signature tune, "On the Good Ship Lollipop," to a chorus of adoring men who shower her with candy. In *Poor Little Rich Girl*, she sits upon her father's knee and croons a love song, begging him to "Marry me and let me be your wife." And in *Dimples* she caresses her grandfather's neck and tearfully sings, "There'd be no me without you, no you without me." *Curly Top* seems particularly egregious in this regard. In this film, a wealthy bachelor adopts her eighteen-year-old sister just so he can bring young Shirley home to live with him, much as Humbert Humbert would marry Charlotte Haze in order to be closer to her daughter, Lolita, in Vladimir Nabokov's novel twenty years later.

When Shirley Temple initially emerged as one of Hollywood's most popular stars, an adult man who did not adore her was perceived as somewhat aberrant. In 1934, one newspaper columnist went in search of the rare man who was not a Temple fan. When he finally found one at the offices of *The New York Times*, readers were assured, "He's normal otherwise, he just doesn't like Shirley Temple."[2] In fact, far from trying to obscure the elements of her films that seem perverse to contemporary audiences—her kissing and cuddling adult costars, crooning love songs to them, rubbing her dimpled cheeks against their grizzled ones—Twentieth Century-Fox deliberately marketed Temple's films as love stories between the girl and middle-aged men, going so far as to portray her as a little seductress who captures the hearts of her adult male coworkers as well as the men in the audience. Newspaper ads for *The Little Colonel* use photographs of Temple and Lionel Barrymore looking lovingly into one another's eyes along with tag lines that describe the pair as though they were star-crossed lovers: "She's a child of the gallant South. . . . He's a crusty silver-haired veteran. . . . Love tears them apart—then brings them together again!"[3] The pressbook offers advertisements that suggest romance as much as they do familial love: "He responds to her and gradually comes to love her, before he learns that she is his grandchild."[4] Likewise, *Dimples* was advertised as a love story between Temple and her costar, Frank Morgan: "A *new* somebody for her to love . . . and what fun he is! She's an irresistible minstrel! He's an incorrigible scamp! And even the rowdy Bowery can't part these sweethearts."[5]

Clearly, men's adoration of Temple was not incidental to her publicity but rather a central element of her stardom. In fact, this aspect of Temple's publicity was a rather formulaic element of child stardom. It is worth examining why male fandom figured so prominently in children's star discourse, what men's pleasure in images of young girls signified to audiences who did not perceive it as a sign of pedophilic desire.

A Very Healthy Sort of Worship

Stories of men's adoration of Shirley Temple suggested that she was an antidote to the licentiousness that attended the aesthetic shift away from sentiment and toward sensation that I discussed in the previous chapter. For example, in *Curly Top*, a wealthy millionaire, Edward (John Boles), returns home after meeting Elizabeth (Temple) at an orphan asylum, where he was charmed by the little girl. In the well-appointed sitting room of the lavish home he shares with his aunt, Edward sits at the grand piano and composes a song, "It's All So New to Me," that describes the surprising effect the child has had on him; she has transformed his life which was "real as can be," into a "wonderland." Humming, he surveys the portraits that adorn the walls of his sitting room. Each is modeled after a well-known portrait of a child: Sir Joshua Reynold's *The Age of Innocence* (1888), Thomas Gainsborough's *The Blue Boy* (1770), Emile Renouf's *A Helping Hand* (1881), and John Everett Millais's *My First Sermon* (1862–1863).[6] And in each of these paintings, Shirley Temple appears in place of the original child. As Edward pauses to admire the paintings, she briefly comes to life, smiles, and waves to him from within the picture frame. These references to eighteenth- and nineteenth-century portraiture work at once to associate Temple with an idyllic past, to suggest that the man's pleasure in her image is similar to the pleasure previous generations of men might have taken in such portraits, and to announce Temple's distance from these old-fashioned children by virtue of her ability to come alive, to turn, smile, and wave at her admirer.

When Millais's *My First Sermon* was unveiled at the Royal Academy in 1863, the archbishop of Canterbury described the beneficent effect of this and similar paintings in a now famous encomium to childhood: "Art has, and ever will have, a high and noble mission to fulfill. That man, I think, is little to be envied who can pass through these rooms and go forth without being in some sense a better and a happier man; if at least it be so (as I do believe it to be) that we feel ourselves the better and the happier . . . when our spirits are touched by the playfulness, the innocence, the purity, and may I not add the piety of childhood."[7] The archbishop's speech famously captures the philosophy that undergirded the Victorian cult of the child. The purity of the innocent child depicted in such portraits was understood to have a transformative effect on the adults in her vicinity, to render them "the better and the happier" for having gazed on her countenance.

With this sequence, *Curly Top* explicitly links Shirley Temple to the Romantic vision of childhood that had been so central to images of children for over a century. What seems so perverse about Temple's stardom—her effect on men both within her films and in the audience—was a vestige of this tradition and an integral aspect of her appeal. While twenty-first-century audiences often find it difficult to imagine that men's love for Temple was not fundamentally erotic, early twentieth-century audiences were accustomed to interpreting popular images of children in very different terms.

As I discussed in the introduction, childhood in the late nineteenth and early twentieth centuries was defined by competing paradigms of innocence. In the United States, a Calvinist view that the child was born into sin and should be rushed toward adulthood and Christian piety as quickly as possible was only gradually displaced by a Lockean conception of the child as a blank slate, characterized by an innocence that was vulnerable to the influence of adult society. The Victorian cult of the child was a manifestation of yet another view of innocence, one developed within the Romantic movement and popularized in sentimental literature. The Romantic view is encapsulated in William Wordsworth's "Ode: Intimations of Immortality from Recollections of Early Childhood":

> Our birth is but a sleep and a forgetting:
> The Soul that rises with us, our life's Star,
> Hath had elsewhere its setting,
> And cometh from afar:
> Not in entire forgetfulness,
> And not in utter nakedness,
> But trailing clouds of glory do we come
> From God, who is our home:
> Heaven lies about us in our infancy![8]

According to this Romantic view, the child is delivered straight from God, "trailing clouds of glory," and offering adults indirect access to a lost realm. Publicity for Jackie Coogan explicitly evokes this image of heavenly childhood, describing the effect he had on audiences: "In the wide childish eyes one feels a wisdom brought from some other world and not yet dimmed by that of this."[9]

Children's performances on the nineteenth-century stage were therefore understood to offer adults an antidote to the ill effects of modern life. As Cedric in *Little Lord Fauntleroy* in the 1880s, for instance, Elsie Leslie led adult

4. Shirley Temple in a tableau of "The Age of Innocence" in *Curly Top*, 1935.

5. Shirley Temple as "The Blue Boy" in *Curly Top.*

6. Shirley Temple in a tableau of "A Helping Hand" in *Curly Top*.

7. Shirley Temple in a tableau of "My First Sermon" in *Curly Top*.

audiences from the hurly burly of city life, offering the theater as a sanctuary from modernity:

> A child like this leads us wild beasts of metropolitan conflict and viciousness straight into the realms of peace and humility. She opens wide her innocent eyes upon our brutality and we are reminded of what we might have been if such an honest gaze had always measured our actions. . . . The angelic cleanness of childhood beams itself over our hard old hearts in a radiance of new hope. We are lifted out of the clatter and clang of metropolitanism, a golden light is glorifying the theater we are in, subtle music is breathing out of the clouds and through the rosy mist that persists in gathering.[10]

The transformative power of the child relies on her "angelic cleanness," her distance from "metropolitan conflict and viciousness" that characterize industrial capitalism. Through a reversal of the gaze, the audience is imagined to see itself through the child's "honest gaze" and recognize its own "brutality." Like the "clouds of glory" Wordsworth described as trailing in the child's wake, Leslie's performance imbued the theater with a "golden light," a "subtle music" that briefly dispels the mists of secular life as it shines on the audience.

As with the child impersonators discussed in the previous chapter, the performing child was understood to have the sort of transformative effect generally associated with religious experience. One reviewer described his rather intense response to Elsie Leslie, for example, in explicitly religious terms: "I'm down on my face, and up above me is a delicious child, with long tangled curls, a pure mouth, and good tender eyes. . . . This is a very healthy sort of worship."[11] The author's vivid description of his lying prone before the child, with her "pure" mouth and "good tender eyes," suggests that he has experienced something akin to religious ecstasy before the child, who has transformed the theater into a space where he can enjoy "a very healthy sort of worship."

Silent-era film, too, offered images of children as an antidote to the ill effects of modern society, suggesting that audiences would be transformed for the better upon looking at a child: "There is a certain sublimity in the faith that a baby puts in the world about it. Its very dependence makes it absolutely independent of all outside influence. Its very trust in humankind robs humankind of any unkindliness. Its very innocence inspires innocence in the immodest. Its very simplicity forces the sophisticated to its knees. All the world loves a baby, and a nude baby is the babiest of them all."[12] In this case, the child's vulnerability is imagined to invite not harm but protective care that would transform audiences for the better—robbing humankind of unkindliness and inspiring innocence in the immodest.

The sentimental child was therefore an antidote to the potential ill effects of the movies; if Jackie Coogan would only stay a child, "We could go to his pictures sure of that appeal to the best in us we all crave and meet with so seldom."[13] The child's innocence was imagined to bring out "the best in us we all crave" for all who came in contact with him, no matter how terrible. When Jackie Coogan met Mussolini, newspapers reported, "The Italian statesman, whose stern glance alone is sufficient to spread terror in opponents, . . . embraced the youngster, lifted him up, and kissed him repeatedly."[14] Similarly, the child seemed capable of transforming even the most disreputable surroundings into something sacrosanct. The *Minneapolis Journal* describes nine-year-old Muriel Cole in her role as "Little Goldie the barroom kid" as having transformed both the imagined bar on stage and the very real theater in which she performed by virtue of her rendition of "Abide with Me" in the 1915 play *The Claim.*[15] And Jane Lee was said to have "tempered the crude metal of many an unlovely theme and smoothed the rough edges of many a grating scene" by virtue of her sweetness.[16]

We should not be entirely surprised, either, to find that Shirley Temple was the object of adult male adulation, like that described by the journalist who admitted, "I feel that I shall go lyrical and slightly maudlin if I tell exactly how lovely Miss Temple seemed to me. And I'm not kidding!"[17] *The New York Times* drew on this language in its tongue-in-cheek assessment that *The Little Colonel* "ought to bring out the best in everyone who sees it" and that her leading men "confess themselves better, nobler chaps since they felt the touch of her little soft hands upon their sin-furrowed cheeks. . . . Thrice has [costar] Mr. Dunn offered up his quivering white body on the altar of Shirley Temple's art."[18]

A New Kind of Love

Men's responses to children's performances were understood not to signal men's propensity for pedophilia but their willingness to be transformed for the better. Boys were often imagined to restore adults to their own youthful innocence, if only for the length of the film. Writing of Francis Carpenter's performance in *Jack and the Beanstalk*, a *Philadelphia Telegraph* reviewer reported that "grownups . . . reveled in the thoughts that carried them back to . . . many a happy childhood hour. See *Jack and the Beanstalk* and you'll be a boy or a girl again for a full two hours."[19] According to another reviewer, Tommy Harper's performance in *The Chimney Sweep* (1916) touched "the spot in the hardest heart in the audience and we recall, perhaps, when we too were 'just kids.'"[20] The *Erie Times* promised that Jackie Coogan's performance, too, could restore men to their youth: "If you want to go back to your boyhood days, go to the Strand and see *Peck's Bad Boy.*"[21] Indeed, films featuring child stars were often described as "a spring tonic" for "the tired business man."[22]

Girls, on the other hand, evoked both nostalgia and a chaste, heterosexual desire. Lotta Crabtree, who would become one of the most popular child impersonators of the stage in the mid-nineteenth century, began her career in California at the age of eight. Publicity for Lotta regularly described her as having been the darling of the California gold miners. Newspaper and magazine stories imagined the striking contrast between the delicate young performer and the coarse men who delighted in her dancing. As the *Chicago Record* described it, "Lotta's sprightliness, her graceful manners, and her natural talent captured the hearts of the rough old miners."[23] According to legend, such was their love for the little girl that they showered her with their hard-won gold nuggets whenever she performed.

In the 1880s and 1890s, such prominent figures as Oliver Wendell Holmes, Sr. and Mark Twain were uninhibited in proclaiming their adoration for the young actress Elsie Leslie, who originated the role of Little Lord Fauntleroy in the United States in 1888. The press described Holmes as a particular fan, and Leslie herself recalled in *Cosmopolitan*, then a family-oriented magazine, that she had received a number of love letters from the poet.[24] Mark Twain was an admirer of young girls in general, surrounding himself in his later years with a bevy of girls, whom he collectively called his "angelfish." Though Leslie was not a member of his "aquarium," Twain publicly declared his love for her in a speech given after one of her performances. He and the playwright/actor William Gillette had each embroidered her a slipper to "express somewhat of the love [they] felt for [her]."[25] The toe of Twain's slipper is decorated with a heart pierced by arrows, "arrows that go in blue and come out crimson—crimson with the best drops in that heart, and gladly shed for love of you, dear."[26] Members of Manhattan's male elite made a particular pet of Elsie Leslie. The Progress Club, a prominent Manhattan men's club, included a contingent of bachelors who invited the girl to give a special performance of *Editha's Burglar* in which she would enact the role of the child, Editha, and club members would take up the roles of her parents and the burglar who is charmed by her innocence. The Progress Club bachelors did not limit the display of adoration for Leslie to the privacy of their club, however, but made a public show of it, attending her performances as a group and sending her a large bouquet of flowers: "200 members of the Progress Club, bachelors all, united their emotions in a block of seats. . . . The chief floral tribute that went down the aisle and crossed the boundary line of footlights between the real and the mimic was the gift of the Progress Bachelor's Club."[27]

Newspaper and magazine articles portrayed young girl stars as miniature versions of the adult divas of stage and screen, their male admirers likened to the young swains who fêted chorus girls or the older gentlemen who made courtesans of them. The press described the girls as being showered with gifts from male admirers. The young actress Corinne, for example, "was sought after everywhere she went, and lovers galore pestered her with attention and ardent epistles of passion."[28]

The press also reported a surprising number of instances in which adult men adopted young girl performers. In the 1880s, Alice Pierce was taken under the wing of a wealthy Boston man, while Zelda Sanders, the "most beautiful child that has ever stepped before the footlights in New York," was swept off the stage by Lucky Baldwin, a California millionaire. According to *Everybody's Magazine*, Baldwin "saw the child, was fascinated by her, and adopting her as his heiress, took her from the stage and placed her in a boarding school. During her holidays she was mistress of a wonderful ranch in California. . . . The aged millionaire idolized the beautiful child."[29] Unfortunately for Zelda, Baldwin was unlucky in business and lost his fortune, and the girl was returned to her family in New York. Gertrude Homan, another of the Lord Fauntleroys of the late nineteenth century, was ten years old when she caught the eye of forty-three-year-old Colonel J. Kennedy Stout, who was a member of the governor's staff in Spokane, Washington. According to *The New York Times*, "he and Gertie became inseparable, and before the company left Spokane he had won from her a promise to correspond with him."[30] After corresponding with Gertie for some time, Stout married the girl's older sister.

Shirley Temple, too, was described as a seductress, flirting with her costars on and off screen: "Shirley Temple always vamps every leading man she works with. Her latest conquest is John Boles, with Dave Butler, the director, as a hot rival."[31] In *Rebecca of Sunnybrook Farm*, she "wins the devotion in rapid succession of the handsome he-man Randolph Scott . . . of Slim Summerville, Bill Robinson, and Dr. J. Edward Bromberg."[32] Thus, adult men's adoration of very young girls was not understood to be dangerous or perverse at all but was considered suitable material for the publicity mill. Newspaper and magazine articles about these girls produced the image of adult men enraptured by the little girls as testimony to the actresses' extraordinary cuteness.

Disciplinary Love

These stories worked not only to demonstrate the considerable charms of girls who could win over even the most churlish of men, but also to celebrate the girls' civilizing influence and their ability to domesticate male desire. In this sense, discourse about girl stars developed out of the nineteenth-century celebration of sentiment, as I discussed in chapter 1. Narratives of white men's love for young girls ultimately worked to reinforce white male rule by assuring audiences that even the coarsest gold miner or the most miserly businessman would prove benevolent when touched by the innocent love of a little girl. In this sense, the child functions symbolically as a corrective to the potential shortcomings of patriarchal rule. Similarly, stories of bachelors awakened to the pleasures of domestic life suggested that child loving, specifically consuming the child star, could have a stabilizing effect on the nation. The child's transformative effect was connected to her ability to elicit tears in the audiences. In producing this bodily transformation on the male audience, it was imagined, the child produced a moral awakening as well; in demonstrating their ability to cry for the helpless child, men demonstrated their capacity to care for the helpless.

In his exploration of the ideological work performed by Temple's star image during the Depression, Charles Eckert argues that Temple represents love incarnate: "Since her love was indiscriminate, extending to pinched misers or to common hobos, it was a social, even a political force, on a par with the idea of Democracy or the Constitution."[33] According to Eckert, the "love" embodied by Temple reinforces economic policies that shifted the burden of the Depression toward private charity rather than government support. In her films, "the child's love functions not only as condensations of all the mid-depression schemes for the care of the needy, but [represses] the concepts of *duty* to give or of a responsibility to *share* (income tax, federal spending). The solution Shirley offers is natural: one opens one's heart . . . and the most implacable realities alter or disperse."[34]

In this sense, the love offered by Shirley Temple serves a similar function to that of little girls in nineteenth-century fiction. Karen Sánchez-Eppler has explored how the child, more specifically the prepubescent girl, functioned as a means of disciplining intemperate fathers in nineteenth-century temperance literature. Over and over again in these formulaic stories, the child's bed is the site of conversion; the girls' kisses transform drunken and often violent men into gentle, temperate fathers. Sánchez-Eppler argues that these scenes reflect a new model of discipline based on love rather than punishment, a form of discipline particularly well-suited to a developing commercial culture, in which restraint is rewarded with the satisfaction of desire. Sánchez-Eppler interprets these scenes of redemption in which adult men crawl into the beds of children and are transformed by the girls' caresses as implicitly incestuous: "The shock of these temperance plots lies in their conflation of [the] categories [of symbolic and actual incest] so that recognizably incestuous acts—however innocently portrayed—yield social order." However, the "recognition" of incest in these stories requires a frame of reference unavailable to nineteenth-century readers or, for that matter, to early twentieth-century filmgoers, one that was only beginning to emerge in the 1930s.[35]

Like the young girls of temperance fiction, the girl performers of the nineteenth and early twentieth centuries served a disciplinary function. In publicity for these young stars, adult male adoration signaled not pedophilia but the disciplining of male sexuality, the channeling of potentially disruptive male desire into a chaste love for the child. The *New York Post* journalist who was overcome by religious ecstasy in response to Elsie Leslie proclaims himself enamored of innocence rather than vice when he announces his love for the girl: "I am only changing positions with some of my contemporaries who once writhed in ecstasy before the Langtry shrine. I remained bolt upright then, and very cold, but now I'm down on my face, and up above me is a delicious child, with long tangled curls, a pure mouth, and good tender eyes. . . . This is a very healthy sort of worship."[36] The author draws a parallel between his adoration of Leslie and other men's devotion to the European courtesan Lillie Langtry to contrast the child's innocence and Langtry's sexuality, and to emphasize that his love, unlike that of his colleagues, is "a very healthy sort of worship." While his description is vividly sensual—the "delicious" child has had a bodily effect on the man who was once cold and stiff but is now "down on [his] face," presumably writhing in ecstasy as his colleagues once did over Langtry—we are not meant to read his writhing as an indication of illicit desire but as an homage to innocence and a celebration of the ecstasy associated with "worshipping" the sacralized child.

Similarly, the men who adopted young girls from the stage are interpreted to be not dirty old men but "children-loving bachelors." Mabel Taliaferro, who made her stage debut in 1890 at the age of three, became the darling of a New York millionaire at the age of twelve: "The little actress has a patron, Mr. Charles H. Wilcox, the millionaire senior member of the firm Wilcox & Gibbs. He gives her silk gowns and American Beauty roses and carte blanche as to cab hire. He wants to back a company, of which she shall be star, supported by a strong company of adult players. . . . Mr. Charles Wilcox, who is a children-loving bachelor, saw Mabel's picture in a photograph gallery."[37] This story echoes the countless tales of adult actresses who have seduced wealthy men away from family and legitimate society, or of wealthy bachelors who have seduced and abandoned chorus girls. It is a story ordinarily characterized by the scandal of uncontrolled sexual desire and invariably accompanied by the ruin of one or more of the participants, as in Emile Zola's 1880 novel of the chorus girl turned courtesan, *Nana.* In the case of Taliaferro, however, the child's youth renders the man's sponsorship—his gifts of silk gowns and roses, his desire to back a play for her, both of which are ordinarily signs of dangerous passion—entirely innocent, even praise-worthy. As in the contrast between Elsie Leslie and Lillie Langtry, by situating the child in the context of the familiar story of the fallen woman and the debased gentleman, this vignette serves to contrast the child's innocence with the wantonness of chorus girls and courtesans who habitually populate such tales. These stories assure readers that, although the bachelor may live outside the bounds of marriage, his adoration of the child demonstrates that he is not ruled by sexual passion but is willing to exercise sexual restraint. And this willingness is inspired by the young stars of the stage.

Likewise, publicity for Hollywood's earliest child stars playfully imagined the girls to have disciplined men to enlist in the war effort. During World War I, *Motion Picture* magazine offered tongue-in-cheek advice to nine-year-old Madge Evans's male admirers: "If you are a mere male and would win your way to the heart of Madge Evans, unspoiled idol of millions, then don khaki—don it quick."[38] The *New York Telegraph* reported that five-year-old Jane Lee enticed men to enlist in the army in much the same manner that a more mature starlet might: "Few men can resist Jane, and when she adopted the policy of kissing each recruit, the enrolling officer lost much of his gravity and actually perspired."[39]

Newspaper and magazine articles that described Temple's popularity with adult men were, likewise, stories of men whose unruly sexuality had been tamed by the love of a child. In 1933, the leading box-office attraction had been Mae West. When independent exhibitors announced that Shirley Temple had displaced West as America's most popular star in 1934, many newspapers celebrated the news as a victory of morality over vice. It seemed cause for rejoicing that the child had won over the nation "without even a sexy inference or a fulsome wiggle of her hips."[40] The fact that "Shirley is no glamorous movie siren, no mysterious foreigner, not even a highly sexed platinum blonde, but just a pretty little girl who is a natural-born actress"[41] was taken as evidence that the nation never really did want the violent gangster films or suggestive sex comedies that Hollywood had been foisting on it: "This 'trying to give the public what it wants' bleat is swept away by the record of Shirley Temple's pictures. For in them is neither overstressed sex nor glamour, nothing but good acting by a remarkably pretty and remarkably intelligent child. Yet that combination brings more money into the box office than the sex-glamour team."[42] The fact that Temple produced more "love," if ticket sales can be taken as a sign of love, than Mae West, and the idea that loving a child proved more popular than erotic love, seemed proof of the moral stability of the nation. Reviewers celebrated Temple's popularity as cause for optimism during the troubled times of the American Depression: "under the leadership of a little child, the cinema is rapidly regaining its faith in the essential nobility of human nature."[43]

A Little Child Shall Lead Them

Over and over again in reviews and publicity for child stars, journalists invoked the biblical phrase "a little child shall lead them" to point to the transformative effect these children had on their elders. The phrase is from Isaiah: "The wolf also shall dwell with the lamb, and the leopard shall lie down with the kid; and the calf and the young lion and the fatling together; and a little child shall lead them." The repeated invocation of the passage points to the role that the sacralized child had in the popular imagination, for it was imagined that she could resolve seemingly irresolvable problems.

Although Shirley Temple's films seldom directly depict the grim effects of the Depression, they often indirectly address issues associated with the social disruption of the 1930s, and they attribute these problems to a failure of patriarchy. At a time when out-of-work fathers were unable to provide for their families, when they had to rely on government relief or wages earned by their wives and children, Shirley Temple's films were peopled by ineffectual father figures. In *Captain January*, she is adopted by an aging lighthouse keeper (Guy Kibbee) who can no longer perform his job and is on the verge of being replaced by a mechanical light. In *Dimples*, she lives with "the professor," her bumbling grandfather (Frank Morgan), who uses inflated language and antiquated social graces to mask his status as an impoverished petty thief and con man. And in *The Little Colonel*, her father is debilitated by pneumonia after being bilked of all his money, while her grandfather (Lionel Barrymore) is an aging southern gentleman who refuses to acknowledge the South's defeat in the Civil War and is unable to prevent his own daughter from eloping with a Yankee. In each case, Temple's character helps to rehabilitate a suffering father figure, securing a job for the Captain, leading the professor away from crime and into a romantic partnership with a wealthy dowager, and inspiring the Colonel to act bravely and selflessly by rescuing his Yankee son-in-law from armed criminals.

More interesting, for the purposes of this analysis, Temple's love also functions to discipline adult male sexuality, driving bachelors to marriage. In *Now and Forever*, Jerry (Gary Cooper) refuses to marry, preferring the peripatetic existence of a con man to the settled life of a husband. However, when he is reunited with his daughter (Temple), he is so taken by the little girl that he has a change of heart and decides to settle down and marry. In *Bright Eyes*, an airline pilot (James Dunn) living in the company of other bachelor pilots is inspired to reconcile with his former fiancée so that he can make a home for an orphan (Temple). In *Curly Top*, the child awakens yet another bachelor to romantic love; a playboy (John Boles) falls for a young girl (Temple) when he spies her singing to her fellow orphans, and once again his love for the child leads the bachelor to marriage, in this case to the child's older sister. And in *Stowaway*, a millionaire playboy (Robert Young) marries so that he can adopt the little orphan girl he met in Shanghai. Initially, the couple plans to divorce as soon as the adoption is finalized, but, naturally, they fall in love and yet another bachelor is awakened to the pleasures of marriage and domesticity through the transformative love of a little girl.

Much of Temple's appeal rested on her apparent ability to reconcile seemingly irreconcilable opponents, both on screen and off; "In fact," crowed a review of *The Littlest Rebel*, "even those who should rightly be enemies become the firmest of friends when Shirley is around."[44] Publicity described her as "the common denominator that takes in all humanity."[45] *Wee Willie Winkie* is a distinctly unfaithful adaptation of a Rudyard Kipling story. In the film, Temple portrays the American granddaughter of a British colonel (C. Aubrey Smith) stationed in Raj Pore near the Khyber Pass. The pass is held by an Afghan rebel, Khoda Khan (Cesar Romero), who is arrested and jailed for arms smuggling. The film suggests that the way out of any political conflict is through the shared recognition of the child's innocence. Winkie befriends Khoda Khan on her arrival in Afghanistan when he loses a religious amulet during a skirmish with the British army officers. She returns the "necklace" to him and wins his gratitude. Later, when Khan is in jail for arms smuggling, Winkie visits him and suggests, "If you told the colonel you're sorry and promised to be good, then he'd let you out of jail." When he replies that he is not sorry, she scolds, "Then you'll have to stay there, Mr. Khan, until you are." In bringing her childish logic to the situation, she exposes what the film imagines is the solution to the political impasse between the British and Afghanis: negotiation.

The film understands the Afghanis to be unreasonably caught in the past, unwilling to enjoy the fruits of modern life. After Khan escapes from jail and kills Winkie's friend, her grandfather tells her: "We want to be friends with Khoda Khan, . . . but if we don't shoot Khoda Khan, Khoda Khan will shoot us." He explains that it is important that the British keep the Khyber Pass open in order to "bring peace and prosperity to everyone." The Afghanis "don't seem to realize

8. Shirley Temple and Cesar Romero in a production still for *Wee Willie Winkie*, 1937. Men's love for Shirley Temple was imagined to be transformative. Author's collection.

that they'd do much better if they planted crops, traded, became civilized." This logic seems clear enough to the child that she determines to go to Khoda Khan's "house" in the mountains to talk some sense into him. But when she explains to Khan and his followers that "the queen wants to protect all her people and make them happy and rich," she is met with laughter, and Khoda Khan refuses to take her suggestion and "talk it over with my grandfather."

The rebel's mind is changed when Winkie's grandfather comes to retrieve her from the rebel stronghold. With the British and Afghani armies poised for battle, the colonel climbs the countless stairs up the mountain where Khan and his followers lie in wait. Khan is impressed by his bravery, inspired by a love for the child that both men share. He stops his soldiers from shooting the Colonel and joins him and Winkie, the three walking hand-in-hand, the two men literally and figuratively joined by their mutual love for the little girl, as the British troops look on in amazement. The film ends with the former rebels joining the British in their outpost, enjoying an exhibition of the soldiers' call to arms. The battle is ended and, presumably, prosperity will soon follow.

Temple's ability to discipline men of all races remained a powerful fantasy even after her career as a child star had ended. In 1941, during World War II, *The New York Times Magazine* reported that one of her fans "thought she could make the Chinese and Japanese see eye to eye" and another "has been urging her to get together with Hitler, Churchill, Stalin, and Roosevelt and make them patch things up."[46]

Something James Barrie Would Understand

Although it would be naïve to assume that audiences *never* responded to child stars in a manner we would identify as pedophilic, it is also a mistake to imagine that men's pleasure in the spectacle of the child typically sought release in the child's violation. Of course, we can never know how individual audience members responded to images of children. However, before the pedophile became fully entrenched in popular discourse, publicity for these child stars produced a discourse that helped men to articulate, and thereby define, their responses to the child in benign terms.

The notion of pedophilia was only beginning to enter popular vernacular in the 1930s. The first of what Philip Jenkins describes as many moral panics over pedophilia did not fully erupt until 1937, and clearly it did not have a significant impact on Shirley Temple's star discourse. Until the 1930s, pedophilia was understood to be accompanied by feeble-mindedness or senescence. Only a particular class of person was subject to sexual desire for the child; the term pedophilia, as it was understood then, therefore did not apply to the vast numbers of healthy men who professed their adoration of the little girl. Indeed, Graham Greene's assertion that Temple's audience—"middle-aged men and clergymen"—were unconsciously aroused by Temple was a "gross outrage" precisely because it suggested that respectable men rather than degenerates were subject to pedophilic impulses.

The nineteenth and early twentieth centuries saw a tremendous explosion of public images of children, not only in theater and film but in advertising as well; clearly, children were extremely appealing to adult audiences. In the absence of a tradition for expressing nonfamilial love for children, publicity for the young stars produced a discourse through which fans could express their unexpected devotion to these children.

Few expressions of adult pleasure in child stars survive outside publicity. However, those that do suggest that the discourse of child loving promulgated by the press helped shape adults' expression of their own pleasure in images of children. Women seem to have had little difficulty associating their responses to child performers in terms of a maternal desire to kiss and cuddle the children. Commercialized images of children developed in tandem with advertising techniques that were designed to lure women into the marketplace. In this sense, Shirley Temple and other child stars were as much a product of what Lori Merish calls "commodity aesthetics" as they were of sentimental literature. As such, they emerged out of a tradition that was explicitly designed to speak to feminine desires.[47] The child's rounded cheeks and limbs, her diminutive size and apparent helplessness, according to Merish, are invitations to touch that produce a desire to possess the child. A journalist for *Motion Picture* magazine expressed much the same idea when she described six-year-old Baby Marie Osborne as "a tiny, wistful-eyed little baby, who seems always begging to be loved and cuddled as it is a baby's right to be."[48] Likewise, a woman writing to the silent-era film star Betty Marsh, who was three or four at the time, writes, "You are the dearest little girl I ever saw. You are just the kind I should like to have if I were married and had children."[49]

Far more complex were men's expressions of love for these children. When men indulged in the pleasures associated with these cute children, they momentarily, and often self-consciously, adopted a subject position far removed from traditional masculinity and the burdens that attend it. Surprisingly, men appear to have had little compunction about publicly expressing what today appear to be obvious attestations of pedophilic desire. As in publicity for child stars, fans of these young girls express their love for the children in exaggerated terms of heterosexual courtship. Betty Marsh received a hand-written letter from a man who identified himself as Frank Kinsella, a "newspaper man, hardened by many years of covering police in a big city." "Being an old bachelor," he writes: "I have never suspected little girls could be so nice and appealing, so I am going to wait until you grow up and then I will lay my heart and fortune at your feet. So you cannot only consider this your first mash note, but also your first proposal. Please, oh please, do not promise to be a sister to me."[50]

In his letter, Kinsella's status as a "hardened" newspaper man, accustomed to covering crime stories in the big city, colors his response to the image of the child, much as the men who once cried over little girls' performances were described in terms of their overt masculinity. This is an articulation of the immense power of the young girl to move men.

Like the reviewer who worshiped Elsie Leslie rather than Lillie Langtry, Kinsella can only express his response to the child's image in the familiar terms of heterosexual desire. His plea that she "not promise to be a sister" turns on the reader's understanding that such a promise would represent a refusal of romantic intimacy in favor of familial love. However, this proposal is framed within his plan to wait until she grows up, which reverses the role of adult and child, he playfully assuming the naiveté and sexual innocence of a child when he proposes to marry her after she has grown. Kinsella clearly does not expect his "proposal" to meet with success. His letter suggests a wink to the adult who would surely need to read the letter to its young recipient. Describing his letter as Marsh's first mash note and her first proposal, Kinsella acknowledges the impossibility of his desire being fulfilled even in the future. And his overblown language—"I will lay my heart and fortune at your feet"—suggests that he is deliberately invoking the language of romantic courtship, pointing to a tradition of chivalry that would be anachronistic in relation to women but seemed charming when addressed to a child. So closely did Kinsella's expression of love conform to publicity for child actors that the letter itself was used as publicity and reprinted in several newspapers throughout the country.

Another unsolicited response similarly draws on the construction of child loving found in publicity for young girls. An exhibitor writing to the *Motion Picture Herald* describes his unexpected response to Shirley Temple: "I am infatuated with this little elf. She left me helpless in a new kind of love. I am wild to be my best girl's father. Something James Barrie, perhaps, can understand, but a terrible *amour* for an old gent like me."[51] As with Kinsella, the writer appears to have been taken by surprise by his response to the young girl, expressing an almost giddy confusion in this "new kind of love." There appears to be no language for him to describe precisely what he feels for Temple; he can only begin to explain it by referring to James Barrie, the paradigmatic child lover and inventor of that eternal child, Peter Pan. It is tempting to simplify the exhibitor's expression of love as the outburst of a man who is unwilling to acknowledge his sexual attraction to a five-year-old girl. His describing her as a "little elf" hints at an unwillingness to recognize her status as a child but to imagine her as a troublesome, magical creature. As with Kinsella, his masculinity is undermined by his love for the child; he is "helpless" in his love, an incapacitated "old gent" who is "wild" for the girl. And, as with Kinsella, he expresses his desire in overblown terms of heterosexual courtship; he is in the grip of a "terrible *amour*." However, his "wild" desire is to be his "best girl's father," a phrase that echoes publicity for girl stars by using the language of courtship even as he positions himself as someone who is *not* driven by sexual passion (an old gent who wants to be her father).

Other fans of child stars describe their desire in terms of romantic friendship reminiscent of Lewis Carroll's friendship with Alice Lytell or James Barrie's with the Davies boys. Betty Marsh received a letter and a gift of books from a man who identified himself as being "Known throughout the South as the children's friend. . . . I am not bragging but only telling you this because I want to number you among my little friends. . . . You must write me and be one of my little friends."[52] The writer goes on to explain that he has had a correspondence with another Los Angeles girl: "I have written two letters [to her] but have received no answers. So by that I suppose she has married for we used to correspond regular."[53] While a correspondence with a young woman might have produced an expectation of commitment, a correspondence with a little girl seems to have fallen within the province of pen pals. These letter writers and their recipients show no signs that they understood a man's love for these children to be potentially perverse, though they are likely to seem dangerously pedophilic to contemporary audiences.

The Female Gaze

Whereas men's responses were often described in terms of a transformation brought on by chaste heterosexual desire, women's responses to these children were primarily framed in relation to motherhood. Cuteness, Lori Merish contends, emerged as a cultural style in the nineteenth century in tandem with the rise of the female consumer, when advertisers relied increasingly on images of children (and, in at least one case, an adult little person posing as a child) to encourage commodity desire. And this desire was aroused by the qualities—the small body, rounded features, and relatively large head—associated with infancy and its attendant helplessness. According to Merish, cuteness "aestheticizes powerlessness" and "stages . . . a need for adult care."[54] One film reviewer nicely illustrates Merish's point when she describes the effect that Jackie Coogan's performance was expected to have on female audience members: "[Every] woman in the audience . . . will yearn to gather him up in her arms and squeeze him good. That fat little face; that baby smile; those pleading brown eyes; the little legs that can run so fast are all assets sure to rouse the mother instinct in any feminine bosom."[55] *The New York Times* was less generous when it described Shirley Temple's performance in *Dimples* as "the latest assault upon the nation's maternal instinct."[56]

Women's responses to children were imagined to be straightforward and maternal: "Every woman, married or not—with children of her own or without—has at some time in her life, pictured to herself the Ideal Child. Often she sees a child player on the films who captures her heart. For instance, many a mother must have been entranced by little Shirley Temple without being any the less fond of her own daughter—for everyone comes under the spell of this fascinating little girl."[57]

However, while men's love for Shirley Temple and other child stars was framed as beneficent, women's love for these children was often perceived as a potential problem. Male spectatorship might be framed in terms of chaste heterosexuality, but, female spectatorship was defined in terms of a covetous, maternal desire that was at risk of becoming out of control.

At best, female fandom was expressed by making one's child over in the image of Shirley Temple or another of the stars. "Good" mothers were proper consumers who helped their children emulate Shirley Temple by buying the products she endorsed. They approached the marketplace as consumers and sought not to exploit their children but to reproduce the ideal child that the marketplace made possible. In this way, discourse about fandom suggested that the proper role for a woman was to train her daughter as a consumer and to teach her to transform herself into the image on screen.

However, women's desire for the child stars was also framed in terms of covetousness. At the height of Jackie Coogan's success, newspapers reported that wealthy society women coveted the boy. The *Los Angeles Examiner* ran a photograph of a very well-dressed woman carrying a basket with a Jackie Coogan doll in it, suggesting that these dolls had become a fashionable accessory for well-to-do women. The caption reads, "Jackie Coogan dolls are the latest. Newport society started the new fad and they are now seen everywhere in the East." And the *Detroit Times* ran a piece describing how Coogan had been "lionized and pampered and petted" by the city's elite. "Mrs. William K. Vanderbilt, Jr. has given him a luncheon at the Ritz Carlton. Mrs. Julius Fleishman has given him a luncheon at the Plaza. Mrs. Charles B. Dillingham has entertained him. Mrs. Henry Russel has given him two spreads at the Biltmore."[58]

Women were reported to engage in frenzied exhibitions of desire for Coogan during the boy's trip to London in the mid-1920s. The *San Francisco Bulletin* reported that a "crowd of women, frantic in their eagerness to have a look at this amazing child . . . pushed their way to the front demanding an opportunity to kiss him."[59] And according to the *Seattle Times*, "women crowded the platforms [at Waterloo station], stairways, street entrance, and fought to get closer to the platform at which the train was due to arrive. The railway police soon were swept away and the metropolitan police . . . had to form a line with linked arms to sweep back the women who fought, scratched, and surged again as soon as the police pressure relaxed. . . . On several occasions the women broke through the line and jumped on the running board and tried to kiss Jackie."[60] Stateside, women and men alike were prone to embrace Jackie. Opera star Enrico Caruso was a fan of the boy, and newspapers reported his holding young Jackie in his arms and exclaiming to the boy's father what a delight he was. The press was less generous to the women who hugged and kissed him, though. Seeing Jackie, women "experience a desire to take the morsel of a star into their arms and sometimes, crowning insult, to kiss him!"[61]

Dimpled Depravity

Even as Shirley Temple reigned as Hollywood's No. 1 star, a new discourse of child endangerment was beginning to emerge. In 1935, Los Angeles area newspapers reported that a twenty-three-year-old man, Maurice Goldberg, had been arrested after demanding to be admitted into the Temple family home.[62] To a nation reeling from the national trauma of the kidnapping and murder of one-year-old Charles Lindbergh, Jr. in 1932, there was increased anxiety over the possibility of public figures being kidnapped for ransom, though as I discuss in chapter 5 these kidnappings were not necessarily understood to threaten the child's sexual innocence.[63] However, Temple's uninvited visitor did not plan to kidnap the young star for ransom. Rather he had hitchhiked from Spokane, Washington, to Santa Monica, California, merely to meet the young star. Upon his arrest, he was turned over to authorities for a psychological examination.[64] Goldberg was one among several men whose adoration of Shirley Temple appeared to signal psychosexual pathology.

According to Estelle Freedman, the figure of the sexual psychopath helped American society adjust to increasingly permissive sexual norms even as it solidified the association of male femininity with sexual deviance: "The concept of the sexual psychopath provided a boundary within which Americans renegotiated the definitions of sexual normality. Ultimately, the response to the sexual psychopath helped legitimize less violent, but previously taboo sexual acts while it stigmatized unmanly, rather than unwomanly behavior as the most serious threat to the social order."[65] Much as the sex psychopath helped to define sexual norms at a time when sexual mores were rapidly changing, accounts of Temple's deranged male fans helped to define normative male pleasure in the child star's image. The men who were consumed by a perverse love for Temple were identified by the sort of overinvestment in her image that has been associated with female fans' devotion to film stars. In 1936, papers reported that a teenage boy who had been jailed for delinquency attempted suicide in his cell after writing a note in which "he told of his despairing affection for the tiny movie star."[66] And in 1937, another man was arrested for exhibiting "strange behavior as he looked at the photograph of [Shirley Temple]."[67] When he admitted having sent Temple two postcards in which he "expressed his great love for her," the Los Angeles Police Department turned him over to the FBI as a suspect in the kidnapping and murder of a young Washington boy.[68] Here, the man's fascination with the image of the child, together with his undisclosed "strange behavior" as he looked at her picture, signaled the possibility that he was dangerous not only to Temple but to all children. While the adoration exhibited by male fans of previous child stars had been celebrated, this man's love for Shirley Temple was not fodder for publicity but taken as a sign of sexual perversity that would ultimately erupt in violence if left unchecked.

This discourse of the dangerous male fan emerged quietly in the 1930s, silenced in part by movie studios that had made a considerable profit promoting the ideal of men's child loving and had little means of profiting from these new fears. However, anxiety about the male sex psychopath—a term that connoted both homosexuality and pedophilia—was mounting outside of Hollywood.[69] In 1937, for instance, FBI head J. Edgar Hoover declared "War on the Sex Psychopath," and national magazines and newspapers ran prominent stories about child molesters and murderers. In the context of this new paradigm, the ideal of men's child loving became increasingly suspect.

Clearly, men's adoration of little girls held quite different meanings for nineteenth- and early twentieth-century audiences than it does for us today. The child-loving bachelor, far from signifying failed masculinity and its attendant threat of perversion and violence, demonstrated white men's ability to put aside their base desires and revel in a "higher sort of love." In celebrating white, middle-class men's adoration of little girls, the press celebrated men's capacity for compassion and protective love for the helpless child.

In 1939, when Shirley Temple lost her position as Hollywood's top-grossing star, several exhibitors attributed her fall to her loss of popularity among men. Bemoaning Temple's plummeting popularity, exhibitors described *A Little Princess* as "The best Shirley Temple picture made," but complained that "our customers, especially the men, are not attending her pictures as they did."[70] While later assessments of Temple's career ascribe her flagging popularity to a variety of causes, it is telling that exhibitors initially identified the problem in terms of a newfound difficulty in attracting adults, especially men, to the child's films. By the end of the 1930s, male sentimentality was no longer valorized as it had once been, and male fandom would not play the same role in the careers of Temple's successors.

CHAPTER 3

IMMACULATE AMALGAMATION

BILL ROBINSON AND SHIRLEY TEMPLE

One man was particularly prominent in Temple's star discourse. The legendary tap dancer Bill "Bojangles" Robinson was featured in four of Temple's films (*The Little Colonel, The Littlest Rebel, Rebecca of Sunnybrook Farm*, and *Just Around the Corner*) and played a significant behind-the-scenes role as her choreographer in a fifth (*Dimples*). Off screen, publicity described the black man as a "devoted slave" to the white girl; he was said to have nicknamed her "Little Darlin'," while she referred to him as "Uncle Billy." The press reported that Robinson had gifts made especially for his young friend: a pair of handmade dancing shoes, with the gilded inscription "To Shirley from Uncle Billy," and a friendship bracelet made of gold and pearls.[1] The pairing appears to have been successful enough that Twentieth Century-Fox sought to reproduce it with other performers; another young, white girl (Joan Carroll) performed alongside Robinson in *One Mile from Heaven* (Allan Dwan, 1937), and when Robinson was hospitalized in 1936, the studio hired another black dancer—Ralph Cooper—to do the choreography for *Poor Little Rich Girl*.[2] And, indeed, white children and black men appeared together on screen with remarkable regularity in the 1930s, particularly considering how rare such meetings were off screen.[3]

As I have argued, the spectacle of white men's child loving was appealing because it seemed to suggest that family and nation were under the stewardship of caring and benevolent men who would eagerly set aside their own desires for the sake of a child. However, black men held very little economic or political power in 1930s America, so the fantasy of a black man's devotion to a white child would have had a very different emotional valence from that of white men besotted by the child. Further, whereas white men's adoration of child stars was often publicized in terms of chaste courtship, Temple and Robinson's affection for one another was described in terms of friendship rather than romance. All this would suggest that the pairing of Temple and Robinson produced quite different meanings than did the pairing of Temple with her white male costars.

This becomes clear through a comparison of Robinson and Temple's performances together to Temple's dancing with Buddy Ebsen in *Captain January.* Their dancing in the "At the Codfish Ball" number evokes the sexuality customarily associated with the dancing of heterosexual couples to comedic effect. The music track signals sexuality with the sound of the "Can Can" when Temple shakes her hips, and it invokes Fred Astaire and Ginger Rogers with the strains of "Dancing Cheek to Cheek" as the man and child press their faces together in the dance. The suggestion of sexuality is made comedic by virtue of the physical disparities between the man and the child. Ebsen's tight sailor's pants emphasize the length and elasticity of his legs; Temple seems impossibly small next to him, barely reaching his waist. This is emphasized when he dances with his hand upon her head or crouched low to the ground, or when he holds the small child in his arms.

Further, while Temple and Robinson invariably dance side-by-side in the style of the challenge dance, Temple and Ebsen's dance mimics the evolution of dance styles that signals the couple's romance in the Hollywood musical. In "I Seem to Find the Happiness I Seek," Richard Dyer considers how the ideal of heterosexuality as "heaven" is produced through the evolution of dance within the musical. The development of the couple's relationship is signaled in the style of their dancing, as they progress from dancing solo or side-by-side to mirroring one another or enacting dependency as the male partner lifts his mate or she leans backward in his embrace. The "Codfish Ball" sequence reproduces this evolution. Temple and Ebsen initially dance side-by-side in a friendly challenge dance. Over the course of the number, they mirror one another, and finally he lifts the child in his arms in an approximation of the stylized dependency Dyer describes. In this way, the number invokes the heterosexual bliss associated with the couple's dance while also signaling the child's absolute innocence; her dependency does not suggest sexual ecstasy but the child's physical dependence on an adult.[4]

By contrast, Temple's dances with Robinson avoid any reference to heterosexual desire. Rather than romance, their dances together recapitulate minstrelsy. They dance side-by-side in the style of the challenge dance, he tapping out a rhythm that she mimics and embellishes upon as in the "Oh Susanna" number in *The Little Colonel.* Or she apes his movements, which are in turn reminiscent of minstrelsy; their mouths open in a wide smile, their fingers splayed, as they enact an awkward cakewalk while busking for tips in *The Littlest Rebel.* Even when Robinson doesn't appear beside her, as in *Dimples,* which he choreographed, we recognize his style reflected in her performance.

A legend of sorts has developed around Temple's dancing with Robinson, a story that appears to have originated with the publication of Shirley Temple Black's

1988 autobiography, *Child Star*, and was repeated often in her obituaries. Black reports that southern audiences objected to the images of Shirley Temple and Bill Robinson holding hands in *The Little Colonel*. According to Black, audiences interpreted their dancing on the stairway of a postbellum plantation home to be suggestive of miscegenation. However, there is no direct evidence to support the claim that southern, or any other audiences for that matter, found the pairing of the black dancer and the white child offensive. *Variety* did express surprise at the film's characterization of a bigoted southern colonel, "in view of Southern play dates."[5] However, the film was approved without eliminations by the Production Code Administration and various state and municipal censor boards. Indeed, southern exhibitors praised *The Little Colonel* as "one of the finest pictures" Fox released in 1934, one that "will please anybody," and reviewers appear not to have interpreted their dancing to be suggestive of pedophilia or miscegenation when they compared the pair to Fred Astaire and Ginger Rogers. Indeed, Robinson's performance of his famous staircase dance for Temple in *The Little Colonel* was repeatedly cited as one of the highlights of Temple's entire career.

As Black's account suggests, and as the surprise expressed by the *Variety* reviewer confirms, *The Little Colonel* was released to a nation that remained divided nearly three-quarters of a century after the Civil War had ended. During the 1930s the Hollywood studios were faced with the difficult task of forging a national audience out of disparate regions that espoused conflicting ethical and aesthetic principles, particularly with regard to maintaining the boundary between black and white populations. As I discuss in chapter 1, early twentieth-century audiences were deeply divided in their tastes. Although sentiment had come to be deemed old-fashioned, many audiences were offended by the lengths Hollywood went to in catering to the new taste in thrills. This taste divide came to a head in the reception of jazz music and dance.[6] "Sophisticated" audiences tended to embrace the new style, but others were deeply troubled by the challenge that jazz seemed to represent to the nation's racial purity. Mae West's career is telling in this regard. West had enthusiastically blurred the boundary between black and white female sexuality in her numerous stage and screen performances. She was often credited with having introduced the shimmy—a frankly sexual dance that she claimed to have "discovered" at a mixed-race cabaret in Chicago's South Side—to white audiences. Further, she regularly performed "hot" blues numbers—"Frankie and Johnny" was one of her signature tunes—that were associated with black female performers. And, though Paramount and the Studio Relations Committee (the precursor to the Production Code Administration) insisted that overt signs of interracial desire be excised from her films, the association of West with black female sexuality was maintained through her suggestive repartee with her black maids.[7]

Far from offending white southern audiences, the pairing of Robinson and Temple was designed precisely to eliminate regional differences and forge a national audience by proposing a solution to the impasse over the place of African Americans in US culture. Fox's casting of Bill Robinson with the studio's most popular star offered a solution to the economic problem of how to capitalize on the talents of a celebrated black performer while minimizing the perceived threat produced by the increased visibility of African Americans in popular culture. At the same time, the pairing conferred the sophistication associated with Harlem onto the child, whose films risked being dismissed as an anachronistic vestige of lachrymose melodrama, an embarrassing throwback to Hollywood's past.

Temple lent Robinson her innocence, and he in turn provided her with a patina of sophistication to counteract the sentimentalism of her films. Her performances with Robinson worked to reinstate the racial ideology that West and others had undermined while still offering the promise of sophistication that had come to be associated with black performers. Temple's appearances alongside Bill Robinson suggested that the meeting of black and white bodies could be fun and exciting without destabilizing racial boundaries. West's performances of such numbers as "Easy Rider" titillated and shocked audiences by proclaiming that West was subject to the same bodily desires as were the black women whose songs and dances she appropriated. Temple, on the other hand, helped to reinstate the ideology of racial difference that was so central to American national identity by demonstrating the intellectual superiority of the white child who could so adeptly mimic the black man's steps while deflecting his sexuality. In pairing Shirley Temple with Bill Robinson, Twentieth Century-Fox helped to counteract fears about the "mongrelization" of American culture by suggesting that jazz music and dance were the product of an immaculate amalgamation rather than a fertile intermixing. In this way, Temple's dancing alongside Robinson helped audiences to imagine away the racial mixing that had contributed to the ubiquity of jazz.

From Harlem to Hollywood

The image of Bill Robinson and Shirley Temple dancing together in *The Little Colonel* was compelling precisely because it represented an interracial exchange without introducing the possibility of miscegenation at a time when the fantasy of American racial purity was felt to be under threat. During the first decades of the twentieth century, the exploding industrial economy had attracted an influx of immigrants from Asia and eastern and southern Europe and had hastened the migration of African Americans from the South to northern cities. Rapid urban growth and technological developments contributed to the proliferation of commercial amusements, from vaudeville and Tin Pan Alley to film and radio, which in turn helped to diversify American public discourse.

In the early decades of the twentieth century, jazz music and dance became a fulcrum for debates about race and American modernity. Although musicologists have demonstrated that jazz developed out of a multiplicity of influences, this amalgamation was minimized in early twentieth-century discussions of jazz. Just as there was little room in the popular imagination to countenance the complexities of identity but to subsume these complexities into broad and presumably self-apparent categories of "black" and "white," so jazz was understood to be the offspring not of a promiscuous mixing of peoples but the discreet meeting of African rhythm with European harmony. Newspaper and magazine articles routinely described jazz as a "primitive" music that had its origins in the "African jungle," a music that threatened the very foundations of American society unless it was tamed to submission by its white interpreters.[8]

At the same time, "sophisticated" white audiences were becoming fascinated by black performance styles. During Prohibition, many white patrons flocked to black neighborhoods, such as Harlem and Chicago's South Side, in search of new thrills. Out of these expeditions emerged what Langston Hughes described as a "Negro Vogue," a fascination with black performance on the part of white audiences.[9] In New York, nightclubs such as the Cotton Club featured black musicians and dancers, including Bill Robinson, performing for white audiences; white vaudeville began to feature black headliners, one of the first of whom was Bill Robinson; and black-cast musicals, including *Blackbirds of 1928* featuring Bill Robinson's famous stair dance, proliferated on Broadway. Robinson was, therefore, a product of the "Negro Vogue," and for many white audiences his name was synonymous with Harlem and the proliferation of black performers in mainstream popular culture.

Hollywood's transition to sound inspired the movie studios to adapt many of the acts that developed out of this vogue for a national audience. A handful of black-cast musicals were released during the early sound era, and individual performers associated with Harlem—including the Nicholas Brothers, Cab Calloway, and Bill Robinson—appeared in short films, many of them produced by Vitaphone to show off their sound technology.[10] However, whereas the Cotton Club, Broadway, and vaudeville were regional venues that catered to local audience tastes, Hollywood film relied on a mass audience. Bringing acts that were so strongly associated with Harlem posed a particular challenge for the studios as they struggled to standardize film to suit the disparate tastes of different regions.

On the one hand, black performers like Robinson were appealing precisely because they evoked the excitement and sophistication associated with Harlem. On the other hand, the cultural and social mixing that Harlem represented provoked fears about the stability of the nation's racial status. The studios quickly developed methods to capitalize on the Harlem vogue without provoking these fears. One approach was to make black performance disappear altogether, and indeed African Americans were relatively scarce in Hollywood feature films. However, from minstrelsy through the jazz age, performances of blackness were central to American music and theater, though African Americans themselves were quite scarce. Further, Hollywood was, as ever, eager to capitalize on headliners like Robinson who had already proven their appeal in other venues.

Another technique for resolving the problem of appealing to an audience committed to racial segregation while still capitalizing on the sophistication associated with Harlem was to limit a given performer's contribution to the film to a specialty number that could be easily excised from prints distributed in southern markets. However, during the sound era the studios sought to standardize their product, not to produce films that needed to be edited to suit the prejudices of specific markets. Further, they felt particularly vulnerable to audience protests during the 1930s, a decade that began with threatened boycotts in response to the perceived violence and licentiousness of Hollywood films.

A third technique for incorporating black performers into films that would appeal to southern audiences was to limit African American performers to broad, stereotyped roles. And, indeed, the studios relied on stereotypes that had been established through nineteenth-century minstrelsy and the ubiquitous Tom show in its delineations of black characters.[11] However, Bill Robinson, who was known for the elegance and precision of his dancing, posed a particular challenge because he was identified with grace and self-control, which were not qualities easily adapted to available racial stereotypes, though his whitened hair and casting alongside a young girl did help to associate him with Uncle Tom, as I discuss later.

Another method for capitalizing on the popularity of Harlem acts was what James Snead describes as a process of "exclusionary emulation," whereby a white star's emulation of a black performer contributes to his or her exclusion from the scene of performance. For example, in *Swing Time* (1936), Fred Astaire pays homage to Bill Robinson in the "Bojangles of Harlem" number, evoking the black performer by donning blackface and putting on Robinson's trademark bowler hat and dapper clothes. However, though the number appears to celebrate Robinson, Astaire's homage actually works to reassert the racial categories that Robinson's success seemed to challenge by reducing the dancer to a sign of hypersexualized, black masculinity. In the process, Robinson's body is removed from the movie screen, replaced with the white dancer's body, and existing categories are reasserted.

This exclusionary emulation was no guarantee that a performance would not offend audiences, particularly when performed by a white woman. Indeed, throughout the 1920s and into the early 1930s, a white woman's exuberant embrace of jazz music and dance was often taken as a sign of her loose morals. For example, in *Our Dancing Daughters* (1928), Diana's (Joan Crawford) disregard for propriety is signaled by her love of jazz dancing; in *Love Among the Millionaires* (1930), Pepper (Clara Bow) deliberately shocks her fiancé with an exuberant jazz performance, "Rarin' to Go"; and in *Honey* (1930), Cora's (Lillian Roth) performance of "Sing You Sinners" conveys her sexual frenzy. It is a testament to Twentieth Century-Fox's success in rendering Robinson safe for national consumption that Eleanor Powell was able to impersonate the dancer by reducing Bojangles to a handful of signs—blackface, bowler hat, tuxedo, and a mobile staircase—in *Honolulu* (1939) without raising the specter of black, male sexuality.

The pairing of Bill Robinson with Shirley Temple represented an effective technique for transforming the black man into a palatable object for national consumption and stripping his image of its troubling meanings. The pressbook for *Just Around the Corner* neatly demonstrates how Robinson functioned as a signifier of urban sophistication while Shirley Temple helped to make him seem reassuringly familiar. In the article, Robinson's devotion to Temple is demonstrated by his nightly ritual of putting her to bed, as he had done in *The Little Colonel*. After performing at "one of the hottest hi-de-ho spots on Manhattan Island," Robinson hurries off stage to make "his nightly New York-to-Hollywood person-to-person call to his friend Shirley Temple." His audience, "blasé New Yorkers" who have been "wowed" to an uncharacteristic show of enthusiasm by his dancing, applauds uproariously, hoping for an encore, but Robinson ignores their flattering calls. Nothing can interfere with his telephoning Shirley: "Whenever Bill's in New York, he invariably calls Shirley just before her bedtime to find out how she is and wish her well. It's just an expression of his sincere friendship of long standing, for it was Bill who first taught Number One how to dance."[12]

Rather than pointing to a troubled history of American race relations—to the legacy of racial violence on the one hand or racial mixing on the other—Temple's innocence guaranteed that their performances together would provide a comforting image of racial harmony and the assurance of racial purity without suggesting miscegenation. The success of this technique for rendering the black, male dancer safe for white audiences can be measured by the relative longevity of Robinson's film career.

Uncle Billy and Little Darlin'

Shirley Temple and Bill Robinson's performances together indicate not a beginning—the first instance of interracial dancing—as some recent accounts would have it, but a new stage in the evolution of the nearly century-old pairing of black men with white girls. For over three-quarters of a century, the most popular stage play in the United States—*Uncle Tom's Cabin*—had featured precisely such a coupling. Linda Williams has demonstrated that since the publication of Stowe's novel, the paired figure of the black man and the white woman or girl has been one of the defining features of the racial melodrama, working to make legible black men's victimhood, as in *Uncle Tom's Cabin*, or their villainy, as in *The Birth of a Nation*.[13] In Stowe's novel, Tom's sojourn in the home of Little Eva is relatively brief, yet the pairing of Tom and Eva quickly became central to

9. Uncle Tom and Little Eva. Images of the pair were reproduced in countless photographs and objects during the nineteenth and early twentieth centuries.

American visual culture. Images of Eva perched on Tom's lap, of Tom holding Eva in his arms, and of the two nestled together in the act of reading or writing circulated widely in illustrated novels, photographs, figurines, and other decorative items that capitalized on the popularity of the tale.[14] Indeed, if anything, Robinson and Temple were less physically intimate than were Tom and Eva. Whereas images of Eva perched on Tom's lap or cradled in his arms had proliferated during the nineteenth and early twentieth centuries, Robinson and Temple generally appeared side-by-side, often holding hands but never sharing the physical intimacy that was so integral to images of Tom and Eva.

Although a number of scholars have pointed to the nineteenth-century fascination with Tom and Eva as a sign of readers' and audiences' cautious fascination with cross-racial desire, Robin Bernstein argues that the physical intimacy between Tom and Eva announces not sexuality but innocence, an innocence that was key to maintaining racial categories. The image of Eva's hand on Tom's thigh "visualized Eva ignoring racial prohibitions and not-imagining sexual congress," Bernstein argues. "Nineteenth-century childhood's ability to assert a state of holy obliviousness while retaining and recapitulating cultural memory was uniquely useful to the construction and maintenance of whiteness" as an unmarked category.[15]

Before "Uncle Tom" became a pejorative in the 1930s, the role was used to render black men safe in the eyes of white audiences. Susan Clark argues that this was the case for Peter Jackson, the heavyweight boxer who played Uncle Tom in the 1890s. According to Clark, one reason for Jackson's accepting the role of Uncle Tom was to counteract the perception that the powerful boxer posed a threat to white society.[16] Jackson's body was implicitly threatening to white audiences by virtue of both his strength and beauty; at least one sportswriter described him as "as nearly perfect as a human being could be: over six feet in height, broad shouldered, with ribs that narrowed in towards hips like the waist of a society belle."[17] The play was amended in order to compensate for Jackson's limited thespian abilities, and Tom did not appear until the third act. As a result, he was introduced not in the context of his eponymous cabin but in the act of embracing Little Eva as he lifted her from her pony.[18]

At the turn of the twentieth century, evocations of Tom's love for Little Eva continued to temper fears about black male violence. In an article in the *Los Angeles Times*, an anonymous writer, who identifies himself as a "Negro," implores African Americans to adopt the example of Uncle Tom to reassure white society that black men posed no danger to white women. The letter conjures the image of the black man as a protector of white womanhood by invoking the image of Tom and Eva alone together: "We must make the humblest white woman in the remotest and wildest part of our country feel as safe in the presence of a Negro as angelic Eva did alone with her Uncle Tom. Let us make the white women of all lands feel that our black arms are ever ready, backed by hearts as pure as truth, as

10. Little Eva helps Uncle Tom write a letter home.

11. Bill Robinson and Shirley Temple in a production still for *The Littlest Rebel*, 1935. Their pose echoes that of Tom and Eva. Author's collection.

guiltless as babes, to defend their honor."[19] Thus the paired figure of Uncle Tom and Little Eva was already well-established as a means of reimagining the powerful black man as pure of heart and "guiltless as babes." So assured were audiences of the purity of Eva in the presence of Uncle Tom that publicity for Universal's elaborate production of *Uncle Tom's Cabin* included a photograph of a white woman, Vivian Duncan, who was then in her early thirties, perched on the lap of the black actor James Lowe, she dressed as Little Eva, he as Uncle Tom, though prohibitions against interracial intimacy between adults were violently enforced at the time.[20]

Uncle Tom's Cabin had long been anathema to white, Southern audiences, and by the 1930s it was felt to be hopelessly outdated, a throwback to outmoded sentimental culture. Nonetheless, by pairing Bill Robinson with Shirley Temple, Twentieth Century-Fox subtly invoked the familiar image of Tom and Eva while updating the pair for modern tastes. Robinson and Temple's first two films together are set on southern plantations, he playing a slave or servant, she the master's child. His hair was whitened in order to make him appear aged like Uncle Tom. And their off-screen nicknames for one another—Uncle Billy and Little Darlin'—echo the loving bond between Uncle Tom and Little Eva. A publicity photograph for *The Littlest Rebel* directly invokes the familiar characters. The pair are posed before a typewriter in antebellum clothing. His hair is whitened, hers in the familiar curls. He is tapping on the typewriter keys as she leans against him, looking over his shoulder, both engrossed in his writing. The pose echoes that of countless "tomitudes" in which Eva helps Tom to write a letter home. During the nineteenth and early twentieth centuries, countless postcards, figurines, and other decorative objects depicted the scene of instruction, the child peering over his shoulders or sitting perched between his legs helping him with his letters. Further, publicity described Robinson as tender and self-sacrificing in the presence of the white child. "In his dancing, he handles Shirley as something very tender and precious—which indeed she is—and he seems mostly concerned with the question of whether she's becoming tired."[21] And just as Tom bravely rescues Eva, dramatically diving into the water to save her from drowning, so publicity assured audiences that Robinson would willingly sacrifice himself for the darling of the Fox lot: "They say around the studio that Bill would lay down his life for little Shirley."[22]

Temple and Robinson's first film together, *The Little Colonel*, worked to update the pairing of the black man and the white girl for audiences in a way that suggested the importance of national unity and imagined a place for African Americans in the modern nation. Ara Osterweil astutely situates *The Little Colonel* in relation to two texts that helped set the terms of ongoing debates about the legacy of slavery—*Uncle Tom's Cabin* and *The Birth of a Nation*—arguing that Temple's films worked to "(insufficiently) suture the festering wound of racial violence that had defined the ideological parameters of American cinema since D. W. Griffith's *The Birth of a Nation*."[23] Like pedophilia, racial violence is a structuring absence in Temple's films. In *The Little Colonel*, a film set in Kentucky during Reconstruction, the Colonel (Lionel Barrymore) threatens to beat his butler, Walker (Robinson), but this is an empty threat that demonstrates the Colonel's irascibility and Walker's acquiescence rather than reflecting the systematic terrorization of African Americans that had been celebrated in *The Birth of a Nation*. While Americans debated the legitimacy of lynching as a means of regulating African American behavior, Shirley Temple's films imagine race relations to be structured by love rather than violence.

The central problem of *The Little Colonel* is not the problem of racial violence but the problem of a nation divided on the question of race, and the film draws on the conventions of melodrama to identify national unity as a moral issue. Drawing on Peter Brooks's argument that melodrama developed in the eighteenth and nineteenth centuries in response to the secularization of European society, Linda Williams argues that Hollywood melodrama orchestrates its characters and narrative situations—its villains and victimized heroes, its nostalgic longing for a "place of innocence," and its "dialectic of pathos and action"—in order to produce "moral legibility," a clear framework for asserting the moral legitimacy of specific values and ideologies.[24] Like Stowe's novel and Griffith's film, and like countless other melodramas, *The Little Colonel* presents us with an idyllic image of home and family only to tear them apart, in this case when the southern colonel's beloved daughter elopes with a Yankee. And, as in *The Birth of a Nation*, the film's climax is a dramatic ride on horseback intercut with scenes of the white family—the Colonel's estranged daughter, her Yankee husband, and their child, Lloyd (Temple)—under threat. Only this time, the family is imperiled not by rapacious black men but by a pair of white swindlers who threaten its economic destruction. Lloyd escapes and runs to her grandfather for help. Recognizing that his family's economic need outweighs his animosity toward the North, the Colonel jumps astride his horse and rushes to rescue his daughter and Yankee son-in-law in a reimagining of the dramatic ride to the rescue made famous by Griffith. In this way, the film works to make what was an economic problem for Hollywood—how to forge a national audience out of diverse regions of varying tastes and ethics—into a moral one, asserting the moral need to realign North and South in order to fight an economic threat.

Through the pairing of Temple and Robinson, Fox assured audiences that, though Bill Robinson might bring with him the sophistication associated with the Cotton Club and the Negro vogue, his presence on screen did not represent a breakdown of the carefully maintained racial barriers that were so central to American national identity. Rather, his pairing with the nation's most beloved child functioned to update the familiar figures of Uncle Tom and Little Eva for a modern, national audience. And, as with white men's love of the young girl, Robinson's adoration of Shirley Temple did not suggest intergenerational desire but rather signaled that his potentially threatening body was guided by a gentle heart.

The Infantile Gaze

Often, Temple functioned as a protective barrier between the image of the black man and his assumed white audience. In their films together, Robinson's dancing is represented as a spectacle not for an adult audience but for the child. In this way, his performances are imbued with cuteness rather than sexuality and audiences are assured that the black man's presence within popular visual culture will not disturb the carefully constructed boundaries that sustained the ideal of white purity against the fact of cultural mixing.

Temple and Robinson's dance on the staircase in *The Little Colonel* set the pattern for their films together, structuring his dancing in such a way that his performance is bathed in the child's innocence. We don't watch Robinson dancing. Rather, we watch the white child, who watches the black man perform the staircase dance that made him famous on vaudeville. In order to distract Lloyd and entice her up the stairs to bed, Walker (Robinson) offers to show her a "brand new way" to climb stairs. She protests, "How could there be a new way to go up stairs?" and he demonstrates his famous dance. Initially, we see his dancing feet

12. Shirley Temple watches Bill Robinson dance in *The Little Colonel*, 1935.

13. Shirley Temple and Bill Robinson in *The Little Colonel.*

in a close-up, point-of-view shot from the child's perspective. Soon, however, the camera pulls back to capture both Walker and Lloyd in the frame, she fascinated by his dancing. In this way, what is "new" is refigured as something familiar—a familiar image of a black man entertaining and comforting a white child—and what had seemed so dangerous—the spectacle of a black man dancing for a white audience—is rendered cute.

Similarly, in *The Littlest Rebel*, Robinson's dancing is introduced through a relay of point-of-view shots that allow the audience to share the gaze of Virgie's (Temple) parents as they adoringly watch their daughter watch the butler, Uncle Billy (Robinson), dance at the child's birthday party. The adults observe as Virgie asks her young guests, "Would you like to see Uncle Billy dance?" The children reply with enthusiastic applause, and with James Henry (Stepin Fetchit) accompanying him on the harmonica, Uncle Billy proceeds to demonstrate his dancing prowess. Interspersed throughout the dance are shot/reverse-shot close-ups in which Billy and Virgie exchange playful hand signals to one another. As in *The Little Colonel*, the spectacle of a black man's dancing is filtered through the innocent gaze of a child, and the audience assumes the spectatorial position of the adoring parents who celebrate the white child's cuteness rather than the black man's art.

14. Bill Robinson dances for Temple and other children in *The Littlest Rebel.*

15. Shirley Temple in *The Littlest Rebel.*

Just Around the Corner, too, offers us the spectacle of Robinson's performing before a crowd of white children, this time in a film set in contemporary Manhattan. And once again, he appears in a spectacle orchestrated by Temple's character, Penny. Penny and her father, a down-on-his-luck architect, live in the basement of an elegant hotel. Penny has enticed the hotel workers to perform for an audience of neighborhood children in order to raise money for "Uncle Sam." The master of ceremonies is a neighborhood tough kid, the opening act a pair of beauticians in uniforms borrowed from the bellboys. And Bill Robinson's number, "Brass Buttons and Epaulets," is performed by the hotel doorman (Robinson) and a chorus line of men from other Manhattan hotels (Café Metropole, the Biltmore, etc.).

The "Brass Buttons and Epaulets" number is remarkable for the manner in which it employs choreographic and cinematic techniques traditionally used to exhibit the female body, in this case adapted to display a chorus line of black men. The men dance in precise unison, in the style of the Tiller Girls or Rockettes rather than the athletic display of physical daring exemplified by the Nicholas Brothers, for example. The performance is even more striking for the series of close-ups on each man's face, a convention familiar from Busby Berkeley musicals in which long shots of decoratively assembled white women are intercut with close-ups of their faces. The effect would be all the more striking had the studio not cut the original lyrics to the song, which urged, "Put a handsome darky underneath your marquee and see all the play he gets."[25] However, the potentially radical image of nine black men dancing in the style developed for the sexualized display of women's bodies is, once again, rendered innocent by virtue of the fact that it is produced by and for white children, and structured through the children's gaze. In this way, the black dancers assume the devalued status of femininity without accruing sexual meanings.

One Mile from Heaven offers a variation on this pattern. Here, the spectacle of Robinson's dancing is tempered by the gaze of black children. In the film, Claire Trevor plays a rookie reporter, Tex, who is sent on a wild goose chase to Maple Heights, an urban black neighborhood, as a practical joke. We share Tex's curiosity as she rushes through the unfamiliar city streets, which are populated exclusively by black men and women. We overhear snippets of conversation that efficiently invoke black stereotypes—two gossiping women complaining about how far they've had to walk, one man urging another to lend him money to invest in a get-rich-quick scheme—for an audience well-versed in such aural stereotypes through nightly radio broadcasts of *Amos 'n' Andy*.

The film assures us that what would ordinarily represent danger—a white woman alone in a black neighborhood responding to the dancing of a black man—is rather adorable. When Tex discovers that she's been made the butt of a practical joke—the body she was sent to find turns out to be the body of a car

16. An audience of children enjoys the dancing of Bill Robinson and a chorus of black, male dancers in *Just Around the Corner*, 1938.

17. A chorus of dancers in *Just Around the Corner*.

in a decrepit junkyard—she is about to return home when she hears the sound of a tap dance. She looks up, smiling, and the film cuts to a close-up of Robinson's feet tapping out a complex rhythm. Like Tex, we hear the staccato of his dancing feet, but we do not see the man who is producing these sounds, though we can infer it is the famous dancer. The film cuts to a montage of black children poking their heads out of brownstone windows and running through alleyways in answer to what appears to be a familiar call. Their feet join Robinson's, shuffling down the sidewalk as Tex follows, curiously looking on. The camera finally pulls back to reveal Robinson surrounded by a bevy of young children. He treats them all to ice-cream cones and demonstrates a dance step. Tex's appreciative smile is a response to the entire scene—the black man demonstrating his steps to an audience of cute, black children—rather than to the image of an agile black man.

It would appear that one reason for Robinson's success in Hollywood was due to the staging of his solo performances in a manner that transformed his spectacularized body from a sign of all the dangers associated with the proliferation of black performance in popular visual culture to one that generated reassuring memories of a familiar performance tradition. And this was largely achieved by filtering his image through the innocent child so that his body connoted cuteness rather than sexuality. One measure of the success of this technique can be found in Robinson's failure to reach audiences in *Café Metropole* (Edward H. Griffith, 1937). In the film, Robinson dances before a sophisticated, white cabaret audience in a scene more reminiscent of the Cotton Club than of Uncle Tom's cabin. After the film was shown to preview audiences, however, the sequence was cut from the film, suggesting that audiences had become enamored of the image of Bill Robinson beside a child and were not eager to be reminded that his live performances connoted sophistication rather than cuteness.

Prophylactic Innocence

Just as the child's gaze functioned as a filter, transforming the meanings of the black man's body, so her body operated as a conduit through which black performances could be imagined to have been transferred to white audiences. In this way, jazz—an art form that was generally understood to represent the mixing of black and white cultures—was imagined not as the product of wanton mixing but as immaculately conceived.

One sequence in *The Little Colonel* stands out stylistically from the others. Whereas the majority of the film is shot on a sound stage using rear projection for exterior scenes, in one sequence Lloyd accompanies her mammy, Mom Beck (Hattie McDaniel), and Walker to attend a baptism on the banks of the river. The sound track is filled with the sounds of a large choir singing "Wade in the Water," a spiritual popularized by the Fisk Jubilee Singers at the turn of the century, and the mise-en-scène is crowded with African American extras. Lloyd is the only white character present for what is framed as an exotic spectacle, and thus she serves as a tour guide of sorts for the film audience. The following day, she reenacts the scene with her two black friends, May Lily (Avonne Jackson) and Henry Clay (Nyanza Potts), the children's innocence eliminating any threat associated with such cultural exchange. The sequence exemplifies the ways in which the white child's innocence functioned to neutralize the dangers associated with African American performance in the context of heightened anxieties about racial mixing.

In *Can This Be Dixie*, too, the white child (Jane Withers) acts as a prophylactic, bypassing Harlem in imagining black performances to have been relocated from the plantations of the South directly to a modern, national audience. Here, jazz is imagined to have developed directly out of the meeting of southern agrarian culture and a modern northern one, and the conduit between these two worlds is the white child. The film is a loosely constructed tale of Doc (Slim Summerville) and his daughter, Peg (Withers), and their attempts to save a southern colonel's plantation from foreclosure. Out of the tired stock figures of melodrama, the film neatly suggests that jazz dance and music spell not the end of white America but its salvation.

The film begins and ends with the image of happily laboring black workers. It opens with the familiar montage of black farm hands stooped in the cotton fields, smiling and singing as they pick cotton. Their children cavort in the fields, and an infant sleeps peacefully on the ground alongside its mother. This nostalgic evocation of the southern plantation as an idealized place in which black workers seem to want nothing more than to serve their white masters was so common to Hollywood films of the period that the sequence may well be derived from stock footage. Indeed, we quickly discover that, though the film has a contemporary setting, these hands are not being paid for their labor. The colonel is too broke to pay his workers, yet they continue to pick his cotton. This is a world apart from the labor unrest and race riots that scarred Depression-era America.

Doc and Peg descend upon the plantation in the hopes of selling their "magic elixir" to the workers. They invite the field hands to engage in a dance competition, and the workers erupt into frenzied dancing, wildly gyrating and mimicking barnyard animals. Later, Peg enters the black workers in a radio competition in order to raise money for the colonel. As the colonel and his family cheer, waving a Confederate flag from the balcony of their plantation home, the strains of "Dixie" playing on the sound track, Peg and the workers embark on their journey north. This journey does not figure in the film, though, and a simple wipe transposes the group from the South to the North. In the next shot, we see Peg, followed by the performing field hands, gazing up at the skyscraper in which they will perform for a radio audience. In this manner, the mixed-race cabarets of Harlem and the South Side are eliminated from the history of jazz, which is reimagined as the sound of the agrarian south relocated to the northern city not by thrill-seeking slummers but by the white child, whose deflective innocence ensures that their songs will be no more dangerous than the cotton they once picked.

Can This Be Dixie goes further, suggesting that the solution to the nation's economic problems lies in the repackaging and marketing of nostalgia, and refiguring jazz music not as a signifier of American modernity but as a vestige of its idyllic past. After the plantation workers, led by Peg performing in blackface,

18. Shirley Temple with Jesse Scott and Thurman Black as the "Two Black Dots" in a production still for *Dimples*, 1936. Author's collection.

win the radio contest, the colonel discovers his plantation is more profitable as a tourist attraction than as a working farm. His grand home is transformed into a nightclub, the workers comprising the floor show, with Peg as its star attraction.

The colonel eventually realizes that he can make even greater profits by literally bottling what the film proposes is the essence of southern living, the mint julep. He buys a factory, operated, of course, by his loyal workers, and mass produces the drink. While Doc's elixir failed to bring the good health he promised, the colonel's mint julep, like the film itself, offers an answer to the question of how the nation might profit from the presence of African Americans on its shores. The film ends with a sequence that echoes the opening scene in order to suggest that the factory is the modern equivalent of the plantation. The same workers once again sing and dance as they perform their labor in the factory. Their syncopated song suggests that jazz music is merely an updated version of the work songs once sung on southern plantations, its rhythms altered to suit the pace of newly mechanized labor.

The film is at once a nostalgic paean to the nation's imagined agrarian past and a celebration of its status at the forefront of modern capitalism. It suggests that the modern phenomena of jazz dance and music have their source in the southern plantations that are such an essential part of the American national mythology and that the black men and women laboring in northern factories are no more threatening than were the field hands for which Hollywood was so nostalgic. And at the center of this comforting narrative is the innocent child, whose ability to safely connect black performers with white audiences is imagined as the linchpin of this cultural exchange.

Similarly, *Dimples* works to reimagine the history of American theater in a manner that imagines the white child as the conduit for racial mixing. Set in antebellum New York, the film features Shirley Temple as the first child to enact the role of Little Eva on stage. *Dimples* begins by inviting its audience to observe the parallels between New York in 1850 and the United States in 1936. Then, as in 1936, the nation was burdened with economic depression and assailed by the empty promises of politicians; an advertisement within the film promises "Vote for Pierce for President: He'll get us out of the Depression by 1852." More specifically, an opening title signals that this will be a film about culture wars: "Little old New York was neither old nor little in 1850 . . . it was a metropolis of half a million, in which decent folks were beginning to tolerate the theatre and young radicals argued against so respectable an institution as slavery." Here, the film identifies an equivalence between southern racial prejudice, which identified slavery as a "respectable institution," and Protestant bigotry against the theater, associated with the North. While the question of slavery was, presumably, safely in the past, the question of propriety in popular culture was at the center of national debate in the 1930s, at least for Hollywood.

The film's concern with the place of black performance in public culture is proclaimed with the introduction of Shirley Temple to the scene. She appears busking for change on the Bowery. She sings and dances, accompanied by an orchestra of young boys playing harmonicas. The children's performance attracts the attention of a wealthy young man, Allen Drew (Robert Kent), who invites the troupe to perform in the home of his aunt, Mrs. Caroline Drew (Helen Westley).[26] There, the dowager smiles benevolently at the sight of Temple tap dancing alongside two young, black boys.

Allen has become enamored of an actress who is attracted to his wealth. In his infatuation, he is determined to produce a play for her, and he settles upon Stowe's novel *Uncle Tom's Cabin* as his vehicle. His aunt is appalled at the idea of a member of her family being involved in the theater. It will be the work of the film to demonstrate that such bigotry—like slavery—has no place in American society. In the end, Mrs. Drew is brought around by the power of Allen's play, her conversion signaled by her tears over Little Eva's death scene much as the readers of Stowe's novel expressed their conversion to abolition by crying for Uncle Tom.

The film ends with a coda that rewrites the history of American theater to imagine minstrelsy as a southern invention brought to northern audiences via the Tom show.[27] And Shirley Temple is at the center of this cultural exchange. On the one-year anniversary of the play's first performance, Allen interrupts the audience's cheers with a shouted appeal to "Wait!" much as Al Jolsen did in his famous spoken dialogue in *The Jazz Singer*. Only this time, rather than the wondrous sound of jazz, the audience is importuned to "wait" to hear a "new form of entertainment" that has come "out of the South." The curtain lifts to a minstrel show, the cast in blackface, all except Shirley Temple who appears in her familiar blond ringlets. In the audience we see the formerly estranged couples reconciled, as though the performance inspired heterosexual couples rather than sexual frenzy. Willie Best performs an imitation of the ignorant black laborer, and Temple performs an imitation of Willie Best as they enact the roles of Tambo and Bones.

Topsy and Eva

Ultimately, Temple's screen persona seems less indebted to little Eva than to the impish Topsy, the unruly slave child who is tamed by Eva's unconditional love in Stowe's novel. Eva's popularity plummeted in the last decades of the nineteenth century, and she was despised by twentieth-century audiences. As I discuss in chapter 1, this was a period of rebellion against nineteenth-century sentimentality. Writing of Marguerite Clark's dual role, the *Los Angeles Times* celebrated her "diablerie" as Topsy and complained, "Eva certainly was a little prig, say what you will, and her death was not untimely."[28] A decade later, Eva was derided as "hopelessly saccharine"[29] and a "monster of sweetness."[30]

While Topsy and Eva initially represented opposites—black and white, goblin and sprite, wicked and angelic, vice and morality—they would increasingly become one, and Little Eva, once sacrosanct in even the most rowdy of Tom shows, became as unruly as Topsy ever was. Prominent among the burlesques of *Uncle Tom's Cabin* was the Duncan sisters' "Topsy and Eva." The play transformed Stowe's story into musical comedy. In it, neither Tom nor Eva dies and the play ends happily with the wedding of Aunt Ophelia. The show toured the country throughout 1925 and 1926, and in 1927 was released as a film. *Topsy and Eva* was dominated by the blackface comedy of Rosetta Duncan, who was the leading female blackface performer of the time and was favorably compared to Al Jolsen and Eddie Cantor. Her antic portrayal of Topsy was described as "distinctly an up-to-date characterization. Her only resemblance to the original is found in the scantiness of her clothing and the blackness of her skin."[31] As "the blooming, buxom, wax-doll 'Little Eva,'"[32] Vivian Duncan was little more than ornamentation, but for her close harmonizing with Rosetta. In their performance, it was not Eva who ascended to the scrim on a wire, but Topsy who ascended, "riding to the proscenium by hanging on to the curtain."[33] In this version, Eva is a spoiled child who threatens to die when she doesn't get her way and comes out of a dead faint to dance wildly with Topsy. The film ends with Aunt Ophelia gratefully tucking Topsy into bed next to Eva.

Similarly, Shirley Temple's persona was updated through invocations of the unruly black child. However, such instances only work to reinforce the distance between little blonde Shirley Temple and the black child she invokes. In *The Little Colonel*, Temple's character is noted for her willful refusal to behave like a young lady. Upon meeting her grandfather, the aging colonel, she splatters him with mud. In *The Littlest Rebel*, Temple blackens up, applying shoe polish to her face in the belief that the Yankee soldiers will treat her cruelly if they know she is white. Of course, they treat her more cruelly when they believe her to be a slave. A villainous soldier demands that she take off his boots, and in her blackface disguise, the impish child tips him onto his back rather than help him undress. And in *Dimples*, when Dimples sighs "I'm so wicked" and offers to sell herself to the aging widow, she is not revealing her wickedness but her virtue. To an audience watching the film in the 1930s, this line would have been an unmistakable reference to Topsy in *Uncle Tom's Cabin*, who was constantly getting into trouble and answered her accusers with "I's so wicked." Mrs. Drew's resemblance to Aunt Ophelia, too, would have been unmistakable. Both are wealthy, middle-aged Yankee women with a strong sense of propriety that is tempered by a soft heart. Temple's line is not meant to suggest that she is actually wicked—in fact she is claiming responsibility for a crime she did not commit in order to protect her grandfather—unlike Topsy, who compulsively steals everything she can get her hands on and vehemently denies any wrongdoing.

Further, within American visual culture, images of white children often work to make white dominance appear natural. According to Rousseau's conception of childhood, the child is a blank slate, unblemished by culture, and therefore a reflection of nature rather than nurture. As Caroline Levander argues, the white child described in political tracts from the Revolutionary through the Civil War eras was naturally freedom loving and rebellious against subjugation, whereas the black child was naturally docile.[34] Likewise, in *The Littlest Rebel*, Virgie's refusal to obey the orders of the Yankee who mistakes her for a slave is contrasted with the behavior of the actual slave child, who cowers in fear. Temple's characters are sensible and unafraid, naturally striving to be fair and honest.

This association of Temple with Topsy, like the pairing of Temple and Robinson, functioned to modernize the adorable white child. *Dimples* very deliberately invokes the history of American theater in order to contrast old-fashioned entertainments with "modern" cinema. In the film, Temple's grandfather, the Professor (Frank Morgan), for example, is a charlatan who had his beginnings on vaudeville. Auditioning for a role in Allen's play, the Professor demonstrates his proficiency at bird calls and Shakespearean dialogue, evoking the sort of outmoded performance that entertained audiences before the advent of the movies.

Similarly, the performance of the play within the film is another opportunity to wink at the audience's presumed memories of the Tom show. During the performance, Dimples, playing Eva, lies dying in her bed while her grandfather is pursued back stage by a pair of policemen. In order to dodge his pursuers, he dons blackface and takes on the appearance of Uncle Tom so that now there are two Uncle Toms. Audiences would recall the absurdities to which the Tom show developed; when two troupes of tommers arrived in the same town, they put on a "double" tom show, in which each of the characters was doubled—so that there were two Toms, two Topsys, two Evas, etc. In this case, there are only two Toms as the professor joins the legitimate Tom on stage in an effort to evade the police.

National Bodies

The pairing of the black man with the white child did more than merely make the black man's performance palatable to white audiences and update the white child's image for twentieth-century audiences. It also worked to assert the black man's unassimilability, the impossibility of his being absorbed into the national body, even as it narrated the process by which jazz became the vernacular of American modernity. While *Uncle Tom's Cabin* and *The Birth of a Nation* paired black men with white girls to radically different ends, both imagined a future in which African Americans were absent. In Stowe's novel, the escaped slave, Eliza, and her family emigrate to Liberia, while Topsy, the unruly slave child, is reformed and grows up to become a missionary in Africa. And Griffith's film begins with the assertion that Africans should never have been brought to

American shores in the first place and ends with a fantasy in which Christ rules over a pristinely white and peaceful American civilization. *The Little Colonel*, on the other hand, literally imagines a place at the table, albeit a separate one, for its black characters. The film begins with a small party in the Colonel's home, with Walker serving drinks to the white guests while the Colonel's daughter plays the harp and sings an old-fashioned air, "Love's Young Dream." It ends with a Technicolor coda in which the Colonel presides over another party at the same home, this time outdoors. The Colonel, his daughter, and his Yankee son-in-law smile adoringly at the sight of Lloyd in a vividly pink dress, and the girl's young black friends joyfully eat ice cream at a separate table. The film's dramatic transformation into Technicolor gives the sequence a fantastical quality, as though to suggest that the "Dream" announced at the film's beginning was realized in this moment in which North and South are reunited, a dream in which African Americans are present though they remain separate from the white family. And the shift from black-and-white to the relatively new Technicolor process lends the scene its associations with progress.

While Temple's films create a fantasy of immaculate amalgamation, they also work to reinstate the black man's exclusion from citizenship, even as they imagine a place for African Americans in the modern nation. African Americans' status as Other has been crucial to maintaining a stable sense of American national identity that is implicitly white. Étienne Balibar suggests that racism is integral to the notion of nation; in order to be identified as a member of the nation one must identify against its outsiders. Michael Rogin and others have demonstrated how immigrants to the United States have identified against African Americans, shedding their ethnic identities—Jewish, Irish, Italian—by establishing the distance between themselves and the black Other.[35] However, the incorporation of Harlem acts into popular discourse posed a threat to this idea of national purity. Robinson's films with Temple worked to affirm black men's status as outsiders by emphasizing the perceived similarities between the white child and the black man.

In Temple's films with Robinson, the white child and the black man are similarly incompetent and helpless within the rational systems of language, capitalism, and justice. The qualities that the black man and the white child were imagined to share positioned both figures beyond citizenship, with the important distinction that the child will one day mature into a citizen whereas the black man will remain beyond the limits of civilized adulthood.

Benedict Anderson describes nations as "imagined communities" whose imagining developed in relation to print capitalism. As printing permitted the wider dissemination of written narratives, larger and larger groups perceived themselves to be members of communities that extended beyond kinship or other established forms of membership and encompassed people one would never see, let alone meet. These communities were bound first by their shared language, a commonality that translated into the idea of nation.[36] Language, then, is integral to determining who is or is not a member of the nation; an immigrant becomes more "American" as he or she becomes more fluent in American English. In this context, the insistence that African Americans speak a language distinct from that of the white nation takes on meanings related to the defining of American citizenship as white, and of blacks as permanent outsiders, an outsider status enforced by slavery, segregation, and incarceration.

Temple's films use language and citizenship to construct an equivalence between the black man and the white girl while also signaling that he will never be incorporated into the nation, whereas she inevitably will. The equivalence between the white child and black adults is made particularly manifest in *The Little Colonel*, when Walker and Mom Beck resort to spelling in order to conceal the meaning of their conversation from the little girl. The joke is that their conversation is riddled with misspellings ("cunel" for "colonel," "fude" for "food," etc.), though Lloyd understands what they are saying all the same. The black adults' and the white child's shared degree of literacy is understood to point to their shared intellectual immaturity. More importantly, Walker and Mom Beck's illiteracy points to their incapacity to become full citizens; Lloyd's illiteracy points to her status as a proto-citizen, a child who will grow up and become a literate member of the national citizenry.

Not only does Temple share the illiteracy of the black characters, her films also emphasize their shared relationship of dependency on the state and ignorance of the justice system. Again, this equivalence signals the black man's status as an outsider and the white child's position as a proto-citizen. This is made apparent in *The Littlest Rebel* when Virgie's birthday party is interrupted by news of the Civil War. Bewildered, Virgie asks Uncle Billy why all her guests have rushed away. He explains that they've gone to fight in a war. She asks what war is, and he replies that it involves "a lot of soldiers and battles where men kill each other with guns." When she again asks why, he answers, "Seems like to me, honey, no one knows why. I heard a white man say there's a man up North who wants to free the slaves." Still not understanding, Virgie asks, "What does that mean, free the slaves?" to which Billy replies, "I don't know what it means myself." Both the white child and the black man are clearly separate from the political action of the film, neither of them completely understanding the doings of white men. However, Virgie has the last line in the scene. Looking contemplative, she mutters to herself, "Hmmm. I wonder?" as though to suggest that in her childish wisdom she can perceive where justice lies despite her ignorance of such human cruelty as war and slavery.

This suggestion that she has an innate sense of justice is confirmed when Virgie and Uncle Billy meet with President Lincoln and beg for clemency for her father, who has been condemned to death for impersonating a Yankee soldier. Lincoln offers the child a slice of the apple he is eating, which she accepts, and then the president takes a slice for himself. As they talk, he distributes the apple between himself and the child. At one point, he inadvertently offers her two slices for his one, and the child points out his error. When he later takes two slices for himself, she reminds him, "No, that one's mine." Lauren Berlant argues that this sequence, in which the child tutors the president on fairness and justice, is emblematic of children's centrality in American political discourse.[37] According to Berlant, the child's naiveté is imagined to operate as a corrective to the cynicism of political life, revivifying adults' belief in a system of justice that has been suffocated by self-interest and a sense of futility. Meanwhile, the black man remains an outsider to this exchange, over-awed in the presence of the man "who wants to free the slaves."

While the white child is shown, in her affinity with the disenfranchised black man, to be a proto-citizen, not external to the system of justice but central to it, the black man is figured as intrinsically an outsider. Even when Robinson plays a police officer, as he does in *One Mile from Heaven*, he fails to function as a representative of the law. Based on a case brought before the juvenile justice court, the film tells the story of a white child (Joan Carroll) whose identity has been hidden and who is being brought up by a black woman (Fredi Washington). The dramatic action turns on a white female reporter, Tex (Claire Trevor), uncovering the lie that the little girl is black. Tex's male competitors challenge her story, producing the child's birth certificate as proof of the child's black parentage. But the document doesn't reveal the truth of the matter; the child whose birth is registered on the birth certificate has died and the black woman has taken the white child under her wing in order to protect her from gangsters. Tex, imbued with the insight and empathy associated with femininity, is able to recognize the "truth" of the child's race, a "truth" that the bureaucracy of the justice system cannot distinguish.

Even as an official representative of the law, Robinson is no more capable of carrying out justice than is the child whose identity is determined by reporters and the courts. Tex combines her female intuition with the ability to navigate the justice system in order to reunite mother and child and ensure, in the words of the judge who presides over the case, that the white child be raised with all the advantages "to which she is entitled as a member of the white race." Not only does Tex's womanly intuition guide her toward the truth that the official records conceal, she is also able to manipulate the court system through subterfuge—disguising herself as a reformer to gain access to the courtroom—and, through empathy to gain the trust of both the child's adoptive and her birth mothers. By contrast, Robinson plays a police officer who knows that the child is white but does not report the lie to the authorities because of his affection for the woman who is raising her.

Thus, even as Temple's and Robinson's performances together stage the meeting of black and white bodies in such a manner as to proclaim their similarity to one another, they do so in a way that affirms the black man's status as Other. The child's innocence played a role in narrating the emergence of jazz in modern life, of erasing its status as an amalgamation of musical styles made possible by cultural mixing, and asserting a history that maintained a chaste distance between the races, imagining children as the carriers of jazz rather than understanding jazz as the progeny of promiscuous cultural exchange. Further, her imperviousness to sexuality or sin served as a filter that helped to purify black culture of its dangerous aspects and make it something to be enjoyed and celebrated rather than feared. In this way, the child's presence alongside black performers functioned to produce an immaculate amalgamation, a mixing without social contact between black and white adults.

CHAPTER 4

BABY BURLESKS AND KIDDIE KABARETS

CHILDREN'S EROTIC IMPERSONATIONS

Shirley Temple began her career at the age of four, when she appeared in a series of short films released as the Baby Burlesks. Unlike the other child-centered comedy shorts of the period—Our Gang, the Mickey McGuire series, Snookums, Buster Brown, Big Boy, and others—the Burlesks did not imagine their cast of children to be typical or place them in what was conceived to be the child's natural habitat, among the neighborhood gang of kids or within the family home. Rather, the Burlesks were innuendo-filled spoofs of popular genre films in which diaper-clad children impersonated Hollywood stars.[1]

In these films, Temple was typecast as a vamp and billed as a "devastating thirty-six-month-old siren."[2] In the second film of the series, *War Babies*, which spoofed *What Price Glory?* (Raoul Walsh, 1926), Temple plays a French barmaid who comes between two American soldiers. The film opens with her character, Charmaine, dancing in a bar, clothed in an off-the-shoulder top and diapers that are clasped with an oversized safety pin. She dances suggestively, watched by a quartet of boy musicians who are clad in diapers and little else. The piano player is so overcome by Charmaine's pulchritude that he lapses into playing "The Streets of Cairo," a musical motif that signals exotic sexuality, until the bass player snaps him back to attention. Leaning against the bar, where he nurses a bottle of milk, Captain Flagg (Georgie Smith) appreciatively watches Temple's dancing and beckons her to join him, offering a lollypop for her attentions. Sergeant Quirt (Eugene Butler) arrives with a girl on each arm, and Flagg and Quirt compete for Charmaine, proffering lollypops in exchange for kisses. When the boys are called away to war, Charmaine embraces one while kissing the other behind his back. And when Flagg shows Quirt the flower Charmaine has given him from her hair, Quirt responds by flourishing the safety pin she has given him from her diapers.

In *Glad Rags to Riches*, Temple is again introduced dancing before an appreciative male audience. This time she plays a showgirl at a tony café, kept by an unscrupulous manager and rescued by a boy from down on the farm. In *Kiddin' Hollywood*, she plays Morelegs Sweettrick (after Marlene Dietrich), who lands a film role when the star, Freta Snabo (Greta Garbo), refuses to perform. Her director and the camera crew are transfixed by her singing, and her costar is so smitten that he prolongs their stage kiss, bending her back in an ardent embrace. And in *Polly Tix in Washington* Temple is introduced in her boudoir, clad in a black lacy bra. This time she is a prostitute hired to seduce a hayseed senator, though in the end he influences her to go straight.

These films seem quite perverse to viewers today, who tend to characterize them as "the mass-mediated sexualizing of little girls," but few Depression-era audiences found anything untoward in them.[3] Exhibitors voiced no complaints

19. Shirley Temple and Georgie Smith in a production still for *Kiddin' Hollywood*, 1933. Author's collection.

about the Burlesks in the pages of the *Motion Picture Herald*, and there is no record that the films were censored.[4] In a 1935 article, Temple's mother, Gertrude Temple, describes them as "good and funny pictures," and notes with pride that her daughter obediently donned her costumes while the other children objected strenuously to the humiliation of wearing diapers and little else; Mrs. Temple bragged, "she would have worn diapers, evening gowns, or nothing with complete indifference."[5]

The perception that these films were "good and funny" rather than perverse reflects the very different understanding of childhood innocence that dominated in 1930s America. Whereas today such mimicry of adult eroticism seems to invite adult desire, a century ago the child's sexual innocence seemed assured. The child's physiological immaturity—her straight torso and flat chest—marked her as incapable of arousing or experiencing sexual desire, no more likely to elicit a sexual response than would the chimpanzees in the Monkey Comedies of the same period.

Likewise, child stars of the time were often imagined to be engaged in miniature love affairs that mimicked the intrigues of their adult counterparts. These impersonations and imaginary intrigues amused audiences because the child was understood to have a purifying effect on even the most scandalous material. When filtered through the body of the sexually innocent child, behavior that would otherwise challenge social mores was transformed into something "clean" and "wholesome." However, in the mid-1930s, new concerns began to emerge in relation to such performances, concerns that baffled the studios and the censors but nonetheless put an end to the practice of children's explicitly erotic imitations.

Playing Grown-Up

Today, scholars tend to describe Temple's performances in the Baby Burlesks as marking the beginning of popular culture's fascination with sexualized girls.[6] However, Temple's early career is better understood as marking the end of an era in which young children's erotic imitations were a staple of both stage and screen entertainments. Far from an anomaly, Temple's appearances in seemingly risqué roles developed over a long period in which children's enactments of adult sexuality had been quite common. During the mid- to late-nineteenth century, all-child productions were a regular feature of British pantomime. In 1867, for example, Charles Dodgson (better known as Lewis Carroll) was a great admirer of the Living Miniatures, whose cast was composed entirely of children. And in the late nineteenth century a vogue for juvenile operettas introduced countless more adult impersonators to the stage; six-year-old Corinne, for example, became a star playing Little Buttercup in *Pinafore.* Such performances inspired debates over children's capacity for expressing the sophisticated ideas and emotions associated with their performances and whether the children were actually interpreting their roles or merely mimicking their elders with no more understanding than a parrot had of the words it spoke. But they did not prompt audiences to question the stability of the child's sexual innocence, which was understood to be absolute.

With increased competition for audiences at century's end vaudeville sought out spectacular novelties to attract spectators, and adult impersonators proliferated on stage. In the 1890s, five-year-old Little Tuesday danced and mimicked famous vaudeville stars. Baby Lil Marks "gave imitations of [male impersonator] Vesta Tilley that were better than Vesta Tilley herself."[7] And Little Ruby and La Regaloncita thrilled audiences with their dancing, which included an assortment of high kicks and back bends, often done en pointe. The *Boston Sunday Herald* describes La Regaloncita as an exotic Spanish dancer: "a turn of her head, a smile, and she is up again with a gay colored fan opened behind her head, which is bent coquettishly to one side."[8] Gus Edwards, one of vaudeville's leading impresarios, developed several troupes of child actors who appeared in all-child variety acts, including "Gus Edwards' School Days" and "Gus Edwards' News Boys." Scores of performers—including Eddie Cantor, the Marx Brothers, and Ray Bolger—began their careers performing in his "Kid Kabarets." Edwards's leading stars, Georgie and Cuddles (the latter would change her name to Lila Lee and enjoy a brief career as a Paramount starlet), were celebrated adult impersonators. Georgie was known for his imitations of vaudeville personalities, including comedian Raymond Hitchcock, African American performer Bert Williams, Ruth Roye, the "Princess of Ragtime," and Eddie Foy, father of the "Seven Little Foys," while Cuddles crooned to her adopted father, Gus Edwards. The *Chicago Tribune* was not alone in praising the young girl "who sings love songs from a box to Mr. Edwards with flashing eye and imploring posture."[9] Florenz Ziegfeld was impressed enough with the pair to propose that they appear in his famous Follies, though Edwards was unwilling to part with his stars.

Off stage, too, children were imagined in adult roles, engaged in chaste romances. These stories imagine heterosexuality without sex, naturalizing gender roles and ethnic stereotypes. La Regaloncita, for example, was reported to be in love with eight-year-old Johnny McKeever, a violin prodigy: "Like all natures of a southern clime, La Regaloncita has commenced early in life to cultivate the grand passion. Already she has had one little love affair."[10] Even the children who embodied more sentimental images of childhood on stage were imagined to be embroiled in romantic intrigue. Gertie Homan, who made a name for herself as Lord Fauntleroy in 1887 at the age of six, was "said to have inspired a passion in the youthful bosom of Tommy Russell [another Fauntleroy], and the courtship of these two pretty children amused the Rialto for a long time."[11] Another of the Fauntleroys, nine-year-old Wallie Eddinger, was portrayed as a "gay Lothario" both on and off the stage:[12]

> Most of the young man's leisure has been spent making love to the various little girls who happen to play with him, and as he is a bright, manly little fellow, and by far the handsomest youngster now on the stage, he has never failed to make a desired impression. But on several occasions he has found some difficulty soothing the indignation of a fair inamorata who has compared notes with her dearest friend. When they both appear before Wallie for an explanation, that young man frankly admits that a man must do a deal of lying to lead two lives, and, before the little girls know where they are, Master Wallie has palavered them into believing that each of them is the best love.[13]

In this description, the young lovers share all the qualities of their adult counterparts, but for the fact that their passion remains chaste. Even this prepubescent Don Juan was seduced into marriage: "after declaring his admiration to several playmates of the gentler sex, [Eddinger] actually, at the age of nine, proposed to Miss Gertie Homan, aged seven. . . . A contract, in the childish handwriting of the little lover and signed by both children still exists."[14] Of course, the fact that Eddinger is enamored of his "playmates" and wrote the contract with "childish handwriting" reminds us that these love affairs are carried out by children whose sexlessness renders their affairs humorous rather than scandalous.

Early Hollywood continued the tradition of casting young children in adult roles, often featuring young girls' impersonations of sexualized women. In Hollywood in 1915, the Franklin brothers developed a troupe of child performers to star in a series of shorts for Triangle Pictures. The oldest member of the group, nine-year-old Carmen de Rue, was best known for her impersonations of Theda Bara. Two years later, Fox studios recruited the Franklin brothers to develop a series of feature-length films that were cast almost exclusively with children. *Jack and the Beanstalk* (Chester and Sidney Franklin, 1917) was the first of a series of extravagant films that showcased the "Fox Kiddies." Four-year-old Virginia Lee Corbin was the female lead opposite three-year-old Frances Carpenter. They were joined by de Rue, Gertrude, Marie, and Buddy Messenger and Violet Radcliffe, a nine-year-old girl who specialized in playing male villains. According to the *New York Post*, adults were particularly taken by Corbin's performance: "Her ecstatic closing of her eyes as Jack kissed her hand . . . appealed to an older part of the spectators."[15] Together the Fox Kiddies also appeared in adaptations of *Aladdin and the Wonderful Lamp* (Chester and Sidney Franklin, 1917) and *The Mikado* (released as *Fan Fan*, Chester and Sidney Franklin, 1918). Budgeted at around $300,000 apiece, the films boasted elaborate miniature sets and lush costumes. Among the set pieces of *Aladdin* is one in which a nude princess (Virginia Corbin) cavorts in her palatial bath, attended by her maid (Gertrude Messenger). Publicity stills for the film show the young girl in harem garb, complete with

20. Virginia Lee Corbin mimics Theda Bara's performance as Cleopatra in a production still for *Aladdin and the Wonderful Lamp*, 1917. Author's collection.

21. Virginia Lee Corbin in a production still for *Aladdin and the Wonderful Lamp*. Author's collection.

22. Baby Marie Osborne. Author's collection.

23. Baby Peggy. Author's collection.

bejeweled bra and slave bracelets, or clothed only in transparent gauze, coyly looking over her shoulder.

Six-year-old Jane and eight-year-old Katherine Lee were also signed by Fox in 1917 and billed as Fox's "Baby Grands." Publicity for the young girls often included photographs of the sisters imitating young lovers. In one photo, for instance, Jane appears dressed as a soldier, kissing Katherine, who is costumed in a Red Cross uniform. Another publicity piece describes Katherine's teaching Jane to make love on stage: "A very dignified one-step ended with a soul kiss, Katherine's stage directing displaying an observant mind. 'Put your arms slowly around my neck. Now bend back—you know this stuff,' and she demonstrated the soul kiss without which no motion picture is complete."[16] And when the sisters did personal appearances wearing grass skirts, they were described as "bring[ing] down the house when they [gave] their version of a hula hula dance."[17]

In 1922, Baby Peggy began her career making Century Comedy shorts for distribution by Universal. Although at first she was little more than a sidekick for Brownie the Wonder Dog, before long the two-year-old was donning elaborate costumes to impersonate the silent film stars of the era in sophisticated spoofs of fairy tales and popular melodramas. In *Carmen Junior* (Alfred J. Goulding, 1923) she mimics Pola Negri and Rudolf Valentino. Reviewing the film, the *St. Louis Post Dispatch* praised her performance in the silent film: "She can't sing the role [of Carmen], but she knows how to put coquetry into it with the aid of expressive eyes, a fan, and a mantilla."[18] In *Too Many Lovers* (also known as *Our Pet*, Herman Raymaker, 1924), Peggy plays an artist's model who sports the "bizarre boudoir costume of [Gloria] Swanson and the jazzy dancing costume of Mae Murray."[19] Likewise, in *Peg o' the Movies* (Alfred Goulding, 1923), she vamps the reigning film stars, while in *Sweetie* (Alfred Goulding, 1923) she transforms herself into Salomé and performs an erotic dance for her parents' dinner guests.

And throughout the 1910s and 1920s, publicity for young, girl stars included glamorous photographs of the girls. Daily newspapers and fan magazines alike featured photographs of children in erotic poses. A nude Baby Marie Osborne clutches a tiger skin to her chest; Jane Lee, in her "Bestest photo," wears a woman's hat, fur stole and muff, and nothing else;[20] seven-year-old Margaret Kosik appears in a bathing suit above a caption proclaiming that she had "such a figure, such grace—Mack Sennett's bathing girls had better look to their laurels!";[21] and Baby Peggy impersonates various Hollywood stars, from Rudolf Valentino to Gloria Swanson.

The advent of sound brought a new style of imitation to the screen as Hollywood recruited vaudeville and radio performers to perform their acts on film. Mitzi Green, for example, had begun her career on the stage at the age of four. Billed as "Little Mitzi, the Child Mimic," she was celebrated for her impersonations of minstrels Moran and Mack, "The Two Black Crows." Her expert

24. Baby LeRoy and Shirley Temple. Author's collection.

imitations were so popular that Paramount signed Green to a three-year contract in 1930. And her mimicry in *Paramount on Parade* (Dorothy Arzner, 1930), *Honey* (Wesley Ruggles, 1930), *Love Among the Millionaires* (Frank Tuttle, 1930), and *Santa Fe Trail* (Otto Brower and Edwin Knopf, 1930) were often singled out as a highlight of these films. Jane Withers, too, was a celebrated mimic, impersonating everyone from Mae West to Greta Garbo, though it was reported that Darryl Zanuck forbade her to give her spot-on imitations of Shirley Temple in public.[22] Baby Rose Marie made her film debut in a Vitaphone musical short, *Baby Rose Marie the Child Wonder*, in 1929 at the age of six. Described as a miniature Sophie Tucker, she sang torch songs in a deep, bluesy voice that belied her youth. In addition to these young stars, Depression-era films were peppered with children's performances of adulthood. Our Gang regularly featured the children putting on a show for the neighborhood kids, with the girls dressed in skimpy costumes, the children imitating various celebrities.

Like their counterparts on the stage, Hollywood's children were imagined to be engaged in miniature love affairs. Young boys were often described as young Lotharios and Don Juans, much as Wallie Eddinger and Tommy Russell had been forty years earlier. In his films, six-year-old Bobby Connelly, star of Vitagraph's "Sonny Jim" series, had several "lovers." According to the *New York Star*, "a film showing him dropping to his knees and kissing [five-year-old Peggy Edeson's] hand with the air of a grand opera lover is one of the treasures of filmdom."[23] Off screen, too, Connelly was depicted as a heart breaker. He was imagined to have jilted Helen Badgely, the "Thanhouser Kidlet," whom he had "proposed" to a year earlier. But Helen had been forgotten: "instead of the impetuous lover, [he] was as fickle as the rest of the men."[24]

Publicity for Jackie Coogan announced that he was in love with a girl from his neighborhood, seven-year-old Patsy Marks, who was described as "a dashing brunet with sparkling black eyes."[25] However, Coogan was imagined to have broken her heart on several occasions when his attentions strayed.[26] And newspapers jokingly reported that La Petite Louise, a French child star who was often costumed as a flapper, intended to seduce Jackie: "La Petite Louise, most popular baby of the French screen, is hardly old enough to talk without lisping, but she has already signified her intention of vamping Jackie Coogan."[27]

Mitzi Green, like many adult comediennes, was portrayed as being unlucky in love: "Mitzi is achieving success—in spite of the fact that her heart beats fast for the dashing Philippe de Lacy, who loves—alas!—another."[28] *Photoplay* described her as suffering from unrequited love for Phillips Holmes, an adult Paramount star. When he stood her up for a lunch date at the studio, the nine-year-old girl was said to have sent him a note asking, "Have my kisses meant nothing to you? I am heart-broken. All is over between us."[29] Spanky McFarland, a popular member of Hal Roach's Our Gang in the 1930s, was similarly portrayed as being besotted with one of the stars on the Twentieth Century-Fox lot: "An idea of his extravagance may be gained from his argument in trying to get [adult star] June Lang to go to the beach amusement pier with him on a date."[30] Baby LeRoy, too, was imagined to have had his heart broken by none other than Shirley Temple. In a photo caption that invokes the scandalous image of Mae West, Baby LeRoy complains, "She was my gal, but she done me wrong." The accompanying interview quotes the toddler as describing Temple as "my idea of the most beautiful woman in Hollywood. . . . She has everything—IT, charm, poise, intelligence, perfect features, brains, brilliant conversation, and a sympathetic understanding for a guy's weaknesses."[31]

Thus, when Shirley Temple made her debut impersonating sexualized adults in the Baby Burlesks, audiences were already quite familiar with children's erotic imitations since young actors had been mimicking their elders on stage for over a century. And when, at age nine, she was jokingly described as "saint and sinner supreme" or it was suggested that she "doubtless has more sweethearts than any one else in history, including Cleopatra" and "for a nine-year-old girl she has done all right with the men," columnists were merely engaging in the sort of tongue-in-cheek publicity that had painted the child stars of stage and screen as miniature versions of the adults whose escapades had scandalized and titillated audiences for nearly half a century.[32]

Kidding Hollywood

Rather than imagining that these young stars had been sexualized by such films and publicity, critics celebrated children's impersonations of sexualized adults as charming and wholesome. The Fox Kiddie films were widely praised as "a welcome relief from the thousand and one vampire films from which [audiences] have lately been suffering."[33] And Baby Peggy's films were repeatedly praised for their wholesomeness. The National Committee for Better Pictures, for example, described them as "not only bright and snappy but clean as well, [their] laughs created by wholesome humor," and the National Board of Review cited Peggy's 1923 film, *Little Miss Hollywood*, as one of the year's exceptional pictures.[34]

These performances were understood not to signal the child's eroticism but, rather, the impossibility of the child's being sexualized. Publicity and films that seem to eroticize these children were understood at the time to celebrate the transformative effect of the child's innocence. Jackie Coogan's innumerable romances, for example, clearly invoke the sex scandals that shook Hollywood in the 1920s, only to provide a means of safely mocking Hollywood's excesses. In the early 1920s, Will Hays, the newly appointed president of the Motion Picture Producers and Distributors of America (MPPDA), responded to a series of Hollywood sex scandals by insisting that a "morals clause" be included in all studio contracts. Publicity for Jackie Coogan and Baby Peggy invoke these

Shirley Temple Mimics Mae West

Has He Got a Friend He Can Bring Along?

Two of the smartest girls in Hollywood are Shirley Temple, sometimes called Wiggle Britches, and Mae West, also known as Diamond Lil. Shirley got her nickname from Gary Cooper. Another of her favorite nicknames is Butch, given to her by an assistant director. Among Shirley's best friends are Jimmy Dunn, who won her heart with a mug of milk; John Boles, and Bill Robinson, who taught her many dance steps. Her autograph book is one of the most valuable in the world.

Greatest box office star in the world. Shirley Jane Temple in 1935 received $69,999 from Twentieth-Century-Fox, and made much more by lending her name to various products. Estimates of her earnings run up to a half-million dollars a year. She was born in Santa Monica, Cal., April 23, 1929, so has just celebrated her eighth birthday. Shirley entered films when 3½ years old, in a "Baby Burlesk" series for Educational comedies. She received $40 to $50 a picture for that early acting . . .

Shirley has 62 golden blond curls, two brothers in college, and a bodyguard. Her father is a broker and her mother makes $500 a week at Shirley's studio helping her. Shirley first walked without help when she was 13 months old. She got her first tooth at the same time. She said her first sentence, "Don't do 'at," when she was a year old. She gets $4.25 each week to spend for herself. She enjoys her work. A special tutor teaches her such subjects as reading, writing and French.

25. Shirley Temple and Mae West. Author's collection.

scandals in order to reverse the image of Hollywood as a city run amok. "Several of our film legal lights are considerably puzzled," announced the *Los Angeles Herald*. "It has just become known that the contracts of Jackie Coogan and Baby Peggy do not contain the morality clause, and there is apprehension that these prominent motion picture stars may get in a scandalous jam."[35] Newspapers tease readers with headlines like "New Hollywood Scandal" and "Scandal! Scandal!" only to report on the imagined imbroglios of child stars:

> Wagging tongues declare a young star has been squandering his money on lollypops for a pretty feminine star. Jackie Coogan . . . refused to make a statement until the out-and-out charge was made that he had "wearied" of Patsy, 7, the little girl who is his neighbor, and had been showering his attentions on Virginia Lee Corbin. Jackie became angered and is quoted as giving this statement: "That's a fib. There ain't nuthin' to it. Patsy's my girl. Virginia's pretty, all right, but she ain't my girl."[36]

Here, the sort of scandal that consumed gossip columns and contributed to the image of Hollywood as an amoral town is turned on its head by the invocation of lollypops and schoolyard slang.

Similarly, girls' impersonations mock sexualized behavior that was scandalous when performed by adults. In *Sadie Goes to Heaven* (W. S. Van Dyke, 1917), for example, Mary McAllister, then eight years old, posed in imitation of a painting, Paul Chabas's *Matinée de Septembre* (*September Morn*; 1912), which had been subject to an indecency suit when it was displayed in Chicago and New York in 1913. Theda Bara's near nakedness in *Cleopatra* (1917) was deemed by censors to be "nasty to the last degree."[37] However, when three-year-old Virginia Lee Corbin reenacted the censored scenes, appearing nude in an elaborate bath in *Aladdin* (1918), the scene was found to be "capitally done."[38] And in *George White's Scandals of 1934* (Thornton Freeland et al., 1934), a young girl performs a fan dance in the style of burlesque dancer Sally Rand, who was arrested for indecent exposure at the 1933 Chicago World's Fair when she introduced the dance to fair audiences. Mitzi Green gave imitations of adult stars who challenged American sexual mores, from Maurice Chevalier to Clara Bow and Mae West. Young girls shimmied and danced the hula, imitating the dances that were the subject of heated debate about the changing nature of American public life. They sang "boop boop a doop" songs in the style of Helen Kane, whose baby-voiced sensuality was the inspiration for Betty Boop. And they mimicked Hollywood's vamps, from Pola Negri to Mae West, stars who helped inspire audiences to effectively threaten Hollywood with boycotts if the studios did not enforce its own Production Code.

Shirley Temple's performances in the Baby Burlesks are clearly an iteration of this tradition, invoking the female stars that had scandalized audiences. In *Kiddin' Hollywood*, Temple sings one of Marlene Dietrich's signature tunes, "Falling in Love Again" from *The Blue Angel* (Josef von Sternberg, 1930), her blonde curls pierced with an arrow, as Dietrich's were in *Blonde Venus* (Josef von Sternberg, 1932), and kisses a legionnaire, in reference to Gary Cooper's role in *Morocco* (Josef von Sternberg, 1930). And in *Polly Tix in Washington* her characterization of Polly, the prostitute, is loosely based on Mae West's star persona. Like West's characters, she is accompanied by a black maid, and when the senator initially resists her charms, she utters one of West's well-known lines from *She Done Him Wrong* (Lowell Sherman, 1933), "You can be had." Her love of jewels and her punning one liners further reference West; when the senator's daughter tells her "You're not a good woman," Polly replies, "You've got to be good to get stuff like this [motioning to her jewels] in these hard times."

Children's impersonations of adult sexuality actually served to emphasize the gulf between adults' and children's bodies. In this way, the films suggest that the child's innocence is biologically determined and immutable, converting debauched behavior into wholesome entertainment. The young girl's décolletage reveals not the breasts of a woman but the flat chest of a child. When the girl lifts her fan or drops her robe, we see not the curve of hips but a straight and slender torso. Although Virginia Lee Corbin appears nude amid the erotic accouterments of Cleopatra's bath, her straight torso is unmistakably prepubescent. And while Temple may sway and strut in the manner of Marlene Dietrich as she sings "Falling in Love Again," her diaper-clad body has all the chubby roundness of a young child, and her piping voice is a far cry from Dietrich's sultry contralto.

In this sense, these performances were rather like nineteenth-century European and American portraiture that made reference to adult female sexuality in order to produce images of childhood innocence. In her examination of representations of children in Western art, Anne Higonnet demonstrates that, since the eighteenth century when the sentimental ideal of childhood as a period of angelic innocence began to emerge in Europe, images of children have reflected a very specific understanding of childhood, one that correlated with the Romantic ideal of childhood innocence: in children's portraits, the child's body is emphasized in such a way as to highlight her corporeal differences from adults. Higonnet identifies five modes in which the Romantic child was regularly portrayed, each emphasizing the child's innocence and bodily difference from the adult: 1) in costumes from the past that made her seem timeless; 2) in the company of small animals, which works to reinforce the association of the child with nature; 3) in the arms of a woman; 4) as an angel, cupid, or fairy, suggesting the child is not entirely human; and, as in the films discussed here, 5) imitating adult gender roles.[39]

According to Higonnet, the children's imitations of adult gender roles emphasize the disparity between the child's sexual innocence and the adult state of knowledge by making veiled reference to the sexuality that will one day come with adulthood. Higonnet's analysis helps to shed light on one of the most popular of the Victorian images of children, *Cherry Ripe* (John Everett Millais, 1879). The portrait of a little girl contains several references to adult sexuality. The title—Cherry Ripe—refers to a poem in which the ripened cherries signal the young woman's sexual maturity. Further, the child holds her hands pressed together in her lap in a manner that brings female genitalia to mind, and her billowing skirts evoke the outline of womanly hips at odds with her flat chest.[40] Rather than shocking audiences with this association of childhood and sexuality, however, Millais's portrait was embraced as an image of childhood purity. The Pears Soap Company purchased the rights to the image, and it became one of the most widely reproduced images of childhood in the nineteenth century.[41]

As with Temple's portrayals of sexualized women, *Cherry Ripe* and other portraits that once connoted innocence have now come to seem perverse. Pamela Reis argues that the signs of adult sexuality within the portrait suggest that its popularity was due, in part, "to its pronounced pedophilic appeal."[42] However, within a nineteenth-century logic, as Higonnet's analysis suggests, these indicators of adult sexuality serve to highlight the differences between the girl and the woman she will become: she is prepubescent and, therefore, according to the logic of the time, presexual. Invocations of adult sexuality point not to the child's desirability but to the distance between the girl and the woman, a distance that, to the nineteenth-century eye, signaled the impossibility of her inviting a sexual response.[43]

Something similar to *Cherry Ripe*'s invocation of the child's absent sexuality can be seen at work in the numerous glimpses we're given of Shirley Temple's underwear. These function not to construct "paedophilic desire" and "reduce Temple to an essentialist position of universal sameness where all female bodies are constructed in like democratic manner," as Nadine Wills argues in her exploration of the crotch shot and the manufacture of femininity in Hollywood musicals.[44] Rather, the child's extremely short skirts and exposed panties highlight her difference from adult female bodies and construct what Lori Merish describes as a "maternal" desire for the cute child.[45]

This transformation of sexual desire into maternal desire is explicitly enacted in the "Baby Take a Bow" number in *Stand Up and Cheer,* which effectively transformed Temple into a movie star. The number begins with an adult man, Jimmy (James Duggan), in top hat and tails, dancing with an adult woman who wears a long, ruffled dress that draws attention to her legs; Jimmy sings of the admiration the woman inspires: "Everybody's asking me,/'Who's that bunch of personality?'" And he invites his paramour, "Baby, take a bow." Jimmy's dance partner is replaced by a bevy of women in short skirts that are hitched up in the back to reveal their ruffled underwear. More chorus girls pour in wearing more elaborate and revealing costumes, and the camera slowly pans their smiling faces in a style associated with Busby Berkley's choreography. The number quite clearly supports Wills's argument that the Hollywood musical "is about gratuitous gender display."[46]

Then the music shifts, and the melody is carried not by the horn section but by bells, evoking the delicate sounds of a music box. The chorus line is transformed into a line of dolls in ruffled, polka-dotted dresses. When the camera tracks back it becomes apparent that the "dolls" are in fact fashioned out of women's legs, the faces painted onto the dancers' knees. Jimmy again takes center stage and stands with his legs wide apart. The sequence reverses the camera work associated with Berkley, in which the camera glides between women's spread legs. Here, the child emerges from between the legs of a male dancer, wearing a ruffled, polka-dotted dress that barely skims the top of her thighs, revealing a profusion of ruffled petticoats and underwear. The child's entrance—announced by the shift in music—emphasizes her difference from the chorus girls and defines that difference in terms of innocence; whereas the women's ruffled underwear was sexy, the child's ruffled underwear is adorable.

The presence of the innocent child transforms the dance number from one connoting sex to one that connotes cuteness. The women, who had once signaled sexual desirability, now suggest maternal desire as they ask of Temple, "Who's that bunch of personality?" And Jimmy's sexual desire is transformed into paternal pride when he instructs the child, "Baby, take a bow." In this way, uncontained desire for countless undifferentiated women metamorphosizes into the desire to cuddle one extremely cute child.

These performances helped audiences adapt to a new commercial culture built around the spectacle of eroticized women. Rather than suggesting that young girls, too, were part of this erotic spectacle, the child's presumed innocence emptied these performances of their dangerous sexuality, making them the object of innocent fun. In this way, children's impersonations of sexualized adults worked at once to render these dangerous aspects of American culture innocuous and to reinforce the idea that the child's innocence was capable of deflecting adult desire rather than being transformed by it. However, unlike Baby Peggy or Virginia Lee Corbin, Shirley Temple would not engage in erotic mimicry in her feature-film performances.

"Nasty Man"

In 1934, as Temple emerged into international stardom, Hollywood began to receive complaints about young girls' erotic imitations rather than the encomiums that had greeted Baby Peggy and the Fox Kiddies' performances. That year, the Catholic magazine *Commonweal* protested against a child's impersonation of Mae West in an unidentified film: "Why do they permit children to be exploited in sophisticated roles? Specifically, on what conceivable theory of taste or morals did they allow two children recently to give a rendering of a scene from *Diamond*

Lil, in which the chubby girl, scarcely more than a baby, with all the convolutions of hip and torso that made the original line famous, invited an equally small boy to 'Come up and see me some time?'"[47] A change was under way in judgments about children's impersonations of adult eroticism, a change that left the studios somewhat flummoxed.

Shirley Temple's emergence as a star coincided with the establishment of the Production Code Administration (PCA), which enforced the Production Code from 1934 until the 1960s. From the first decade of the twentieth century, when film emerged as a popular form of public entertainment, various groups had protested what they perceived to be the deleterious influence of the movies on the morals of young people and immigrants. In an effort to stave off government censorship, the Hollywood studios agreed to abide by a set of guidelines, the Production Code, that promised to temper the sex and violence in their films. However, it wasn't until the studios were threatened with boycotts in the early 1930s that they developed a system for enforcing the Code. The Production Code Administration, headed by Joseph Breen, vetted the studios' films in order to preclude the distribution of material that might be found objectionable by censors and audiences in the United States and abroad. Breen and his staff strove to predict the objections that myriad groups might have whether or not they personally found the material objectionable. This involved a process of tracking the eliminations that had been made by various censorship boards, reading film reviews, and fielding complaints from both studios and audiences.

Shortly after the PCA was established, Breen began to receive complaints about a child's eroticized performance in *George White's Scandals.* In his capacity as head of the PCA, Breen had assured Will Hays that there was nothing objectionable in the sequence. He had approved the film's script and the release print. Censors in Chicago, Kansas, Maryland, Pennsylvania, and Virginia echoed his assessment when they approved the film with only minor alterations. However, by June of 1934, *George White's Scandals* was among sixty-three films banned by the Legion of Decency and was subsequently withdrawn from distribution. There was a litany of objections to the film. Most of the complaints centered on the film's vulgar humor, which referred to toilet seats and breastfeeding among other things. However, the sequence that generated the most outrage was the one in which a young girl of roughly five years performs a fan dance, mimicking the erotic play of concealment and exposure that Sally Rand had introduced the previous year at the Chicago World's Fair. In the film, the child shimmies and jerkily arches her back in an awkward approximation of Rand's infamous dance, singing to an imagined "nasty man," "I know you're hoping I'll drop my fan. Go ahead, stare all you can." She concludes the number by lifting the fan to reveal that she is naked but for a pair of white cotton underwear.

Breen was surprised to receive word that some audiences found the sequence objectionable, particularly in light of the fact that there were no objections to

26. Shirley Temple and Buddy Ebsen in a production still for *Captain January*, 1936. The sequence in which Temple performed a hula was cut from the release print due to audience protests. Author's collection.

Alice Faye's singing the same song. An internal PCA memo painstakingly identifies the source of audiences' concern: "The real objection was wholly on the basis of having a child do the fan dance and sing the song, "Oh! You Nasty Man!" In short, the objection was not to the dance or the song, per se, but to having a little child perform them in combination."[48] Similarly, when the East Coast office of the PCA raised objections to a Warner Bros. short, *Trouble in Toyland* (also known as *Kiddie Review*), in which a young girl performs a rhumba singing "La Cucaracha," the studio was baffled by the response. Initially, the PCA asked that the film be edited to eliminate "only that very short sequence where the child imitates an adult's wiggling of torso."[49] However, when the office was provided with a translation of the lyrics, which included references to Pancho Villa's chest and to marijuana, it determined that the number should be eliminated altogether. Vitaphone found the cut so outrageous that they wrote a letter of protest: "We feel that some of the suggestions made by your office are very unreasonable. . . . Aside from asking us to take out the little Spanish girl in the kiddie picture, which I thought was ridiculous, there have been many other occurances [*sic*]."[50] And Warner Bros. complained that they could not "understand how you can take exception to a small child doing the Hula and the Rhumba in a picture." The studio felt that, because the dances were performed by a child rather than an adult, they were entirely innocent. "If it were a grownup you might have some reason to object, but this is a kiddie review."[51]

The protesters were rather vague about the reasons for their concern. It is not clear that they, like audiences today, objected to these performances because they seemed to invite audiences to take erotic pleasure in the child's image. Unlike Graham Greene's assertions that Temple's performances appealed to audiences who remained ignorant of their own desire for her "well shaped and desirable little body," these protests do not rest on a Freudian understanding of repressed desire. Rather, discomfort was framed in terms of the "bad taste" of such performances: "When the appeal of children is exploited in an objectionable song and dance, and an evident six year old stages a pathetic imitation of a fan dance one feels that the depths of bad taste in screen entertainment have been reached."[52]

One reason for the shift in interpretation of these performances may have had to do with the introduction of sound technology—which allowed children to verbalize adults' words rather than miming them. Virginia Lee Corbin and Baby Peggy had merely pantomimed their erotic desire. The fan dancer in *George White's Scandals*, by contrast, actually spoke offensive dialogue. Writing of *George White's Scandals*, a representative of the General Federation of Women's Clubs complained, "A chorus of small children, wholly innocent of its meaning, is used to exploit the offensive song, 'Oh, You Nasty Man.'. . . When . . . you . . . put into the mouths of little children what would be repulsive coming from adult actors we feel we have the right . . . to protest."[53] The complaint doesn't explicitly suggest that the child has been sexualized, and it asserts her continued innocence in noting her apparent ignorance of the song's meaning. Similarly, in its protest against a child's impersonation of Mae West, *Commonweal* cited the child's voicing West's famous double-entendre, "Come up and see me some time," in combination with "the convolutions of hip and torso that made the original line famous" as objectionable.

In 1936, Breen warned Twentieth Century-Fox that the studio would need to tone down one of Shirley Temple's performances in *Captain January* (David Butler, 1936) because "any . . . ribald quality in such a character done by a child might bring on a storm of protest."[54] Ultimately, Breen found "little, if anything, that is reasonably censorable" in the film and approved a sequence in which Temple impersonates a sailor with a girl in every port, singing "lines about China, France, Hawaii, etc., illustrating each with mannerisms and characteristic dance steps."[55] According to the *Hollywood Reporter*, so many women protested the sequence in previews that it was cut from the release print.[56] Contemporary audiences have attributed this censorship to audiences' objections to Temple's being sexualized.[57] However, only six months earlier Temple had performed a hula dance in *Curly Top*—wearing a grass skirt, a lei, and nothing else—in a sequence that appears not to have offended the public and was, in fact, recycled in *Young People* (Allan Dwan, 1940) for a montage depicting Wendy's (Temple) childhood as a stage performer. It seems more likely that, as Breen predicted, it was the ribaldry of the song's lyrics that audiences found objectionable.

The emergence of complaints about children's erotic imitations after 1934 might also be attributed to the fact that the Production Code Administration offered a new, centralized venue for fielding such responses. Prior to the establishment of the PCA, censor boards had, in fact, cut some film sequences in order to eliminate images of children's genitalia. Virginia Corbin's bathing scene in *Aladdin* and Mary McAllister's recreation of the painting *September Morn* had both been subject to cuts by Chicago censors. (The same censor board insisted on eliminating shots of nude statuary and references to dirty diapers.) However, these scenes were not cut in their entirety, but only censored to eradicate views of the girls' exposed genitals. The bathing scene in *Aladdin*, for example, was cut "from the time she drops drapery until she is seen in the pool," thus retaining references to adult eroticism while eliminating any view of Corbin's nudity.[58] Indeed, the Production Code included a clause that prohibited such exposure, and the fan dancer in *George White's Scandals* remains partially clothed, unlike Corbin or McAllister. The PCA and the studios attributed protests against children's erotic performances not to the bad taste or suggestiveness of the films but to opposition to child labor in general, as I discuss in the next chapter.

It appears that a change was under way. The very type of erotic imitation that had once been celebrated by organizations like the National Board of Review were now beginning to raise complaints from similar organizations. It appears that these performances no longer signaled the inviolability of childhood innocence. The objections to *George White's Scandals of 1934* points to the emergence of a new discourse about children's vulnerability. However, the perplexity of the PCA suggests that this was a period of transition and that the terms of this new discourse were not yet well-established.

"When I Grow Up"

Following the controversy over *George White's Scandals of 1934*, the Production Code Administration would pay closer attention to young children's imitations of adult eroticism, though with little understanding of the concerns these performances aroused. Temple's career was shaped, in part, by an understanding that such impersonations would be met with condemnation rather than the encomiums that had greeted Virginia Corbin's turn as Cleopatra and Baby Peggy's as Salomé. When Temple did impersonate adults during her time with Twentieth Century-Fox, the films carefully sidestepped any hint at the references to illicit sexuality that had been so central to the performances of earlier child stars.[59] In *Poor Little Rich Girl*, for example, rather than mimicking sexualized vamps, Temple impersonates Bing Crosby, a crooner who was associated with Catholicism and fatherhood, and she does so in a cute, ruffled dress. And in *Stowaway*, she likewise remains in her childish togs when she sings "You've Got to S-M-I-L-E (to Be H-A-Double P-Y)" in the style of Al Jolson, Eddie Cantor, and Ginger Rogers and Fred Astaire. Further, rather than inviting salacious looks from a "nasty man," the song's lyrics are indisputably chaste, exhorting audiences to the childish optimism that was her trademark.

Similarly, in *Curly Top*, when Elizabeth (Temple) performs "When I Grow Up," she imagines herself as "sweet sixteen" in a frilly, virginal gown, in a white wedding dress at twenty-one, and when she is "very, very old" she appears as Whistler's mother before exuberantly lifting her skirts and dancing off stage. Each image of adult womanhood is defined by virginity or celibacy, and the lyrics make it clear that she is imagining herself in the adult roles she has seen depicted in her picture books, not the sexualized women who populated Hollywood movies. Unlike her erotic imitations in the Baby Burlesks, her performance of adult femininity in *Curly Top* and *Captain January* present what is meant to be a child's fantasy of adulthood, a fantasy as chaste as the child's mind is imagined to be.

Even when she wasn't explicitly impersonating adults, however, Temple's performances often invoked adult sexuality. But rather than sexualizing Temple, the association of Temple with illicit sex helped to make sexualized women and other challenges to American mores the object of fun, much as Virginia Corbin, Jane Lee, and Baby Peggy had done in the silent era. In *Stowaway*, for example, the popular cycle of fallen woman films is reimagined in relation to the child. In *The Wages of Sin*, Lea Jacobs argues that the Code developed, in part, to counteract the perceived ill effects of what she terms the fallen woman film, films in which a woman trades on her sexuality. Jacobs argues that, while Mae West may have been a touchstone for film industry critics who demanded that Hollywood curtail its erotic imagery, complaints about her films were part of a longstanding concern that Hollywood would corrupt female audiences. Specifically, reformers feared that girls watching films about gold diggers and other venal women would learn to perceive their sexuality as a bartering chip rather than the foundation of marriage and family.[60]

As with the impersonations of sexualized women, *Stowaway* uses the figure of the child to turn the controversial elements of the fallen woman film into a benign joke. The film opens with a series of gags in which the child's body quite literally substitutes for that of the fallen woman. Here, Shirley Temple plays Ching Ching, the orphaned daughter of missionaries who has been separated from her guardians during a rebel uprising. Alone and penniless in Shanghai, Ching Ching happens upon a carefree bachelor, Tommy (Robert Young), who is buying a souvenir from a Chinese vendor. Pamela Robertson Wojcik analyzes this and other scenes in which Temple walks the streets (her hitchhiking in *Bright Eyes* and being chased by a policeman through the foggy streets of Victorian

London in *A Little Princess*) to demonstrate how Temple's films worked to reimagine the street walker, a figure that generally signifies the dangers of uncontained female sexuality in the modern city, to render her benign.[61] In *Stowaway*, Temple "picks up" Tommy; he treats her to lunch at a restaurant and takes her along in his car when he goes to meet his friends at a bar frequented by Anglo-American tourists. What would be the scene of moral downfall if Ching Ching were not a child—the penniless woman's charming the dissolute playboy so that she might cadge lunch off him—instead instigates Tommy's moral redemption.

The film reinforces this analogy between Ching Ching and the absent fallen woman through its jokes, which rely on Temple's ability to invert the figure of the venal woman. Tommy's friends invite him to join them for a drink, but he refuses, joking that he is "under the spell of a good woman." They naturally assume that he has formed a romantic attachment and ask to meet the "good woman." Tommy brings the group to the car where he has left the child to wait for him, warning his friend to monitor his "Rabelaisian" language in front of her. However, he is surprised to find the child is gone, the car empty. "At least she left you the car," his friend consoles him. "Sometimes they don't even do that." And the friend launches into a reminiscence about a woman he picked up in Kansas. Here, once again, the figure of the fallen woman is substituted with that of the innocent child, the friends continuing under the mistaken impression that Tommy has been jilted and robbed by a woman he picked up on the streets of Shanghai.

Later, Ching Ching inadvertently becomes a stowaway on the luxurious ship that is transporting Tommy to Bangkok. When the captain discovers her, he takes Ching Ching and the woman she has befriended, Susan (Alice Faye), to see "Uncle" Tommy, but Tommy is asleep: "Mr. Randall never gets up before 2:00, sir," Tommy's valet informs the captain. When the captain insists that Tommy be woken, the valet nervously interrupts his employer's sleep: "I'm sorry, sir, but there's a young lady to see you." Tommy grumbles, so the valet adds, "She is beautiful." "That's not so bad," responds Tommy. "She has a child," continues the valet. "That's bad." "And the captain." "That's very bad." Again, Tommy's playboy past has led to a misinterpretation, and Ching Ching's presence, this time with the captain, is imagined to be a sign of Tommy's past indiscretions. Tommy grabs his checkbook and starts writing out a check to the woman he assumes must be there to demand child support before he realizes that the child in question is Ching Ching. What would be a salacious story of abandonment and blackmail is transformed into a joke by virtue of Temple's presence.

Unlike previous girl stars, Temple did not build her stardom around erotic mimicry. Although Mae West played an important role in Temple's stardom, as I discuss in chapter 2, the child would not continue to imitate West, Garbo, Dietrich, or Hollywood's other scandalous women while she was with Twentieth Century-Fox. During Shirley Temple's career, forces were already gathering that would help bring an end to the child-star era. Freudian ideas proliferated during the post-World War II era, eventually dominating discourses about childhood and adult sexuality. This ideology tapped into and helped to explain audiences' emergent nervousness about girls' eroticized performances, a nervousness that was as yet inchoate during Shirley Temple's own career.

CHAPTER 5

ECONOMIC INNOCENCE

THE PARADOX OF THE PERFORMING CHILD

In 1934, when the Production Code Administration began to receive complaints about children's impersonations of eroticized women, the Code administrators were somewhat at a loss to explain to the studios what it was that audiences found objectionable in these performances. Whereas religious groups and women's club members may have understood that the child who performed a fan dance or a hula represented a challenge to the ideal of childhood innocence, this challenge was not readily apparent to Joseph Breen and the Hollywood studios.

As I discuss in the previous chapter, Breen and his colleagues clung to the well-established view that children's sexual mimicry could only highlight the inviolability of the child's innocence. The PCA interpreted audiences' objections to such performances as a response not to the children's eroticization—an eroticization that seems so apparent to twenty-first-century audiences—but to the child's economic exploitation. Rather than attribute complaints to a rather new interpretation of children's erotic mimicry as dangerous, the Production Code Administration perceived these complaints to be an outgrowth of longstanding concerns about child labor. Writing of audience objections to the young girl's fan dance in the "Nasty Man" number in *George White's Scandals of 1934*, one administrator wrote, "It must be remembered that we have one group of critics who are opposed in principle to having children appear in professional acts and, of course, they are always looking for situations of this kind to justify their point of view."[1]

Whereas the child's sexual innocence seemed assured to Production Code administrators, another equally important aspect of childhood appeared to be put at risk by children's performances. What was at stake, it seemed, was not the child's sexual innocence but her economic innocence. By the 1930s, mandatory schooling and labor laws had all but eliminated children from the workforce and relocated them to the classroom. Viviana Zelizer describes this as part of a larger shift whereby children became "economically useless"—no longer vital contributors to the family economy—but "emotionally priceless," their emotional value demonstrated in the exorbitant amounts parents would pay for a child's funeral or be paid in a suit over the wrongful death of a child. Although the economic depression of the 1930s sorely challenged the ideal that white children of every social class should be protected from labor, and Shirley Temple's tremendous success inspired countless parents to pursue acting jobs for their children, Temple's films invariably rely on and reinforce the ideal of the child's economic innocence.[2]

The sentimental ideal of childhood innocence developed hand-in-hand with industrial capitalism. As the marketplace expanded to incorporate more and more aspects of American life, childhood was imagined as a precapitalist Eden, a repository for all that had been lost to modernity. The child's innocence provided a respite from the alienating effects of the marketplace. Indeed, this was the source of the rejuvenating effect the child was understood to have on adults, an effect that was integral to many of the theatrical and film performances that featured children, as I discuss in chapter 2.

However, the performing child was an abomination of the sentimental concept of childhood. Enacting innocence on screen, she is tainted by the very things that children are meant to be protected from. "Children on the stage created a curious paradox," writes Zelizer. "They were child laborers paid to represent the new, sentimentalized view of children. They worked to portray the useless child."[3] The performing child exists not in the private realm of the family but is the object of a public gaze, consumed and adored by a mass audience. Unlike the child of nature, she is highly artificial. Her hair is dyed and curled, her face painted, and she is trained by adults to portray cuteness and innocence, though these qualities are imagined to become obnoxious if they are enacted consciously rather than spontaneously. Finally, she is a laborer, often responsible for the economic welfare not only of her family but of her employers and coworkers as well, inverting the parent–child relationship and the ideal that the child should remain separate from the marketplace, an ideal that is, ironically, the very basis of her appeal.

This paradox—the conflict between her enacting economic innocence on screen and her status as a child laborer off screen—was far more troubling to Depression-era audiences than were any of the aspects of her career that seem so pedophilic to us now. The child's ignorance of and immunity to the marketplace were key elements of Temple's appeal. And yet this economic innocence seemed constantly under threat by virtue of her status as a laboring child.

Come and Get Your Happiness

Temple's stardom corresponded with a period in which American capitalism was profoundly under threat. The market crash of 1929 and the lingering depression that followed had left many Americans wondering whether American prosperity would ever be restored. Within this context, the child's economic innocence—her supposed inability to recognize let alone understand the workings of the capitalist marketplace—made her ideally suited to an audience that wanted to escape the implications of the apparent collapse of that marketplace.

Temple's films actively work to establish her status outside capitalist circuits of exchange and characterize the child as incapable of understanding the abstract value of money. Often in her films, sweets are playfully substituted for money, as when Temple sells her kisses for lollipops and bribes a senator with cake in the Baby Burlesks. And eating spinach is a stand-in for labor in *Poor Little Rich Girl.* When Temple joins Jack Haley and Alice Faye's singing "You've Gotta Eat Your Spinach, Baby," the child enacts the role of union organizer when she sings that she "represents all the kids of the nation" in protesting the green.

More common are the instances when her characters display a charming naiveté in relation to a corrupt marketplace, a naiveté that is carefully maintained by the adults around her. In *Poor Little Rich Girl*, for example, Barbara (Temple) comes across a "read your weight" machine at the train station and tries to put a penny in the wrong slot. Her governess inserts the money for her, and the machine releases a ticket with her weight and fortune, "You will be married within a year." Rather than let on that the machine is a sham, the governess substitutes a more accurate prediction: "You're going away on a long trip and will meet a lot of strange people." In this way, the governess preserves the child's faith in the machine's magical abilities while sharing the audience's cynicism over a marketplace designed to hoodwink innocent consumers.

Within her films, Temple has a transformative effect on the captains of industry, who are inspired to open their wallets once they have been seduced by the little girl. According to these narratives, economic growth is stymied by the miserliness of aging men. In *Just Around the Corner*, whose title refers to President Herbert Hoover's empty promise that prosperity was "just around the corner," Penny (Temple) plays the daughter of an architect who has hit hard times. She and her father live in the basement of a tony Manhattan apartment building in which they once occupied the penthouse. When Penny asks about their changed circumstances, her father shows her a cartoon image of Uncle Sam and explains that everyone is demanding help from Uncle Sam, and he's done everything he can for them but it's still not enough. Temple views the situation with childish simplicity and asks, "Why doesn't somebody try to help Uncle Sam?" Later, when she spots a gray-haired, bearded man being mobbed by reporters outside her apartment building, Penny mistakes him for Uncle Sam and convinces the neighborhood kids to put on a talent show to raise money to "help" the man who turns out to be a stingy millionaire. The man is so charmed by her innocent generosity that he loosens his purse strings enough to hire Penny's father to design a building and thereby help revive the household economy.

Tellingly, the rare instance in which Temple plays a child who is savvy about money is in *Stowaway*, in which she adeptly negotiates the presumably irrational marketplace operated by Chinese street vendors. On the streets of Shanghai, she overhears an American tourist, Tommy (Robert Young), struggling to explain to a vendor that he wants to buy a dragon's head mask. Ching Ching agreeably steps in as translator, explaining to the vendor exactly what it is that Tommy is looking for and telling Tommy the price. However, when Tommy reaches to pay for the mask, Ching Ching stops him. "No," she says, pointing to a figure written in Chinese. "He's trying to cheat you. The price is $5." Ching Ching's innocence leads her to insist on an honest exchange within what the film imagines to be an irrational, unregulated marketplace outside US borders.

The child's economic innocence is further developed in the songs Temple croons in her films, many of which express a pious preference for love over material possessions. While the crooners and torch singers whose voices dominated film and radio during the 1930s generally sang songs of romance and love gone awry, Temple often sang about money, or rather its immateriality. *Stowaway* ends with Ching Ching standing in front of a Christmas tree, singing to her wealthy adopted parents that she doesn't want expensive gifts—electric trains or "twenty-dollar aeroplanes"—but only the love of her friends and family. Likewise, in *Captain January* she tells her adopted father, "You may have a bankful for which to be thankful," but that happiness will only come with the "right somebody to love." And to demonstrate the point, although she is surrounded by a roomful of mechanical toys, gifts from her wealthy aunt and uncle, she prefers the simple doll the captain has made for her. And singing "Come and Get Your Happiness" in *Rebecca of Sunnybrook Farm*, Temple reminds audiences that happiness is free and bountiful, unlike money. In these songs, the child's economic innocence is evoked to help recalibrate American values and remind audiences that the important things aren't bought and sold in the capitalist marketplace.

More than providing a humorous or comforting fantasy of life beyond the reach of the marketplace, however, Temple's economic innocence offered a means of critiquing the values promoted by modern capitalism without criticizing capitalism itself. In Temple's earliest films she was often paired with criminals, men who were characterized by economic guilt of one sort or another. In *Little Miss Marker*, she is taken in by a band of gangsters; in *Now and Forever*, her father is a con artist who tries to sell her to her uncle; in *Baby Take a Bow*, her father is an ex-con, a jewel thief who goes straight for the love of a woman; and in *Dimples* she is cared for by her grandfather, a pickpocket and petty thief. However, rather than glorifying these criminals for their refusal to recognize the sanctity of private property, these films suggest that the child's economic innocence can function as an antidote to the corrupting influence of modern capitalism.

In *Little Miss Marker*, Temple plays Martha Jane, or Marky, a young girl whose father has left her with a miserly bookie, Sorrowful Jones (Adolph Menjou), as a marker on a bet. The bet is lost, the father kills himself, and Sorrowful finds himself saddled with the orphaned little girl. However, the child's innocence inspires a transformation that results in Sorrowful's embracing marriage and family and turning away from crime, a transformation signaled by his new willingness to spend money on others rather than hoard it for himself. Sorrowful is not alone in this transformation. His entire cohort of small-time gangsters is inspired to embrace an ethos of sentiment and caring rather than cynicism and self-interest in response to the child.

The film suggests a tug-of-war between traditional and modern values. Sorrowful and his cohort are held together not by any sense of brotherhood but by their shared economic interests. They inhabit a subculture—an underworld of small-time criminals—in which sentiment is considered a handicap because relationships are built on economic self-interest rather than any sense of caring or community. This is a world in which everyone is a con artist looking for the next sucker; even a blind panhandler proves to be working a scam, pretending to be blind in order to inspire generosity. The only heterosexual relationship we see, between Bangles and Big Steve, is one based on the exchange of goods—diamond bracelets, an expensive apartment, a maid—for sex. The characters' valuation of cash over sentiment is established in the opening scene, when Steve demands that the gang pay him $1,000 apiece in exchange for his guaranteeing that his horse, Dream Prince, will lose in the next race. If he doesn't receive their payoffs, he threatens to give the horse a shot of adrenaline to ensure it will win, though the "speed ball" is certain to kill the animal. "Are you sentimental about Dream Prince, Steve?" asks one of the men. "No," Steve answers. "I'm short on cash. . . . I can't afford to kill him today."

In its depiction of a cynical and cut-throat world, the film reflects anxiety about an increasingly corporate economy in which deals are made between strangers and are based not on trust but on cash in an exchange that seemed to be a zero-sum game, each party striving to get the better of the other. Rapid urbanization and immigration in the 1920s meant that families and communities were scattered, a condition exacerbated by the economic depression of the 1930s. Meanwhile, the proliferation of commercial media—radio, newspapers, magazines—contributed to a cacophony of advertisements that strove to part suckers from their money. If one wasn't on guard—if one wasn't cynical—one risked being taken advantage of by strangers who had little regard for the needs of others.

In this cynical world, the child is assessed according to her economic value rather than her sentimental appeal. When the gang is introduced to Marky, each man in turn picks her up and holds her, not in response to her consummate cuteness but in order to place a bet on her weight. When Sorrowful initially agrees to take the girl as a marker on a $20 bet, his morose assistant, Regret, disapprovingly observes, "She ought to melt down for that much," though Sorrowful assures him that the girl is "worth that much any way you look at her." When the girl's father fails to pay his debt, Sorrowful does, indeed, find a way to profit off the child with a scheme whereby Big Steve will transfer ownership of a horse to Marky so that the two men can manipulate the odds on the race and share in the $100,000 take.

Marky invokes a very different ethos and a different brotherhood of men through her fascination with the tales of King Arthur and the Knights of the Round Table. Marky's mother had read Arthurian tales to her daughter before she died, and audiences in 1934 would have recognized this as a mother's strategy for imparting good moral values to the child.[4] Marky initially mistakes Sorrowful's gang for the knights of the round table, dubbing them with Arthurian nicknames. The men's dismissal of these characters as "fairies" points to their rejection of the principles—chivalry, piety, selflessness—upheld by the Knights of the Round Table as unmanly; after all, chasing a quick buck is antithetical to the Arthurian quest. However, by the end of the film, the men willingly (if grudgingly) transform themselves to conform to Marky's image of ideal manhood, staging an elaborate party for the young girl in which they impersonate the characters from the stories of King Arthur, although their round table is shaped like a horseshoe.

Initially, however, it appears that Marky will be transformed by these men rather than vice versa, that she will lose her faith in fairy tales and become as cynical as they are. She loses interest in tales of chivalry when she discovers that she has been conned and that the horse Sorrowful and Big Steve gave her isn't really hers at all. The nightclub singer, Bangles, suggests the trajectory that Marky will take if her faith in men is not restored. The physical resemblance between Marky and Bangles is striking. When the girl and the woman lie together in Marky's bed, their profiled faces are mirrored on the pillow they share, and Marky's tousled blonde curls are matched by Bangles's carefully marcelled and bleached hair. In a blues lullaby, Bangles warns the child, "You got some tough nights ahead." Her song suggests that women suffer a disadvantage, made vulnerable to a world in which "it's all a racket" and "the cards are stacked against you" because, unlike men, women are "born with a heart."

The outcome of this battle of values has consequences beyond the child's personal development, for the values awakened by the men's love for the little girl are demonstrated to be necessary to a civilized society. When Sorrowful and Big Steve recognize that they value Marky for sentimental rather than economic reasons, their treatment of horses and women also changes. As Marky lies close to death on the operating table, Sorrowful has a spiritual reawakening and prays to God for the child's survival, vowing that he won't allow the horse to be killed, and crushing the vial of adrenaline in his fist. Further, although he had earlier proposed an illicit affair with Bangles, he now proposes marriage so that the couple can create a proper home for the child. Steve, too, is visibly transformed by his desire to protect Marky. Watching the small, helpless child begin to revive, Steve discovers that it is far more thrilling to give life than to take it. Although he has come to the hospital to have it out with Sorrowful for having an affair with Bangles (in fact, Bangles had fallen asleep in Marky's bed while singing the girl to sleep), after the girl's survival is assured, his interest in vengeance and horse racing vanishes. In this way, the film suggests that child loving represents more than the transient pleasure of gazing upon the cute antics of a little girl. The child's economic innocence is imagined to help men to reconnect with the traditional values that are essential to a civilized society, values that seemed to be threatened by industrial capitalism.

In *Now and Forever* Temple appeared opposite Gary Cooper and Carole Lombard in another film about criminals that relies on the child's innocence of the value of money. This time, she plays Penny, the daughter of a peripatetic con artist. Initially, Jerry (Gary Cooper) is happy to have his daughter stay in the care of her conservative, New England uncle so that he can continue his carefree life, traveling the world with Toni (Carol Lombard), paying his hotel bills with stolen money, and catching the next train, plane, or boat before the police can catch up with him. When the uncle tracks down Jerry to demand that he be given custody of Penny, Jerry travels to Connecticut, where he intends to give his former brother-in-law custody of the child in exchange for $75,000. However, while in Connecticut, Jerry indulges in an afternoon of play with the young girl, searching for "pirate's treasure" on an "island" in a Connecticut lake. Jerry realizes that Penny's uncle is overly strict with the child, demanding obedience and refusing to engage in her fantastical games. Jerry has a change of heart and decides to bring Penny to Paris with him. There he struggles to go straight and support Toni and Penny on the salary he earns as a real estate agent, though he is drawn back into crime by a blackmailing jewel thief.

In Paris, Penny charms a wealthy dowager who is so taken with the child that she asks Jerry to allow her to adopt the girl. Initially Jerry resists, enjoying the simple home life he has built with Penny and Toni in Paris. However, he fears that he will soon be arrested for writing a bad check. Worse, the jewel thief threatens to expose his involvement in a crime. With the threat of jail looming over him, Jerry reluctantly agrees to steal a necklace from the dowager. He gets away with the crime, but Penny discovers his guilt and is heartbroken that her father has lied to her. In an attempt to redeem himself in his daughter's eyes, Jerry demands the necklace back from the jewel thief. The thief pulls his gun and shoots Jerry, but not before Jerry has shot him. The thief dies, but Jerry survives, covering up his injury long enough to return the jewels and consent to have the dowager adopt Penny. He remains conscious long enough to see Penny off to boarding school. The film had two endings. In one, Jerry dies in Toni's arms. In the other, he wakes in a hospital bed with the police on hand to arrest him, but either way, in the words of one reviewer, Jerry is "regenerated through love for his daughter."[5]

Now and Forever suggests that Jerry is trying to escape his responsibilities within the capitalist marketplace, to assume the position of a child and live on fantasy rather than cash. However, he learns he must abide by the rational laws that govern financial relations so that Penny may enjoy the fantastical pleasures of the imagination and remain unconcerned with money. The film's original title, "Honor Bright," refers to the code Penny's mother had taught her in order to distinguish between her fantasy life and "what's honest-to-goodness true." For example, pirates are "true" but not "honor bright true."

Jerry is arrested in childhood. He has not learned to properly differentiate between fantasy, which the film relegates to the realm of children, and reality, which is the proper concern of adults. He plays imaginative games rather than observing the rational rules of law and finance. The film opens with Jerry and Toni enjoying a late breakfast in a Shanghai hotel room, surrounded by evidence of the previous night's celebrations. Jerry engages in a game in which he is the emperor of all China. When the reality of the hotel bill interrupts this fantasy, he slides easily into another role, playing at being the man of business who runs off to "bring home the bacon" and asks Toni what she plans to cook for dinner. The film suggests that this sort of fantasy play will lead to crime. Paying the hotel bill involves Jerry in an elaborate charade, in which he impersonates an auditor inspecting the hotel's accounts. In this role, he collects very real money from other guests who are past due on their accounts. Later, he infuriates his brother-in-law by making an origami bird of the contract he has drawn up for Penny's adoption and using Chinese and British coins as props in the game of buried treasure. The ultimate sign of Jerry's irresponsibility, though, is his eagerness to sell something that does not belong in the marketplace: his child. When Jerry proposes trading custody of his daughter to her uncle in exchange for $75,000, Toni begins to question their relationship.

Although Jerry is determined to live a carefree life of fun and play, he is repeatedly drawn back into the rational world of money that is necessary to support his extravagant lifestyle. The film abounds in references to bills and checks, conveying the precise amounts Jerry owes and collects, from an $805 hotel bill, to the $75,000 that he demands from Penny's uncle, the $5,000 he collects in exchange for a fictitious gold mine, and the $2,000 check he has bounced when he has only $35 in his wallet. These concrete numbers contrast with Jerry's playful attitude toward work and money.

As in *Little Miss Marker*, Temple's character is in danger of losing her economic innocence through her association with the criminal. Money figures prominently in Penny's life, too. Her name, Penny, points to this association, as does her engaging her father in the playful search for pirate's treasure and the small purse she carries with her on the boat from New York to Paris. The film suggests that what is most troubling about an irresponsible father is the effect he has on his daughter. When Jerry first takes custody of Penny, the two enjoy the sort of irresponsible fun that characterizes Jerry's life with Toni. He buys his daughter ice cream and hot dogs, and takes her on a bus ride through the city. However, the child becomes ill from this irresponsible consumption. Worse, she appears to have learned too well how to weave stories in the service of real gain. While in Paris, Jerry and Toni overhear the child bartering with a young boy, offering him a handful of rocks in exchange for his roller skates, claiming that the rocks are in fact gold. The boy makes the trade, but Jerry insists that Penny return the skates after she admits that the rocks are not "honor bright" gold. Later, the tables are turned when Penny impersonates a detective and interrogates her father about the stolen jewels. "Did you steal the jewels, Mr. Day?" she asks. When he replies, "No," she wags her finger at him and demands, "Honor bright?" Later, when Penny discovers that her father had stolen the jewels after all, it is his breaking the code of "honor bright" that shakes her faith in him. And it is in his effort to restore this faith that Jerry is shot. Both *Little Miss Marker* and *Now and Forever* rely on the child's status outside the cynical and rational world of the capitalist marketplace in order to critique the values associated with modern capitalism, in the case of the former, and attest to the necessity of men's responsibly upholding the rational laws of the marketplace in the latter.

Similarly, Temple's characters were imagined to provide a welcome relief from the hardship of capitalist labor. In *Curly Top*, for example, Elizabeth's (Temple) adopted father, Edward, is a captain of industry. A newspaper article informs us that his "holdings include stocks and bonds, real estate and industrial properties, and one of the world's most valuable art collections." With his father's death, Edward also takes "control of banking and [his father's] industrial empire." As Edward toils at the office, Elizabeth and her sister frolic at the beach of his summer house. Seated at his desk in his city office, Edward looks over the bills for the toys he has purchased for Elizabeth, and each bill is associated with a delightful image of himself and the girls engaged in fun. The bill for the rental of an aquaplane prompts him to remember waterskiing with Elizabeth and Mary; one for a pony cart leads to a flashback of Elizabeth riding the cart; and one for a hula dancing costume and ukulele reminds him of her dancing for him and her friends. In this way, Shirley Temple's innocence is spread to those around her, and the audience is invited to share in her existence beyond the reach of capitalism.

"An Inverted Patriarchal System"

Economic innocence was as central to Temple's screen persona as was her sexual innocence. Ironically, however, Temple herself was most decidedly engaged in modern capitalist exchange, both as a laborer and a commodity. By the time Shirley Temple appeared on film, the question of children's theatrical labor had already been the subject of prolonged debates that were resolved, for the most part, with the enactment of laws to ensure that child performers would receive an adequate education. However, Hollywood introduced a new challenge to the innocence of the performing child. Whereas concerns for stage children had centered on the question of whether they would be properly prepared to lead productive adult lives, debates over Hollywood's child stars centered on the question of whether they were valued for their sentimental or their economic worth. In this sense, the child's economic innocence was central to discourse about Hollywood's laboring children.

What Zelizer terms the "sacralization" of childhood was easy enough to enact in painting, theater, and literature, and even in the lives of middle-class children who were protected from labor. It was more difficult to maintain in relation to working-class childhood. Indeed, as Zelizer points out, age was not introduced as a criterion for wage labor until the late nineteenth century, and as late as 1899 most US states were without minimum age requirements for employment.[6] The late nineteenth and early twentieth centuries witnessed a struggle between working-class parents, for whom the child's wages often contributed significantly to the family economy, and middle-class reformers who sought to secure childhood as a period of education and play for all classes of children.

Beginning in the 1870s, children's labor, including their labor on stage, was overseen in New York by the Society for the Prevention of Cruelty to Children, known popularly as the Gerry Society for its founder, Elbridge Gerry, and less popularly as "the Cruelty" for its propensity to remove children from their working-class homes and into the care of the state. The Gerry Society had successfully lobbied for legislation requiring stage managers to acquire a permit for performances by children under the age of sixteen, and such a permit would be denied to a child who sang, danced, or turned cartwheels on the stage, a provision designed to curtail the careers of young Italian acrobats.

Early debates over children's stage labor hinged on the child's status as a protocitizen. Proponents of child performers argued that stage acting offered children excellent preparation for adult life and a far safer environment than the airless apartments and city streets on which other working-class children spent their youth. The Gerry Society, on the other hand, was concerned for the moral health of young thespians fueled by a Protestant distrust of the theater. Drawing on the language that condemned the exploitation of children in factories and coal mines, Gerry painted the life of a child performer as physically dangerous: "a child of tender years is forced to sing and dance at night, half clad in scanty theatrical costume [in a theater] where the draughts are incessant and where the exertion of the performance constantly overheats the system so as to render the exposure still more dangerous."[7] Gerry further warned that children's immersion in the immoral atmosphere of the theater and their being habituated to a life of glamour and excitement would leave them ill-prepared to become productive adults.

Gerry's efforts against children's stage appearances were decidedly unpopular, and stories abounded of audiences jeering and booing when it was announced that a child had been denied a permit to perform. Parents and managers openly flouted the law, and children often performed without a permit. It was well known that ten-year-old Juliet Shelby, for example, had assumed the name of a deceased cousin, Mary Miles Minter, who would have been seventeen at the time, in order to evade the Gerry Society and star in a stage production of *The Littlest Rebel* in 1912. However, debates over the status of child performers in the theater were all but resolved by 1920, when it was determined that children's theatrical performances would be exempt from the prohibitions on child labor provided that working hours were limited and the child's education assured.

Hollywood worked to forestall similar criticism that it exploited child performers by actively promoting the illusion that the child was unaware of her status as a laborer—that she remained economically innocent despite the fact that she worked for pay—and that the perils of stage life had been obviated by film. Indeed, numerous publicity pieces touted the improved conditions enjoyed by the children who performed for the movies rather than the theater. Hollywood children did not face the same hazards that stage children did, publicity asserted, since they performed before the camera rather than live audiences. Rather than dancing on a "draughty" stage, they cavorted in the California sunshine, and they were not subject to the same travel and performance schedules that characterized the careers of stage children. Film work represented "the happy, healthy new profession of children. . . . They don't learn lines. They don't have any set routine for the day. They don't have to be up at night or undergo any strenuous fatigue. All they have to do is play, as they would at home in their own back yard."[8]

Further, audiences were assured that children's film labor was carefully regulated by the state of California, which mandated the number of hours the performing child was to spend in front of the cameras and in front of her school books. The studios kept tutors on hand to see to the children's education. Publicity for Shirley Temple trumpeted the fact that she had a tutor all to herself, in addition to a private bungalow in which to rest during her state-mandated breaks.

Although the studios promised to see to the health and education of Hollywood's performing children, there remained quite a bit of concern for the children who so publicly labored in the movies. Hollywood introduced a new hazard to performing children: the astronomical salaries paid to the child stars. "Fortunes have fallen on the shoulders of children," remarked one journalist in response to the announcement that Jackie Coogan had been offered $2,500 a week to appear on stage, "but this is the first time that a child has ever made a fortune through his or her work."[9] Jackie Coogan was repeatedly referred to as a "miniature Midas" or "the boy Croesus."[10] "Almost everything he touches turns to gold. Not only does he make money in the movies, but he has commercial enterprises through connections with big manufacturers who pay him handsome royalties on articles bearing his name. . . . In short, he's a demi-John D. Rockefeller, the splitpint J. P. Morgan of the world."[11]

Debates about whether children should be permitted to perform on stage had centered on the question of whether young actors received the proper foundation to grow into good citizens. Concerns about children in the movies, on the other hand, centered on the apparent disruption of the family and loss of parental authority triggered by large paychecks. For the most part, the high salaries paid to child stars were taken as a sign of the public's love for these children. It was imagined that every dollar earned came directly from the pocket of the adoring fans, the children's economic valuation thus serving as testament to their sentimental value.

However, the children's salaries also threatened to invert the normative family structure, making adults dependent on children. In the words of one journalist, the child star's astronomical salary "inspires a vision of some inverted patriarchal system under which babes and sucklings might heap riches on their elders."[12] The child's earning power was understood to corrupt the child as well as the adults who depended on him; an extended story about the problem of the child prodigy relayed the story that "one youthful actor ran his mother out of the house one evening in a fit of rage, exclaiming that he 'was tired of supporting the whole family.'"[13]

Numerous newspaper stories bemoaned the child's film labor as a form of "white slavery," and journalists figuratively wrung their hands over stories of child prodigies left penniless because their parents had taken all their earnings. Such stories contradicted the fantasy that the children's salaries were merely a manifestation of their sentimental appeal by suggesting that their cuteness was a sign of economic rather than sentimental value. Virginia Lee Corbin took her mother to court in order to claim the salary she had earned as a child. And custody battles raged over Edith Fellows and Freddie Bartholomew, who were both in the care of extended family members when they became stars, only to have their absent parents emerge to demand a share of the children's new wealth and celebrity. Finally, in 1938, Jackie Coogan engaged in a well-publicized battle with his mother and stepfather over the money he had earned as a child. Although the public supported Jackie in his attempts to claim the money, the law held that a child's earnings were the property of the parent.[14]

Newspaper stories about these young children reflect larger concerns about capitalism run rampant and the capacity of the government to see to the interests of a helpless American populace. In these stories, the government and the Hollywood industry alike were imagined as a benign patriarch, looking after the interests of the young and helpless. This discourse reasserts the ideals of childhood innocence and of patriarchal authority while also suggesting that the capitalist state provides an adequate safety net should individual fathers fail in their duty toward these children. The studios were imagined to be benefactors rather than employers to the young stars. When a producer formed Mission Productions to exploit the talent of eight-year-old Gloria Joy, his business venture was described as "the magic wand that transformed the little Cinderella, Gloria Joy, into a bright and shining star."[15] Baby LeRoy, best known for his performances opposite W. C. Fields, was "discovered" while in the care of the Salvation Army. Rather than pointing to this fact to suggest the failure of the family ideal, newspaper stories about the boy's background imagined his as a Cinderella story, with Hollywood fame and fortune descending on the deserving young boy. When Baby LeRoy emerged from "retirement" at the age of seven, audiences were assured that the boy's absence from the screen had had nothing to do with the child's decreased market value but rather concern for the child's well-being. During that time, Paramount was reported to have kept the child on the payroll and "supervised his education, his training." When Baby LeRoy fell ill, "Paramount worried as much as any parent ever did."[16] And lest audiences worry that his earnings made him vulnerable to adult exploitation, readers were assured that the courts were looking out for his interests. Since LeRoy's sixteen-year-old mother was also a child, the boy's contract was signed by his grandfather under the beneficent gaze of a judge. Similarly, when it was determined that Baby Marie Osborne's parents "did not do their duty by their remarkably gifted little daughter," the child was brought "before a kindly old judge" who appointed a guardian to look after her. "Thus her moral and material welfare will be conserved, and the baby will have the chance that every child should have, with the additional advantage of a great earning power. . . . As to her physical welfare—the studio officials are seeing to that."[17]

Audiences were assured that Shirley Temple's father, a bank clerk, was overseeing the child's wealth, which would become available to her when she reached adulthood.[18] Shirley Temple herself was "innocently unaware of her importance to the world" and "unaware that if she needs toys she can well afford to buy them."[19] Temple's charm appeared to rest on her economic innocence, yet that innocence seemed tenuous, something that would need to be carefully maintained to prevent it from being corrupted by the knowledge of her spectacular economic value. Newspapers warned that "everyone knows that on the day when Shirley becomes conscious of her great charm, then on that day will her charm disappear."[20]

Restoring Innocence

While the idea that the child existed outside capitalism made for a very powerful fantasy, it was also one that was very difficult to maintain. Shirley Temple, it was widely acknowledged, was an industry unto herself. Her image adorned advertisements for everything ranging from oatmeal and flour to cars and radios. There were Shirley Temple clothes and Shirley Temple dishes, and many, many Shirley Temple dolls. Shirley Temple's films inspired sales of books and sheet music as well as movie tickets. "Motion picture and insurance executives become jittery if an intimate friend of the family picks her up and holds her in his arms," remarked the *Boston Globe.* "She represents an investment running well into the millions. Hundreds of technicians, extras, actors, and studio employees depend upon her for employment."[21] In this sense, her stardom was built on a contradiction. While the economic innocence attributed to childhood was central to her screen persona, audiences were very aware that Shirley Temple had a high dollar value. Much of Temple's film work was, therefore, devoted to erasing her status as a child laborer and promoting the illusion that, like any other innocent child, the only currency she recognized was love.

In *Child-Loving,* James Kincaid makes the compelling argument that the pedophile was invented as a means of disavowing our culture's erotic investment in the child.[22] However, Philip Jenkins argues that moral panic over pedophilia did not begin to take shape until the mid-1930s.[23] Therefore the pedophile was only beginning to emerge as a scapegoat to contain anxieties about children's vulnerability, and Shirley Temple's stardom was little affected by the figure of the predatory pedophile.

Nonetheless, there were on hand two figures that functioned as scapegoats to contain fears about the fragility of childhood innocence: the kidnapper and the stage mother. Given that it was her economic innocence, not her sexual innocence, that seemed under threat, the scapegoats that emerged spoke to these anxieties in a way that the pedophile could not. The kidnapper, who took children for economic rather than sexual gain, was a prominent figure in the early 1930s following the kidnapping and murder of the Lindbergh baby in 1932.[24] The studios understood Shirley Temple and other child stars—particularly Jane Withers and Freddie Bartholomew—to be at risk from kidnappers. It was for this reason that Temple was assigned a chauffeur who doubled as a body guard.

In several of Temple's films the child is given a monetary value in a manner that suggests that the worst violence that can be done to a child is to imagine her worth in economic rather than sentimental terms. In *Heidi* (Allan Dwan, 1937) a cruel governess attempts to sell Heidi to gypsies. In *Little Miss Marker,* she is used as a marker on a bet. In *Now and Forever,* her father proposes selling her for $75,000. In *Dimples,* her character sells herself to a wealthy dowager in order to pay off her grandfather's debts. And in *Poor Little Rich Girl,* her character is threatened by a man who tries to kidnap her for ransom. Recent accounts have identified the kidnapper as a pedophile, which is a testament to the power of the pedophile in the contemporary imagination. However, the film suggests that the man's interest in the child is economic rather than sexual. When he first sees Barbara, she is standing alone at dusk outside the basement apartment of a working-class Italian family. She's an incongruous sight: a well-dressed and well-groomed child standing alone outside a tenement apartment. Later he tries to coax her into telling him her name by offering to buy her some candy, and again, at the end of the film, he wheedles, "I'll buy you a pretty present if you tell me who your father is." The man is a disturbing presence in an otherwise cheerful film. And the camera work emphasizes his threatening presence; we are repeatedly shown ominous shots of him spying on the girl. However, within the logic of a film that is preoccupied with the question of the child's economic exploitation—Barbara is in the care of two performers who enjoy unprecedented success when they incorporate the child into their act—the kidnapper's fiendishness is attributed to his failure to recognize the economic sanctity of the child.

Ultimately, however, the figure of the stage mother functioned as the most effective scapegoat for managing concerns about the child star's economic innocence. To her were attributed all the qualities—particularly greed and ambition—that did not conform to the ideal of childhood innocence. Newspapers told horror stories of greedy women's attempts to monetize motherhood. Stage mothers were vilified for becoming "predatory females, ruthless, mean and insanely jealous of another child's preference over theirs. They become travesties, too, of the mother sentiment."[25] Much as newspapers and magazines had once warned of the plight of the young women who had flocked to Hollywood to find work in the movies during the silent era, the press abounded with stories about unscrupulous women who attempted to profit off motherhood: "the offices of Central [Casting] are besieged daily by overdressed and over-made-up youngsters whose mothers drag them to the registration window and order them to perform."[26] Hollywood film, too, portrayed the stage mother as monstrous. In *Stand-In* (1937), an efficiency expert (Leslie Howard) takes temporary control of a movie studio. In one scene, he is horrified by a mother who plays the harmonica while her daughter shimmies and sings a bawdy song. He cuts the pair off before the child can perform her "Mae West number." Similarly, in Nathanial West's 1939 novel *The Day of the Locust*, the child actor, Adore Loomis, is the monstrous progeny of an aspiring stage mother.

Just as the figures of the kidnapper and the stage mother worked as scapegoats to help audiences disavow the child's presence in the capitalist marketplace, Shirley Temple's films worked to disavow the child's labor. Temple starred in twenty-two films while under contract at Twentieth Century-Fox. In six of these she plays a professional performer, and she performs in amateur productions in an additional four. It isn't surprising that she would portray performers in so many of her films, given that she was known for her singing and dancing. However, Temple's backstage musicals differ significantly from those of her adult counterparts. For one thing, whereas rehearsals often constitute a significant site for song and dance in the traditional backstage musical, Temple's characters do not rehearse their numbers.

Often, Temple's films self-reflexively invoke the child's status as a performer in a manner that encourages the audience to celebrate rather than condemn her professional status. The films invoke the commercial aspects of Temple's career—the fact that her singing brought in a great deal of money through the sale of sheet music and records as well as movie tickets—to suggest that her singing and dancing before audiences is not labor at all but rather represents the fulfillment of the child's own desires. In *Poor Little Rich Girl*, for example, she sings lines from "The Good Ship Lollipop" and "Animal Crackers in My Soup," two of her previous hits, during her radio audition.[27] The references to these hits make no sense within the context of the film; they refer to Shirley Temple's stardom though her character is meant to be inexperienced before the microphone. Rather, her singing serves to merge her character with her off-screen persona within a plot that encourages us to hope she will be a commercial success. Similarly, *Rebecca of Sunnybrook Farm* breaks the fourth wall when Rebecca (Temple) makes her radio debut with a medley of Shirley Temple's previous hits—"On the Good Ship Lollipop," "Animal Crackers in My Soup," "When I'm with You"—interspersed with chatter ("I never will forget my grandest thrill, the very first time that I sang this song . . ."). Within the film she sings the songs live on radio as part of a show sponsored by Crackly Grain Flakes and ends the performance with an advertisement for the imaginary product. *Young People*, too, evokes nostalgia for Temple's career. In this, the last of Temple's films for Twentieth Century-Fox, the film provides a montage of Temple's previous film appearances in what is meant to be an overview of her character's career as a stage actress. Together these films allow audiences to celebrate rather than condemn the child's commercial success.

And Temple's films repeatedly associate the condemnation of child labor with outmoded values that are often associated with a meddling spinster. In film after film, Temple represents a young girl who wants nothing more than to charm adult audiences by performing publicly. And, as I discuss in chapter 1, in film after film, misguided spinsters stand between her and the stage, frustrating Temple's desire to perform and the audience's desire to see her sing and dance. The romance narrative that accompanies these plots reinforces the sense that the child belongs in front of an audience. As with many backstage musicals, Temple's triumphant stage success is accompanied by the resolution of the romantic plot. However, due to Temple's extreme youth, romance is displaced onto the adult characters. In *Dimples*, *Rebecca of Sunnybrook Farm*, and *Little Miss Broadway*, the men who produce the shows in which Temple's characters triumph are rewarded not with the fame and wealth produced by the child's labor, but by the satisfaction of their romantic desires. Indeed, the lovers are invariably united at the very moment that the child appears before an admiring audience of adults. In this way, the performance represents the satisfaction of all desire.

These techniques for mollifying audience members who might be troubled by Temple's professional status were not always successful. For example, Graham Greene was as appalled by the economic exploitation of Shirley Temple as he was by her sexualization. "Watch the way she measures a man with agile studio eyes, with dimpled depravity," he wrote. In describing Temple as a bit of a whore—a "complete totsy," in his words—Greene did not blame the child for the unseemly intermingling of commerce and sex; rather he attributed her corruption to the adult machinations of the studio. In its suit against Greene, the studio claimed that he had described them as Shirley's pimp (Greene had actually likened them to "leaseholders"), which contradicted the paternalistic image the studio promoted of itself. For Greene, Temple's knowingness is a product of her professional training, displayed in the "way she measures a man with agile studio eyes."[28] Like Dietrich and Colbert, she is a product of the star machinery that has been constructed to serve the erotic interests of adult audiences. It is the competence of that machinery that has made her so horrifying to him.

Whereas Temple's sexual innocence seemed assured enough that audiences read men's love for the child as benign and considered her erotic imitations a charming joke, it was her economic innocence that seemed in peril to early twentieth-century audiences. By contrast, upon the death of Shirley Temple Black in 2014, countless obituaries noted the apparent threats to her sexual innocence—describing her performances in the Baby Burlesks, citing the controversy over Graham Greene's reviews, and repeating Black's description of MGM producer Arthur Freed's exposing himself to her when she was twelve years old. However, rare was the acknowledgment in these obituaries that the child whose dimpled smile had enraptured audiences around the world for half a decade had been economically exploited. When Shirley Temple Black received a reckoning of her earnings in 1951, she discovered that of the over $3 million she had earned between the ages of three and sixteen, less than $90,000 was hers, and half of that was in the form of a dollhouse valued at $45,000. "My rate of salvage," she writes in her autobiography, "was less than 3 percent over nineteen years of effort."[29] The rest belonged to her parents.

While today we might see children's precocious performances as posing a threat to the child's sexual innocence, in the early twentieth century the child's sexual innocence seemed inviolable, capable of transforming adults rather than being transformed by them. It was the child's economic innocence that was understood to be at risk. This would suggest that, despite the fact that sexual mores were changing radically in the early twentieth century, the rapid development of industrial capitalism and the commodification of all aspects of American life were felt to be more threatening to children than were the changing rules of sexual behavior. By contrast, today we are relatively reconciled to the perils of modern capitalism, while other threats loom large in our minds.

EPILOGUE

In 1944, *Time* magazine published a review of *National Velvet* that reflects a markedly different paradigm of innocence than the one that shaped Shirley Temple's career. The magazine described the film as "an interesting psychological study of hysterical obsession, conversion mania, pre-adolescent sexuality. Twelve-year-old Elizabeth Taylor . . . is probably the only person in Hollywood who could bring this curious role its unusual combination of earthiness and ecstasy."[1] Writing in *The Nation*, James Agee likewise identifies a sexual undertow to Taylor's performance. He begins his review with the sort of declaration of helpless love for the child that was once common, describing himself as incapable of evaluating Taylor's work with dispassion: "Frankly, I doubt I am qualified to arrive at any sensible assessment of Miss Elizabeth Taylor. Ever since I first saw the child, two or three years ago . . . I have been choked with the peculiar sort of adoration I might have felt if we were both in the same grade of primary school." Unlike the reviewers who found themselves in the grip of a "peculiar" adoration for previous generations of child stars, however, Agee goes on to describe Taylor's performance in terms of her latent sexuality, praising the child's ability to convey "two or three speeds of semi-hysterical emotion, such as ecstasy, an odd sort of pre-specific erotic sentience, and the anguish of overstrained hope, imagination, and faith."[2]

These interpretations of Taylor's performance rest on a Freudian paradigm for understanding childhood sexuality and male spectatorship. Drawing on the language of psychoanalysis—hysterical obsession, conversion mania, pre-adolescent sexuality—the reviewers seemingly expose the film's subconscious, revealing *National Velvet* to be not merely a film about a girl's love for her horse but also about the polymorphous perversity of girlhood. And rather than trumpeting his adoration of the "rapturously beautiful" child as a victory of innocence over vice, Agee's confession that he is overcome by a "choked" admiration for the girl is an "unpleasant unveiling." However, rather than cast his response to Taylor as perverse, Agee identifies it in terms of his own regression to a preadolescent stage of development characterized by "peculiar adoration," much as earlier audiences had enjoyed the juvenating effect of child impersonators like Mary Pickford in previous decades.

Unlike Greene's reviews of Temple's films, these assessments of *National Velvet* did not prompt libel suits on the part of the studio (MGM). Nor were they deemed by the courts to be a "gross outrage" against the child. For one thing, the descriptions of Taylor's sensuality maintain that the girl remains innocent, contrary to the "dimpled depravity" that Greene had encountered in Temple's performances. Further, in the years during and immediately following World War II, psychoanalysis became the dominant paradigm for understanding sexuality and childhood development. During this period, Hollywood itself helped to popularize Freudian ideas, incorporating pop psychology into films of every genre. For postwar audiences, Freud's theories of childhood sexuality had become pervasive and now seemed credible rather than outrageous. Indeed, Rachel Devlin has compellingly demonstrated that girlhood was so thoroughly defined in terms of Oedipal desire during the postwar period that a girl's erotic interest in an adult man was taken to signify her normative sexual development, a belief that helped shape countless film narratives about adolescent girls, including those starring a teenaged Shirley Temple.[3]

Freud's understanding of childhood sexuality and repressed desire did not challenge the images of childhood promoted by Hollywood in films of the 1940s and after but, rather, helped to shape these images. Whereas Shirley Temple's star persona was built around the longstanding ideal of childhood as a semi-divine state, the most popular child star of the 1940s, Margaret O'Brien, was based on something else entirely. O'Brien was eight years old when she appeared in the No. 9 spot on Quigley's list of top box-office stars in 1945, the second youngest child, following Temple, to appear on the list. O'Brien represented a marked departure from Temple. Temple was known for her blonde ringlets; O'Brien's brown hair was habitually tied back in braids. Whereas Temple was celebrated for her singing and dancing, O'Brien was a dramatic actress with a remarkable gift for crying. More importantly, Temple's persona was built on the sentimental ideal of childhood innocence that imagined the white child to be an emissary from God, "trailing clouds of glory" in her passage from heaven to earth. By contrast, O'Brien was a "delightful imp of Satan."[4] In his consideration of Vincente Minnelli's films, James Naremore argues that O'Brien's performance as Tootie in *Meet Me in St. Louis* "problematizes the very idea of innocence": "here as everywhere else, [O'Brien] is the antithesis of Shirley Temple, not only because she seems less weirdly accomplished, but also because she delights in forbidden games." Citing Robin Wood's contention that O'Brien foreshadowed the demonic children who would populate horror films of the 1970s, Naremore suggests that O'Brien's performance "introduces a certain Freudian element into the film."[5]

Margaret O'Brien's career points to a shift in the terms of child stardom in Hollywood. Temple and the other girls of the child-star era were celebrated for their ability to uplift audiences and transform men for the better. However, O'Brien often played characters who were themselves in need of transformation. And whereas Temple and her predecessors were, often disparagingly, described as embodying "sweetness and light," O'Brien more often portrayed the unruly id who disrupts the ordered lives of those around her. O'Brien made her film debut at the age of four in *Babes on Broadway* (1941), starring Judy Garland and Mickey Rooney. She had a bit part in the film, playing a child actor who auditions for a role with an enthusiastic interpretation of the lines "Don't send my brother to the chair! Don't let him burn!" This macabre bit of humor was developed further in *Meet Me in St. Louis*, in which Tootie (O'Brien) embodies all that is repressed in the apparently tranquil world of turn-of-the-century St. Louis. Tootie is preoccupied with violence and death. She is heartbroken, for instance, when her attempt to derail a trolley misfires and no one dies. Similarly, in *The Unfinished Dance*, her character actually does cause grave harm. Here O'Brien plays an aspiring dancer who jealously sabotages a ballet performance, causing a renowned dancer to injure herself severely, ending her career.

Temple's transformative innocence repeatedly worked to rehabilitate men both on and off screen. In O'Brien's films, on the other hand, it is often childhood that is in a precarious state, in danger of being lost prematurely. Often what is threatened is the child's sense of wonder. In *Lost Angel* (1943), for example, O'Brien plays Alpha, a girl who has been brought up in a laboratory as a scientific experiment. During an interview, a newspaper reporter introduces her to a world of magic and fairy tales. Sensing that she has missed out on an essential aspect of childhood, Alpha runs away from her home in the clinic to find the reporter and experience childhood for herself. In *Tenth Avenue Angel* (1948), she plays Flavia, a child of the slums who clings to her belief in the superstitions her mother has taught her, that a white mouse will turn into money, for example. When she discovers this isn't true, Flavia angrily runs away, indirectly causing her mother to fall and miscarry. With her mother on her deathbed, the child goes in search of a miracle and has her faith in God restored. Similarly, in *Miracle on 34th Street* (1947), starring eight-year-old Natalie Wood, a child who has been raised to favor rationalism over wonder is transformed when she meets Santa Claus.

In *Big City* (Norman Taurog, 1948), O'Brien's character, Midge, is understood to be vulnerable to adult influence because she is being raised outside the bounds of the normative nuclear family and therefore prematurely exposed to adult sexuality. Midge is an orphan who has been taken in by a Jewish cantor (Danny Thomas) and his mother as well as a Protestant clergyman and an Irish Catholic policeman. In one sequence, the three men watch in horror as the child impersonates a nightclub singer (Betty Garrett). So dismayed are they by the performance that they determine to end their shared custody of the child so that Midge can enjoy the protective parenting of a heterosexual couple.

Thus Shirley Temple's career marked the end of a long period in which childhood innocence was celebrated as inviolable. However, it would be several decades before her appeal would be widely read as pedophilic. In 1966, film critic Andrew Sarris described Temple as the "Lolita of Depression audiences," and eight years later Molly Haskell characterized her as "an ideal post-Production code sex kitten, her attraction politely shrouded in the natural interplay of family feeling."[6] Such assessments clearly rest on a Freudian paradigm (Sarris's review is titled "Freudian Fantasy") and they are indebted to Vladimir Nabakov's giving form to the child seductress with the publication of his novel *Lolita* in 1955. No longer was the white child defined by her inviolable innocence. She now seemed imperiled, vulnerable to adult desire. And it is this paradigm of innocence that has shaped reassessments of Temple's career as well as more recent performances of girlhood.

NOTES

ABBREVIATIONS

AMPAS	The Margaret Herrick Library, Academy of Motion Picture Arts and Sciences
BRTC	Billy Rose Theatre Collection, New York Public Library
HTC	Harvard Theatre Collection, Harvard University
RLC	Robinson Locke Collection, Billy Rose Theatre Collection, New York Public Library
UCLA	Performing Arts Special Collections, Charles E. Young Research Library, University of California, Los Angeles
USC	Archives of Performing Arts, Cinema Library, University of Southern California

INTRODUCTION: SEX AND SHIRLEY TEMPLE

1. "Peewee's Progress," *Time*, April 27, 1936, 42.
2. Robert C. Jennings, "Her Eyes Are Still Dancing," *Saturday Evening Post*, June 5, 1965, 95. Roosevelt's words have been repeated in numerous recent sources. However, the earliest citation I have been able to find is from Norman J. Zierold, *The Child Stars* (New York: Coward-McMann, 1965), 69.
3. At nineteen, Mickey Rooney was the next youngest star to reach the No. 1 spot in 1939. Margaret O'Brien was eight when she was named among the top-ten box-office stars in 1945 and appeared there again in 1946. Other children who appeared among the top ten were Jane Withers, Tatum O'Neal, and Dakota Fanning, and Judy Garland and Sandra Dee appeared among the top ten as teenagers.
4. James R. Kincaid, *Erotic Innocence: The Culture of Child Molesting* (Durham, NC: Duke University Press, 1998), 114.

5. For extended analyses of Temple's pedophilic appeal, see Valerie Walkerdine, *Daddy's Girl: Young Girls and Popular Culture* (Cambridge, MA: Harvard University Press, 1997); Ann duCille, "The Shirley Temple of My Familiar," *Transition*, 73 (1997): 10–32; Kincaid, *Erotic Innocence*; Ara Osterweil, "Reconstructing Shirley: Pedophilia and Interracial Romance in Hollywood's Age of Innocence," *Camera Obscura*, 72 (2009): 1–39.

6. Lynn Sacco, *Unspeakable: Father–Daughter Incest in American History* (Baltimore, MD: Johns Hopkins University Press, 2009).

7. Sex offenses vary from state to state; in a number of states, public urination is classified as a sexual offense, as is consensual sex in public.

8. Lee Edelman, *No Future: Queer Theory and the Death Drive* (Durham, NC: Duke University Press, 2004).

9. Ibid., 29.

10. I use the term "pedophilia" to suggest an explicitly sexual interest in children, the ultimate expression of which results in the violation of the child. I use the term "child loving" to denote a broader, more amorphous range of pleasures, erotic and otherwise, produced by the child and celebrated in the nineteenth and early twentieth centuries.

11. Thomas S. Kuhn, *The Structure of Scientific Revolutions*, 3rd ed. (Chicago: University of Chicago Press, 1996), 150.

12. During Shirley Temple's career, white children alone possessed this transformative innocence. Black children occupied a completely different category from their white counterparts. Dehumanized as pickaninnies, black children were understood not to produce the same response as the cute white child did. While the proper response to the white child's cuteness was a longing to protect and caress the child, as I discuss in chapter 2, Robin Bernstein has demonstrated that nineteenth-century American material culture encouraged quite different responses to black children. Robin Bernstein, *Racial Innocence: Performing American Childhood from Slavery to Civil Rights* (New York: New York University Press, 2011).

13. Graham Greene, "*Under Two Flags, Captain January*," *The Spectator*, August 7, 1936. Reprinted in *The Graham Greene Film Reader: Reviews, Essays, Interviews & Film Stories*, ed. David Parkinson (New York: Applause, 1993), 128.

14. Graham Greene, "*Wee Willie Winkie, The Life of Emile Zola*," *Night and Day*, October 28, 1937. Reprinted in *The Graham Greene Film Reader*, 234.

15. Greene, "*Wee Willie Winkie*," 234.

16. F. Scott Fitzgerald, *Tender is the Night* (New York: Charles Scribner, 1962), 86.

17. The incident would come to haunt Greene two decades later when he was among the first critics to publish a positive review of Vladimir Nabakov's novel *Lolita*. His admiration for the novel was attributed to his harboring a desire for young girls, and his reviews of Temple's films were taken as an early indication of his pedophilia.

18. James Kincaid, *Child-Loving: The Erotic Child and Victorian Literature* (New York: Routledge, Chapman & Hall, 1994); Kincaid, *Erotic Innocence*.

19. Philip Jenkins, *Moral Panic: Changing Concepts of the Child Molester in Modern America* (New Haven, CT: Yale University Press, 2004).

20. Lauren Berlant, *The Queen of America Goes to Washington City: Essays on Sex and Citizenship* (Durham, NC: Duke University Press, 1997).

21. Bernstein, *Racial Innocence*, 41.

22. Gaylyn Studlar, *Precocious Charms: Stars Performing Girlhood in Classical Hollywood Cinema* (Berkeley, CA: University of California Press, 2013), 236.

23. Karin Calvert, *Children in the House: The Material Culture of Early Childhood, 1600–1900* (Boston: Northeastern University Press, 1994).

24. William Wordsworth, "Ode: Intimations of Immortality from Recollections of Early Childhood," in *The Oxford Book of English Verse*, ed. Sir Arthur Thomas Quiller-Couch (Oxford: Clarendon, 1919, [c.1901]); Bartleby.com, 1999. www.bartleby.com/101/

25. Gary Cross, "Wondrous Innocence: Print Advertising and the Origins of Permissive Child Rearing in the US," *Journal of Consumer Culture,* 4:2 (2004): 192.

26. Gail Bederman, *Manliness and Civilization: A Cultural History of Gender and Race in the United States, 1880-1917* (Chicago: University of Chicago Press, 1995).

27. Daniel Cook describes the explosion of consumer goods for children during this period. Daniel Thomas Cook, *The Commodification of Childhood: The Children's Clothing Industry and the Rise of the Child Consumer* (Durham, NC: Duke University Press, 2004), 7–13.

28. W. T. Stead, "The Maiden Tribute of Modern Babylon I: The Report of Our Secret Commission," *Pall Mall Gazette,* July 6, 1885. Reprinted on W. T. Stead Resource Site, http://www.attackingthedevil.co.uk

29. Catherine Robson, *Men in Wonderland: The Lost Girlhood of the Victorian Gentleman* (Princeton, NJ: Princeton University Press, 2001), 156–157. Elsewhere in the book Robson suggests that the shift was not as sudden as she implies here.

30. Carolyn Steedman, *Strange Dislocations: Childhood and the Idea of Human Interiority, 1780–1930* (Cambridge, MA: Harvard University Press, 1995), 140.

31. Quoted in ibid., 140.

32. Quoted in ibid., 140–141.

33. As originally cast, the role of young Lord Fauntleroy alternated between a boy and a girl, Elsie Leslie and Tommy Russell, though girls tended to be preferred in the role, in part because they were understood to be more tractable, and thus easier to control, than boy performers.

34. "Denounced by Mr. Gerry," *The New York Times,* January 26, 1892, II3.

35. Ibid.

36. Elbridge T. Gerry, "Children of the Stage," *North American Review,* July 26, 1890. Children on the Stage: Laws, HTC. Claudia Johnson argues that Gerry's increasingly virulent campaign against the employment of children on the stage arose out of his personal distaste for the profession as well as pragmatic reasons; factory owners and businessmen made for more formidable opponents than did theater managers.

37. Gerry, "Children of the Stage."

38. I borrow the term "child star era" from Diana Serra Cary's lively history of Hollywood's child stars, *Hollywood's Children: An Inside Account of the Child Star Era* (Dallas, TX: Southern Methodist University Press, 1997). As a child, Serra Cary was known as Baby Peggy Montgomery, one of the most popular child stars of the 1920s.

39. Richard Butsch, "Bowery B'hoys and Matinee Ladies: The Re-Gendering of Nineteenth-Century American Theater Audiences," *American Quarterly,* 46:3 (September 1994), 374–405.

40. Lori Merish, "Cuteness and Commodity Aesthetics: Tom Thumb and Shirley Temple," in *Freakery: Cultural Spectacles of the Extraordinary Body,* ed. Rosemarie Garland Thomson (New York: New York University Press, 1996), 185–203.

41. Evans began her film career at the age of five in 1914 and was one of the rare child stars who successfully made the transition to adult stardom, as one of MGM's leading ladies in the 1930s.

42. Richard Dyer, *Stars* (London: British Film Institute, 1979), 49; Richard Dyer, *Heavenly Bodies: Film Stars and Society, Second Edition* (New York: Routledge, 2004), 156–159.

43. Fox merged with Twentieth Century in 1935, forming Twentieth Century-Fox. *Curly Top,* which premiered in December of that year, was the first of Temple's films to be released under the studio's new moniker. For the sake of brevity, unless I am referring specifically to one of the five films she made for Fox (*Stand Up and Cheer, Baby Take a Bow, Bright Eyes, The Little Colonel,* and *Our Little Girl*), I will refer to her studio as Twentieth Century-Fox.

CHAPTER 1 — AMERICA'S SWEETHEARTS

1. Delight Evans, "Mary Pickford, the Girl," *Photoplay*, July 1918, 111.
2. Pickford went so far as to do color screen tests for the role. Ultimately, the project was shelved when Paramount threatened to sue for copyright infringement.
3. After leaving Twentieth Century-Fox, Temple appeared in one more role associated with Pickford, that of Annie Rooney in *Miss Annie Rooney* (1942), her first teen role. Several publicity photos of Pickford and Temple together helped to cement the association between America's two favorite sweethearts.
4. Unidentified clipping, Shirley Temple: Clippings, BRTC. See also, "Shirley Temple: The Most Popular Girl in the World," unidentified clipping, Shirley Temple: Clippings, BRTC.
5. Gaylyn Studlar, "Oh, 'Doll Divine': Mary Pickford, Masquerade, and the Pedophilic Gaze, *Camera Obscura* 16:3 (2001): 197–227.
6. Richard Dyer, *Stars* (London: BFI, 1998), 31. In *Heavenly Bodies*, Dyer expands his observation that Monroe successfully embodied these two opposed terms—sexuality and innocence—into an analysis of mid-century discourse about Monroe.
7. Ann Douglas, *Terrible Honesty: Mongrel Manhattan in the 1920s* (New York: Noonday Press, 1995), 4.
8. Edward Elgar, Letter to Alice Stuart-Wortley, September 18, 1917. Reprinted in *Edward Elgar, the Windflower Letters: Correspondence with Alice Caroline Stuart Wortley and Her Family*, ed. Jerrold Northrop Moore (New York: Oxford University Press, 1989).
9. Rev. of Jarrett and Palmer's production of *Uncle Tom's Cabin*, March 2, 1878, *Uncle Tom's Cabin*, File No. 2, HTC.
10. Rev. of *Uncle Tom's Cabin, Boston Globe*, March 2, 1880. Reprinted in Stephen Railton, *Uncle Tom's Cabin and American Culture: A Multimedia Archive* (Charlottesville, VA: University of Virginia, 1998–2004), March 31, 2005, http://www.iath.virginia.edu/utc/
11. "The Passing Show," *Boston Courier*, August 22, 1897, *Uncle Tom's Cabin*, File No. 2, HTC.
12. "Uncle Tom in Ragtime," *Boston Journal*, May 8, 1900, *Uncle Tom's Cabin*, File No. 5, HTC.
13. Unidentified clipping, March 10, 1907, *Uncle Tom's Cabin*, File No. 2, HTC.
14. Andreas Huyssen, *After the Great Divide: Modernism, Mass Culture, Postmodernism* (Bloomington, IN: Indiana University Press, 1986), 53.
15. Douglas, *Terrible Honesty*.
16. Francis Hackett, "Sweetness Without Light," *The New Republic*, March 13, 1915. *Daddy Long Legs:* Clippings, HTC.
17. Edward Wagenknecht, "Lillian Gish: An Interpretation" (1927), reprinted in *The Movies in the Age of Innocence* (Norman, OK: University of Oklahoma Press, 1962), 251.
18. Lea Jacobs, *The Decline of Sentiment: American Film in the 1920s* (Berkeley, CA: University of California Press, 2008), 22.
19. Raymond Williams, *Marxism and Literature* (New York: Oxford University Press, 1978).
20. Unidentified clipping, *New York Spirit of the Times*, December 2, 1876, Lotta Crabtree, RLC.
21. This practice was aided by the fact that, prior to the 1930s, young people were categorized according to their social role rather than chronological age. In the early twentieth century, the term "youth" was used to describe a young person who was no longer a dependent but not yet a parent; a fifteen-year-old factory worker, a nineteen-year-old college student, and twenty-three-year-old newlyweds might all be ascribed to the same category of "youth."
22. Christine Gledhill, "Mary Pickford: Icon of Stardom," in *Flickers of Desire: Movie Stars of the 1910s*, ed. Jennifer M. Bean (New Brunswick, NJ: Rutgers University Press, 2011), 53.

23. John C. Tibetts, "Mary Pickford and the American 'Growing Girl,'" *Journal of Popular Film and Television*, 29:2 (Summer 2001): 50–62.
24. Grace Kinsley, "Flashes: New Griffith Star," *Los Angeles Times*, November 19, 1920.
25. Horatio Bottomly, "The Meaning of Mary," *Sunday Pictorial*, June 27, 1920, Mary Pickford Scrapbook, 1920, AMPAS.
26. W. Livingston Larned, "Mary Pickford," *Review Portrait Tours*, No. 7, Mary Pickford: Clippings, BRTC.
27. Florence M. Carter, "To Miss Mary Pickford," *Motion Picture*, November 1914.
28. "Players' Checkerboard: Curly-Haired Mary," *Exhibitors Film Exchange*, June 24, 1915, 31.
29. Morduant Hall, Review of *Little Annie Rooney, The New York Times*, October 19, 1925, 26.
30. R. H. Davis, "The Garden of Eyes," unidentified clipping, Mary Pickford: Clippings, HTC.
31. See, for example, Grace Kingsley, "Mary Pickford's Story," *Los Angeles Times*, January 24, 1915, III3; and Gertrude M. Price, "Sun Never Sets on Face of Popular Mary Pickford," *New Orleans Statesman*, March 19, 1915, Mary Pickford: Clippings, RLC.
32. W. G. Faulkner, "The Real Mary Pickford: A Woman's Heart in a Child's Body," *London Daily Mail*, June 22, 1920, Mary Pickford Scrapbook No. 33, AMPAS.
33. Gaylyn Studlar, *Precocious Charms: Stars Performing Girlhood in Classical Hollywood Cinema* (Berkeley, CA: University of California Press, 2013), 360.
34. Twells Brex, "A Mary Pickford 'First Night,'" *London Daily Mail*, October 13, 1919. Mary Pickford Scrapbook, 1919. AMPAS.
35. Harry Birdoff, *The World's Greatest Hit: Uncle Tom's Cabin* (New York: S. F. Vanni, 1947), 328.
36. "Grand Opera House: *Uncle Tom's Cabin*," unidentified publication, April 2, 1907, *Uncle Tom's Cabin*, File No. 5, HTC.
37. Ralph Eugene Lund, "Trouping with Uncle Tom," *The Century*, January 1928, *Uncle Tom's Cabin*, File No. 3, HTC.
38. W. Livingston Larned, "Review Portrait-Tours No. 7, Mary Pickford," Unidentified clipping, Mary Pickford: Clippings, RLC.
39. Review of *The Antics of Ann, Exhibitors Herald*, December 1, 1917, 27; "Oh, the Joys of Puppy Love," Unidentified clipping, Lila Lee: Clippings, RLC.
40. "Oh, the Joys of Puppy Love."
41. Unidentified clipping, *Photo Play Journal*, September 1919, Bessie Love: Clippings, BRTC.
42. Katherine Synon, "The Unspoiled Mary Pickford," *Photoplay*, September 1914.
43. Vachel Lindsay, *The Art of the Moving Picture* (New York: Macmillan, 1916), 27–29. Studlar points to this passage as evidence that Pickford invited a "pedophilic gaze" (*Precocious Charms*, 29).
44. Edward Wagenknecht, Letter to Mary Pickford, *Sunday Tribune Magazine of Books* (1955). Reprinted in Wagenknecht, *The Movies in the Age of Innocence*, 138.
45. Unidentified clipping, *Picture Play Magazine*, c.1919, Mary Pickford Scrapbook, 1919. AMPAS.
46. Nancy F. Cott, *The Grounding of Modern Feminism* (New Haven, CT: Yale University Press, 1987).
47. Joanne J. Meyerowitz, *Women Adrift: Independent Wage Earners in Chicago, 1880–1930* (Chicago: University of Chicago Press, 1991). See also Kathy Peiss, *Cheap Amusements: Working Women and Leisure in Turn-of-the-Century New York* (Philadelphia: Temple University Press, 1986).
48. Paula Fass, *The Damned and the Beautiful: American Youth in the 1920s* (New York: Oxford University Press, 1977).
49. Prior to 1909, the names of the actors appearing in films were not known to audiences. And Biograph, where Pickford made her first film in 1909, did not start releasing the names

of its performers until 1913. Richard DeCordova, *Picture Personalities: The Emergence of the Star System in America* (Champaign, IL: University of Illinoi Press, 2001).

50. Richard Dyer, *Heavenly Bodies: Film Stars and Society* (New York: Routledge, 2003).

51. Robert Grau, "The Highest Paid Woman in the World," *Boston Herald*, February 28, 1915, Mary Pickford: Clippings, RLC.

52. "Mary Pickford Weds Douglas Fairbanks," *Boston Post*, March 31, 1920, Mary Pickford: Clippings, HTC.

53. Idah M'Glone Gibson, "Mary Pickford Tells Her Own Story Over Life from Cradle to—Now," *Toledo News Bee*, March 22, 1915, Mary Pickford: Clippings, RLC.

54. Unidentified clipping, Mary Pickford: Clippings, HTC.

55. Grace Kingsley, "Mary Pickford, Producer," *Los Angeles Times*, December 8, 1918.

56. Faulkner, "The Real Mary Pickford: A Woman's Heart in a Child's Body."

57. Barbara Hudson, "Femininity and Adolescence," in *Gender and Generation*, ed. Angela McRobbie and Mica Nava (London: Macmillan, 1984), 53.

58. Hudson, "Femininity and Adolescence," 34.

59. Catherine Robson, *Men in Wonderland: The Lost Girlhood of the Victorian Gentleman* (Princeton, NJ: Princeton University Press, 2001); Kenneth Kidd, *Making American Boys: Boyology and the Feral Tale* (Minneapolis, MN: University of Minnesota Press, 2004). Kelly Schrum argues that girls were the "first teenagers" in relation to the emergence of a consumer culture, which began to target female high-school students as early as the 1920s. However, more research is needed to determine whether these girls, too, were caught between the discourses of femininity and masculinity. Kelly Schrum, *Some Wore Bobby Sox: The Emergence of Teenage Girls' Culture, 1920–1945* (New York: Palgrave Macmillan, 2004), 19.

60. Lillian Montanye, "When Bessie Was Lost in New York," *Motion Picture*, April 1918, Bessie Love: Clippings, BRTC.

61. Paul Hubert Conion, "Three Little Amazons," *Los Angeles Times*, August 8, 1917, II3. The film does not appear to have survived.

62. "Marguerite Clark in *The Amazons*," *Exhibitors Herald*, August 11, 1917, 25.

63. "Miss Peter Pan: The Screen Star Who Refuses to Grow Up," *Photo Play Journal*, July 1917, Bessie Love: Clippings, BRTC. The identification of Love as "Miss Peter Pan" further enforces this association between childhood and masculinity.

64. "Pickford in Mott Street," *Boston Transcript*, September 30, 1925, Mary Pickford: Clippings, HTC.

65. Martha McKelvie, *Motion Picture Classic*, July 1918.

66. Mollie Merrick, "Fine Piece of Publicity," *The Spokesman-Review*, March 30, 1932, 5.

67. Adele Rogers St. John, "Janet Gaynor," *Liberty*, August 2, 1930, 22.

68. Grace Kingsley, "Western Film Activity Due," *Los Angeles Times*, March 30, 1932, 6. Gaynor's refusal contributed to her falling out with Daryl Zanuck following the merger of Fox with Twentieth Century and to the studio's eventually dropping her contract.

69. B. R. Crisler, "Footnotes on Pictures and People," *The New York Times*, October 4, 1936, X5. Prior to Shirley's appearing in the role, Anne Shirley had been played by silent film star Mary Miles Minter.

70. Today, Anne Shirley is best remembered for her role as Laurel, Stella's daughter in *Stella Dallas*.

71. "*Anne of Green Gables* Gentle Homespun Tale," *Los Angeles Times*, December 14, 1934, 7.

72. Richard Watts Jr., Review of *State Fair*, unidentified clipping, c.1933, Janet Gaynor: Clippings, BRTC.

73. Edwin Schallert, "Sugar Classic Waxes Ultra," *Los Angeles Times*, January 31, 1933, A7.

74. Ibid.

75. Edwin Schallert, "Character in the Forefront," *Los Angeles Times*, January 25, 1932.

76. L. N., "*Rebecca of Sunnybrook Farm* Sings Her Simple Song Again at the Paramount Theatre," *The New York Times*, July 30, 1932.

77. "The Wizard of Oz," *Film Indexes Online: AFI Catalog*, http://film.chadwyck.com/framesets/afi_frameset.htm

78. John Fricke, "Oz and Judy," *Memories*, August/September 1989, *The Wizard of Oz*: Clippings, AMPAS.

79. "Culture with a Capital K," *The New Yorker*, April 2, 1949. *Portrait of Jennie*: Clippings, AMPAS.

80. Pressbook, Production Files: *Dimples*, AMPAS.

81. "Pathos Can Still Make Him Cry," *Little Colonel* Pressbook, *Little Colonel*: Production files, AMPAS.

82. Ibid.

83. Delight Evans, "Mary Pickford, the Girl," *Photoplay*, July 1918, 111.

84. Cal York, "Cal York's Gossip of Hollywood," *Photoplay*, January 1938, 41.

85. Graham Greene, "*Under Two Flags, Captain January*," *The Spectator*, August 7, 1936, reprinted in *The Graham Greene Film Reader: Reviews, Essays, Interviews & Film Stories*, ed. David Parkinson (New York: Applause, 1993), 128; Gilbert Seldes, "Two Great Women," *Esquire*, July 1935, 86.

86. The designation "bunk" or "hokum" was widely used to disparage sentimental culture.

87. Seldes, "Two Great Women," 86.

88. Mae West, too, might be understood to have embodied the tensions between old-fashioned tradition and modern mores. She was known for her anachronistic silhouette—the corseted curves of her breasts and hips, which evoked the Gay Nineties—as well as her very modern approach to sexuality. Pamela Robertson argues that, "Rather than nostalgically evoking the past, West used [invocations of the 1890s] to expose the ideological contradictions of women's roles in the 1930s." Pamela Robertson, *Guilty Pleasures: Feminist Camp from Mae West to Madonna* (Durham, NC: Duke University Press, 1996), 27.

89. Kathryn Fuller-Seeley, "Shirley Temple: Making Dreams Come True," in *Glamour in a Golden Age: Movie Stars of the 1930s*, ed. Adrienne L. McLean (New Brunswick, NJ: Rutgers University Press, 2011), 46–49.

90. Ibid., 48.

91. See the "Exhibitors Report" and "Showmen's Reviews" columns in the *Motion Picture Herald*. Including February 2, 1935, 85; February 16, 1936, 69; March 23, 1935, 61.

92. "Exhibitors Report," Herman Brown (Nampa, Idaho), *Motion Picture Herald*, October 6, 1934, 79. Quoted in Fuller-Seeley, "What the Picture Did for Me," 200.

93. Fuller-Seeley, "Shirley Temple," 47.

94. Ibid.

95. "Hollywood Preview," *Motion Picture Daily*, March 9, 1938, PCA Files: *Rebecca of Sunnybrook Farm*, AMPAS.

96. Review of *The Little Colonel*, *Variety*, February 27, 1935.

97. *Time*, October 19, 1936.

98. John V. A. Weaver, Story Outline for *Baby Take a Bow*, April 11, 1934, Scripts: *Baby Take a Bow*, UCLA. Emphasis in original.

99. Ibid.

100. "Permanent Parents for Shirley Temple," *Los Angeles Times*, September 15, 1934. See also, "A Child among Gangsters," *Flushing [NY] Journal*, August 25, 1934, Shirley Temple: Clippings, AMPAS.

101. "Tap Dancing Shirley," *Wall Street Journal*, March 29, 1938, 13.

102. Review of *Rebecca of Sunnybrook Farm, Motion Picture Herald*, March 12, 1938, Rebecca of Sunnybrook Farm: Production Files, AMPAS. While critics celebrated Temple's sophisticated appeal, some audiences complained that Fox was playing a game of bait and switch, luring audiences to the theater with the promise of old-fashioned entertainment only to deliver something else entirely. In 1938, the Federal Trade Commission threatened Twentieth Century-Fox with a cease-and-desist order, accusing the studio of deliberate fraud in

advertising Temple's films under the names of familiar stories. Audience members complained that *Rebecca of Sunnybrook Farm*, for example, bore little resemblance to Wiggin's well-known story or its characters. Douglas W. Churchill, "Hollywood on the Spot," *The New York Times*, April 17, 1938, 143. Other films that met with similar objections included *Heidi, Wee Willie Winkie* (both starring Temple), *Davie Balfour*, and *Kidnapped*, which starred Freddie Bartholomew.

103. Allison McCracken, *Real Men Don't Sing: Crooners and American Culture, 1925–1933* (Durham, NC: Duke University Press, forthcoming).

104. James Kincaid makes precisely this assertion. *Erotic Innocence: The Culture of Child Molesting* (Durham, NC: Duke University Press, 1998), 113.

CHAPTER 2 — "A TERRIBLE AMOUR"

1. Molly Haskell, *From Reverence to Rape: The Treatment of Women in the Movies* (Chicago: University of Chicago Press, 1987), 123.
2. George Lewis, "Cinematters," *Post Record* [Los Angeles], December 13, 1934, Shirley Temple: Biographical File, AMPAS.
3. *The Little Colonel* Pressbook, Production File: *The Little Colonel*, AMPAS.
4. Ibid.
5. *Dimples* one-sheet, *Dimples:* Production File, AMPAS.
6. My thanks to Jim Herbert for helping me to identify these portraits.
7. John Guille Millais, *The Life and Letters of Sir John Everett Millais: President of the Royal Academy* (New York: Frederick A. Stokes Co., 1899), 378.
8. William Wordsworth, "Intimations of Immortality from Recollections of Early Childhood," *Tintern Abbey; Ode to Duty; Ode on Intimations of Immortality; The Happy Warrior; Resolution and Independence; and On the Power of Sound* (Ann Arbor, MI: University of Michigan Library, 1901) 20.
9. Samuel Goldwyn, Untitled, *Minneapolis Journal*, April 30, 1924, Jackie Coogan Scrapbook, AMPAS.
10. CMS McLellan, *New York Press*, December 9, 1888, *Little Lord Fauntleroy* (American Performances): Clippings, HTC.
11. Unidentified clipping, C.M.S. McLellan, *New York Post*, December 9, 1888, *Little Lord Fauntleroy* (American Performances): Clippings, HTC.
12. "The Nude on the Screen," unidentified Clipping, Jackie Coogan Scrapbook, AMPAS. Perhaps this explains why Jackie Coogan's bathing scene in *My Boy* (1921) was repeatedly cited as one of the highlights of the film.
13. Mae Tinee, "If You're in Trouble—See Jackie Coogan in *Trouble*," *Ft. Wayne Journal Gazette*, June 25, 1922, Jackie Coogan Scrapbook, AMPAS.
14. "Jackie Coogan Has Great Time with Mussolini," *Rochester Times*, October 1, 1924, Jackie Coogan Scrapbooks, AMPAS.
15. "Chat with Child Actress," *Minneapolis Journal*, May 6, 1915.
16. Allen Corlis, "Captains Kiddie," *Photoplay*, May 1916.
17. James Montgomery Flagg, "Shirley Temple Angel to Artist," *Boston Traveler*, September 11, 1941, Shirley Temple: Clippings, HTC.
18. Leonard Hall, "Shirley Temple Sheds a Tooth," *The Stage*, August 1935. Shirley Temple: Clippings, HTC.
19. Unidentified clipping, *Philadelphia Telegraph*, October 19, 1917, Francis Carpenter: Clippings, AMPAS.
20. Review, *The Chimney Sweep, Exhibitors Herald*, July 22, 1916, 21.
21. "*Peck's Bad Boy* Is Gloom Chaser," *Erie Times*, September 7, 1921, Jackie Coogan Scrapbook, AMPAS.

22. Marion Russell, "Peck's Bad Boy," *Cincinnati Billboard*, May 7, 1921, Jackie Coogan: Clippings, AMPAS.

23. Unidentified clipping, *Chicago Record*, July 11, 1909, Lotta Crabtree: Clippings, BRTC.

24. Elsie Leslie, "Children on the Stage," *The Cosmopolitan*, September 1909, Children on the Stage: Clippings, HTC.

25. "A Wonderful Pair of Slippers," *St. Nicholas: An Illustrated Magazine for Young Folks*, February 1890, 309.

26. Ibid., 312.

27. *New York Star*, December 4, 1888, *Little Lord Fauntleroy* (American Performances): Clippings, HTC.

28. "A Chat with Mlle Corinne and John R. Rogers," *The Era*, date unavailable, Corinne: Clippings, HTC.

29. Alexander Hume Ford, "Children of the Stage," *Everybody's Magazine*, date unavailable, Children on the Stage: Clippings, HTC.

30. "Her Photograph Won Him," *The New York Times*, October 24, 1892, 10. Gertrude later married Edwin Thanhouser, founder of the Thanhouser Film Company.

31. Unidentified clipping, Shirley Temple: Clippings, BRTC.

32. "*Rebecca* Charming Vehicle for Shirley Temple's Wiles," *Hollywood Reporter*, March 5, 1938, Production Files: *Rebecca of Sunnybrook Farm*, AMPAS.

33. Charles Eckert, "Shirley Temple and the House of Rockefeller," in *Stardom: Industry of Desire*, ed. Christine Gledhill (London: Routledge, 1991), 68.

34. Ibid., 67.

35. Gaylyn Studlar also draws on Sánchez-Eppler's argument to understand Shirley Temple's appeal, though she links this to a nineteenth-century tradition of coddling that does not account for Sánchez-Eppler's understanding that such narratives were implicitly incestuous. Gaylyn Studlar, *Precocious Charms: Stars Performing Girlhood in Classical Hollywood Cinema* (Berkeley, CA: University of California Press, 2013); Karen Sánchez-Eppler, "Temperance in the Bed of a Child: Incest and Social Order in Nineteenth-Century America," *American Quarterly*, 47:1 (1995): 1–33.

36. Unidentified clipping, C.M.S. McLellan, *New York Post*, December 9, 1888, *Little Lord Fauntleroy* (American Performances): Clippings, HTC.

37. Unidentified clipping, "The Child Star of Zangwill's Play," October 22, 1899. *Vanity Fair*, too, reported on Wilcox's patronage in December of 1899 (page and title unknown), Mabel Taliaferro: Clippings, BRTC.

38. *Motion Picture* (unidentified clipping), June 1918, Madge Evans: Clippings, BRTC.

39. "Miss Pearson and Little Lees Help in Bond Campaign," *New York Telegraph*, June 10, 1917, Jane and Katherine Lee: Clippings, BRTC.

40. Al Sherman, "Shirley Temple Passes Mae West at Box Office Sans Resort to Sex," *Morning Telegraph*, June 3, 1934, Shirley Temple: Biographical file, AMPAS.

41. "Clean Movies Make Money," *Gloversville [NY] Herald*, July 5, 1934, Shirley Temple: Biographical file, AMPAS.

42. Ibid.

43. ELH, "Shirley Temple in *The Littlest Rebel*," *Boston Herald*, December 21, 1935, *The Littlest Rebel:* Clippings, HTC.

44. Unidentified clipping, Production Files: *The Littlest Rebel*, AMPAS.

45. "Shirley Temple's Swift Rise Puts Her among Ten Best Screen Stars," *The Little Colonel* Pressbook. Production File: *The Little Colonel*, AMPAS.

46. Frank S. Nugent, "Now It's Miss Temple," *The New York Times Magazine*, November 2, 1941, Shirley Temple: Clippings, HTC.

47. Merish's choice of the word "maternal" points to the degree to which this response is gendered feminine. Lori Merish, "Cuteness and Commodity Aesthetics: Tom Thumb and

Shirley Temple," in *Freakery: Cultural Spectacles of the Extraordinary Body*, ed. Rosemarie Garland Thomson (New York: New York University Press, 1996), 185–203.

48. Roberta Courtland, "Filmdom's Tiniest Star," *Motion Picture*, September 1917, Marie Osborne: Clippings, BRTC.

49. Phyllis Crawford, letter, undated. Betty Marsh, Vertical File Collection, Folder 32, Betty (Marsh), AMPAS. Betty Marsh was the younger sister of Mae Marsh, one of D. W. Griffith's early leading ladies.

50. Frank Kinsella, letter, May 14, 1915, Vertical File Collection, Folder 32, Betty (Marsh), AMPAS.

51. "What the Picture Did for Me," *Motion Picture Herald*, February 16, 1935, 69.

52. John A. Newman, letter, August 18, 1915, Vertical File Collection, Folder 32, Betty (Marsh), AMPAS.

53. Ibid.

54. Merish, "Cuteness and Commodity Aesthetics," 187.

55. Mae Tinée, "Only Six, Girls, but He's Champion He-Vamp of Screen," *Chicago Tribune*, June 2, 1921, Jackie Coogan Scrapbook 1, 289. AMPAS.

56. Frank Nugent, "Miss Temple Plays Little Eva in *Dimples* at the Roxy," *The New York Times*, October 10, 1936, 21.

57. "A Star at Ten," unidentified Clipping, July 6, 1935.

58. Fay Stevenson, "New York Society's Latest Lion Is a Cub, Little Jackie Coogan, and He Isn't Spoiled by Princesses' Favor," *Detroit Times*, May 16, 1921, Jackie Coogan Scrapbooks, AMPAS.

59. "Mob Psychology," *San Francisco Bulletin*, September 16, 1924, Jackie Coogan Scrapbooks, AMPAS.

60. "Jackie Coogan and Press Agents Are Rescued from London Mob," *Seattle Times*, September 14, 1924, Jackie Coogan Scrapbook, AMPAS.

61. "Jackie Coogan—Famous at Five," *Movie Weekly*, undated clipping, 23, Jackie Coogan Scrapbooks, AMPAS.

62. "Shirley Temple Annoyer Is Held for Examination," Los Angeles *Herald*, October 4, 1935, Shirley Temple: Biographical clippings, AMPAS.

63. Bruno Hauptmann was executed for the kidnapping and murder of Baby Lindbergh in April of 1936, after a trial in January and early February of 1935.

64. "Shirley Temple Annoyer Is Held for Examination."

65. Estelle B. Freedman, "'Uncontrolled Desires': The Response to the Sexual Psychopath, 1920–1960," in *Passion & Power: Sexuality in History*, ed. Kathy Peiss and Christina Simmons (Philadelphia: Temple University Press, 1989), 201.

66. "Pens Shirley Temple Love Note, Tries Death," Los Angeles *Herald*, January 30, 1936, Shirley Temple: Biographical clippings, AMPAS.

67. "Transient Held as Cards Said Mailed to Star," Los Angeles *Citizen News*, March 5, 1937, Shirley Temple: Biographical clippings, AMPAS.

68. "Suspect Held in Shirley Temple Case," Los Angeles *Examiner*, March 5, 1937, Shirley Temple: Biographical clippings, AMPAS.

69. Philip Jenkins, *Moral Panic: Changing Concepts of the Child Molester in Modern America* (New Haven, CT: Yale University Press, 1998).

70. Paul Harrison, "Some Rumblings," *Boston Transcript*, June 1, 1939, Shirley Temple: Clippings, HTC; emphasis added.

CHAPTER 3 — IMMACULATE AMALGAMATION

1. Read Kendall, "Around and About in Hollywood." *Los Angeles Times*, January 18, 1936, A7; Read Kendall, "Odd and Interesting," *Los Angeles Times*, November 15, 1936, C4.

2. Today, Cooper is best remembered as the master of ceremonies at the Apollo theater and the man who introduced Ella Fitzgerald's first public performance.

3. See for example, Bobby Breen in *Way Down South* (1939) and Paul Robeson in the British production *Big Fella* (1937).

4. Richard Dyer, *In the Space of a Song: The Uses of Song in Film* (New York: Routledge, 2011). I am grateful to Pamela Robertson Wojcik for pointing me to Dyer's work on the musical.

5. "The Little Colonel," *Variety*, March 27, 1935, PCA File: The Little Colonel, AMPAS.

6. I use the term "jazz" in the sense that it was popularly known in the early twentieth century to denote popular music.

7. See Pamela Robertson Wojcik, "Mae West's Maids: Race, 'Authenticity,' and the Discourse of Camp," in *Camp: Queer Aesthetics and the Performing Subject, a Reader*, ed. Fabio Cleto (Ann Arbor, MI: University of Michigan Press, 1999), 393–408.

8. Karl Koenig, *Jazz in Print (1856–1929): An Anthology of Selected Early Readings* (Hillside, NY: Pendragon Press, 2002). Early 1930s' Betty Boop cartoons featuring Cab Calloway and Louis Armstrong exemplify this discourse. See, for example, *I'll Be Glad When You're Dead, You Rascal You* (Max Fleischer, 1932).

9. Langston Hughes, *The Big Sea* (New York: Hill and Wang, 1940). Langston Hughes himself capitalized on this vogue when he was hired by Sol Lesser to write a film, *Way Down South* (1939), for the child star Bobby Breen.

10. Alice Maurice, "Cinema at Its Source: Synchronizing Race and Sound in the Early Talkies," *Camera Obscura*, 17:149 (2002): 31–71.

11. Thomas Cripps, *Slow Fade to Black: The Negro in American Film, 1900–1942* (Oxford: Oxford University Press, 1977).

12. *The Little Colonel* pressbook. Production Files: *The Little Colonel*, AMPAS.

13. Linda Williams, *Playing the Race Card: Melodramas of Black and White from Uncle Tom to O.J. Simpson* (Princeton, NJ: Princeton University Press, 2001).

14. Jo-Ann Morgan, *Uncle Tom's Cabin as Visual Culture* (Columbia, MO: University of Missouri Press, 2007).

15. Robin Bernstein, *Racial Innocence: Performing American Childhood from Slavery to Civil Rights* (New York: New York University Press, 2011), 7.

16. Susan Clark, "Up Against the Ropes: Peter Jackson as 'Uncle Tom' in America," *The Drama Review*, 44:1 (Spring 2000): 170. According to Clark, it was not uncommon for well-known boxers to perform in stage plays for curious audiences at a time when boxing was outlawed in many states.

17. A. G. Hales, *Black Prince Peter* (London: Wright and Brown, 1931), 15. Quoted in Clark, "Up Against the Ropes," 170.

18. *San Francisco Chronicle*, February 28, 1893, 3. Quoted in Clark, "Up Against the Ropes," 171.

19. "A Negro on Lynching," *Los Angeles Times*, September 12, 1897, 26.

20. Lowe starred in *Uncle Tom's Cabin* in 1927 and Duncan played Eva against her sister Rosetta's Topsy on both stage and screen in a sister act that ran until the 1950s.

21. George Lewis, "Cinematters," *Post Record*, December 13, 1934, Biographical File: Shirley Temple, AMPAS.

22. Edith Lindeman, "The Real Miss Temple: Report Finds Shirley Lovable, Modest, Girlish," *Richmond Times Dispatch*, 1936. Reprinted in A. C. Griffith, *Richmond Then and Now: Old Newspaper Articles*, http://richmondthenandnow.com

23. Ara Osterweil, "Reconstructing Shirley: Pedophilia and Interracial Romance in Hollywood Age of Innocence," *Camera Obscura*, 24:3 (2009): 2.

24. Linda Williams, "Melodrama Revised," in *Refiguring American Film Genres: Theory and History*, ed. Nick Browne (Berkeley, CA: University of California Press, 1998), 42–88. See also Linda Williams, *Playing the Race Card: Melodramas of Black and White from Uncle Tom to O.J. Simpson* (Princeton, NJ: Princeton University Press, 2001) and Christine Gledhill,

"Rethinking Genre," in *Reinventing Film Studies*, ed. Christine Gledhill and Linda Williams (London: Edward Arnold), 221–243.

25. "Brass Buttons and Epaulets" lyrics, PCA File: *Just Around the Corner,* AMPAS.

26. It is no coincidence that the family's name, Drew, is also that of one of the theater's most prominent theatrical families.

27. The association is not unfounded. The Tom show incorporated a number of conventions that had originated in minstrelsy during the postbellum period.

28. Antony Anderson, "*Uncle Tom's Cabin*: Marguerite Clark in Roles of Topsy and Eva," *Los Angeles Times*, July 30, 1818, II3.

29. Hal K. Wells, "Uncle Tom's Hollywood Bungalow," *Motion Picture Magazine* (1927), *Uncle Tom's Cabin*: Production files, AMPAS.

30. Richard Watts, Jr., "The Theaters," *New York Herald Tribune,* October 30, 1936, *Sweet River:* Clippings, HTC.

31. "Duncan Sisters at the Colonial," *Boston Globe,* May 12, 1925, *Topsy and Eva:* Clippings, HTC.

32. Sherwin Lawrence Cook, "New Lamps for Old at the Colonial: Mystery Revival at the Copley," *The Boston Review,* May 16, 1925, *Topsy and Eva:* Clippings, HTC.

33. Harry Birdoff, *The World's Greatest Hit: Uncle Tom's Cabin* (New York: S. F. Vanni, 1947), 328.

34. Caroline Levander, *Cradle of Liberty: Race, the Child and National Belonging from Thomas Jefferson to W.E.B. Du Bois* (Durham, NC: Duke University Press, 2006).

35. Etienne Balibar, "Racism and Nationalism," in *Race, Nation, Class: Ambiguous Identities*, ed. Etienne Balibar and Immanuel Wallerstein (London: Verso, 1991), 37–68; Michael Rogin, *Blackface, White Noise: Jewish Immigrants in the Hollywood Melting Pot* (Berkeley, CA: University of California Press, 1996).

36. Benedict Anderson, *Imagined Communities: Reflections on the Origin and Spread of Nationalism, Revised Edition* (London: Verso, 2006).

37. Lauren Berlant, *The Queen of America Goes to Washington City: Essays on Sex and Citizenship* (Durham, NC: Duke University Press, 1997).

CHAPTER 4 — BABY BURLESKS AND KIDDIE KABARETS

1. In all, there were eight films in the series. The first, *The Runt Page* (Ray Nazarro, 1932), was a ten-minute reenactment of the popular Broadway show *The Front Page*, with adults voicing the dialogue, much like the Monkey Comedies of the same period, in which chimpanzees enacted human roles. In the remaining seven Burlesks, though, the children speak their own lines, which gently mock popular Hollywood genre films of the period. *War Babies* (Charles Lamont, 1932) spoofed the war film *What Price Glory?* (Raoul Walsh, 1926); *Pie Covered Wagon* (Charles Lamont, 1932), a play on *The Covered Wagon* (James Cruze, 1923); *Glad Rags to Riches* (Charles Lamont, 1933); *Kiddin' Hollywood* (Charles Lamont, 1933); *The Kid's Last Fight* (Charles Lamont, 1933), which mocks fight films; *Polly Tix in Washington* (Charles Lamont, 1933); and *Kid 'n Africa* (Jack Hays, 1933), a play on *Tarzan the Ape Man* (W. S. Van Dyke, 1932). While Shirley Temple was the only star to emerge from the series, Philip Hurlic, a black child who was billed as Dynamite, also went on to have a career beyond these short films. Indeed, Hurlic was the first of the children to be signed for the series, suggesting that Hays was, indeed, inspired by *Our Gang*, which had initially been developed around the talents of a black child, Sunshine Sammy, who had gained the attention of exhibitors with his unbilled appearances alongside Baby Peggy in her Century comedies.

2. "Educational's Latest Baby Burlesk," Educational Pictures publicity material, July 14, 1933, Baby Burlesks: Clippings, BRTC.

3. Ann duCille, "The Shirley Temple of My Familiar," *Transition*, 73 (1997): 14.

4. As should become clear, it is likely that these films would not have been approved by the Production Code Administration had they been released a year or two later.

5. Gertrude Temple, "Bringing Up Shirley," *American Magazine*, February 1935, 27.

6. See DuCille; Bret Wood, "Lolita Syndrom," *Sight and Sound*, 4:6 (1994): 32–34; Marianne Sinclair, *Hollywood Lolita: The Nymphette Syndrome in the Movies* (Medford, NJ: Plexus Publishing, 1996).

7. "Little Stars of the Stage: They Twinkled in Tony Pastor's Theatre Yesterday," Date and publication unknown, Children of the Stage (1880–1890): Clippings, HTC. Tilly herself began her stage career at the age of three.

8. "The Child Drama Revived," *Boston Sunday Herald*, September 4, 1882, Children on Stage: Clippings, HTC. La Regaloncita's dancing has been preserved on an Edison film from 1894, *Cupid's Dance*, in which she appeared with her sisters, who were billed as La Graciosa and La Preciosa.

9. Percy Hammond, "At the Varieties: Gossip of the Stage," *Chicago Tribune*, July 10, 1913, Gus Edwards: Clippings, BRTC.

10. Arthur Hornblow, "The Children of the Stage," *Mumsey's*, October 1894, Children on the Stage: Clippings, HTC. Although publicity for La Regaloncita often described her as a Latin American spitfire from Chile, when her mother was brought to court for allowing the seven-year-old to perform in New York without a permit, newspapers began to refer to her birth name, Mildred Ewer, and identify her as the granddaughter of an Episcopal bishop.

11. The role of Cedric in *Little Lord Fauntleroy* was regularly played by both boys and girls. The role was originated on the American stage by Elsie Leslie and Tommy Russell, who performed on alternating nights, though Leslie appears to have been the favorite of most audiences. Arthur Hornblow, "The Children of the Stage."

12. Alexander Hume Ford, "Children of the Stage," *Everybody's Magazine*, Children on the Stage: Clippings, HTC.

13. "Lord Fauntleroy On and Off the Stage," *Boston Herald*, May 15, 1892, *Little Lord Fauntleroy:* American Performances, HTC.

14. Ford, "Children of the Stage."

15. "Jack and the Beanstalk," *New York Post*, July 31, 1917, Virginia Lee Corbin: Clippings, RLC.

16. Unidentified clipping, Jane and Katherine Lee: Clippings, RLC.

17. "Lee Kids in New Photoplay," Publication unknown, July 29, 1917, Jane and Katherine Lee: Clippings, RLC.

18. Unidentified clipping, *St. Louis Post Dispatch*, February 25, 1923, Virginia Lee Corbin: Clippings, RLC.

19. In a strange twist, she also imitates Mary Pickford imitating a young girl. "Baby Peggy to Be Seen as Imitator of Screen Stars," *Exhibitors Trade Review*, January 6, 1923, 309, Baby Peggy: Clippings, BRTC.

20. "Here's Jane Lee's 'Bestest' Photo," *Toledo News*, October 12, 1917, Jane and Katherine Lee: Clippings, BRTC.

21. "Not Flapper—Early Model Sand Bather," unidentified clipping, Jackie Coogan Scrapbooks, AMPAS.

22. Paul Harrison, "Members of Movie Colony Spend Idle Hours on Same Amusements as Other Folks," *Washington Post*, May 9, 1934, TR3.

23. Unidentified clipping, *New York Star*, April 5, 1916, Bobby Connelly: Clippings, BRTC.

24. "Helen Found Bobby as Fickle as Any of His Sex," *New York Telegraph*, October 7, 1917, Bobby Connelly: Clippings, BRTC.

25. "New Hollywood Scandal," *Cincinnati Times*, June 7, 1922, Jackie Coogan Scrapbooks, AMPAS.

26. See, for example, "Patsy in Tears as Jackie, Welcomed by Throng, Overlooked Tiny Fiancée," *South Reno News Times*, July 7, 1921, Jackie Coogan Scrapbooks, AMPAS; Winifred

van Duzer, "Six-Year-Old Movie Star Says His Love for Girl of Five Made Him Succeed," *Pittsburgh Press*, April 10, 1921, Jackie Coogan Scrapbooks, AMPAS; "New Hollywood Scandal," *Cincinnati Times Star*, June 7, 1922, Jackie Coogan Scrapbooks, AMPAS.

27. "Look Out Jackie! This Baby Vamp of French Films Is After You," *Danton Repository*, August 20, 1922, Jackie Coogan Scrapbooks, AMPAS.

28. Elaine Ogden, "Mitzi Has Boy Trouble," *Photoplay*, 1930, 41.

29. Unidentified clipping, *Photoplay*, March 1930, 111, Jackie Coogan Scrapbooks, AMPAS.

30. Kolma Flake, "Spunky Spanky," typescript 9, Hal Roach papers box 1, USC.

31. Grace Wilcox, "At Last—Little Baby LeRoy Confesses!" *Screen and Radio Weekly*, September 23, 1934, 4, Baby LeRoy: Clippings, AMPAS.

32. Kirtley Baskette, "A Goddess Grows Up," Unidentified clipping, Shirley Temple: Clippings, BRTC.

33. "The City of Beautiful Nonsense," *Vanity Fair*, September 1917.

34. "National Committee for Better Pictures Praises Century," *Exhibitors Trade Review*, April 1, 1922, 1252, Baby Peggy: Clippings, BRTC; "Peggy's Latest Commended," *Exhibitors Trade Review*, August 25, 1923, 551, Baby Peggy: Clippings, BRTC.

35. Unidentified clipping, *Los Angeles Herald*, June 15, 1922, Jackie Coogan Scrapbooks, AMPAS.

36. "Scandal! Scandal!" *Cleveland Plain Dealer*, March 8, 1922, Jackie Coogan Scrapbooks, AMPAS.

37. "Censors Demand Bare Legs Barred at Picture Shows," *Ames Tri-Weekly Tribune*, February 26, 1919.

38. "Wonderful Child Actors Seen in Aladdin Picture," *New York Bulletin*, Unidentified clipping, Violet Radcliffe: Clippings, RLC.

39. Anne Higonnet, *Pictures of Innocence: The History and Crisis of Ideal Childhood* (London: Thames and Hudson, 1998), 33–34. Not surprisingly, publicity photographs, films, and stage plays drew on all five of these modes of representation.

40. Pamela Tamarkin Reis, "Victorian Centerfold: Another Look at Millais's *Cherry Ripe*," *Victorian Studies,* 35:2 (Winter 1992): 201–206.

41. Higonnet, *Pictures of Innocence*, 51.

42. Reis, "Victorian Centerfold," 201. Gaylyn Studlar draws on Reis's analysis to argue that Elizabeth Taylor's appeal likewise lay in her ability to convey both innocence and sexuality. However, as I will discuss briefly in the epilogue, Elizabeth Taylor emerged within a very different ideological context, one shaped by Freudian ideas of repression and the unconscious. Gaylyn Sudlar, *Precocious Charms: Stars Performing Girlhood in Classical Hollywood Cinema* (Berkeley, CA: University of California Press, 2013), 144.

43. Higonnet identifies the indexical qualities of photography as the source of twentieth-century anxieties about the eroticization of childhood. However, this does not take into account the shifts in representations of childhood that took place outside portraiture, in theater and film for example, which I attribute to the postwar hegemony of Freudian thought.

44. Nadine Wills, "'110 Per Cent Woman': The Crotch Shot in the Hollywood Musical," *Screen,* 42:2 (Summer 2001): 130.

45. Lori Merish, "Cuteness and Commodity Aesthetics: Tom Thumb and Shirley Temple," in *Freakery: Cultural Spectacle of the Extraordinary Body*, ed. Rosemarie Garland Thomson (New York: New York University Press, 1996), 186.

46. Wills, "'110 Per Cent Woman,'" 138.

47. *Commonweal*, February 23, 1934, 452.

48. Memorandum to Mr. Hart, August 23, 1935, Production Code Files: *George White's Scandals of 1934*, AMPAS.

49. Ibid.

50. Letter from Sam Sax to Vincent Hart, MPPDA, December 12, 1935, Production Code Files: *George White's Scandals of 1934*, AMPAS.

51. C. E. Millikan, Memorandum to Joseph Breen, August 23, 1935, Production Code Files: *George White's Scandals of 1934*, AMPAS.

52. Memo to the file, no date, PCA Files: *George White's Scandals of 1934*, AMPAS.

53. Letter to Mr. Winfield Sheehan, Fox Studios, from Mrs. William Sporborg, Chairman, East Coast Preview Committee, March 7, 1934. PCA Files: *George White's Scandals of 1934*, AMPAS.

54. Joseph Breen, Letter to Colonel Jason S. Joy, Twentieth Century-Fox, October 17, 1935, PCA Files: *Captain January*, AMPAS.

55. Joseph Breen, Letter to Colonel Jason S. Joy, Twentieth Century-Fox, February 27, 1936, PCA Files: *Captain January*, AMPAS; Sam Hellman and Gladys Lehman, "Captain January, Second Draft," August 5, 1935, Scripts: *Captain January*, UCLA.

56. "No Shakes for Shirley," *Hollywood Reporter*, March 16, 1936, Shirley Temple: Biographical Files, AMPAS. A similar sequence in *Curly Top* (Irving Cummings, 1935) does not appear to have raised objections, perhaps because in this film she wears a bathing suit.

57. Bret Wood, "Lolita Syndrome," *Sight and Sound*, 9:6, 32–34.

58. "Official Cut-Outs Made by the Chicago Board of Censors," *Exhibitors Herald*, November 17, 1917, 33. On the elimination of the *September Morn* pose in *Sadie Goes to Heaven*, see "Official Cut-Outs Made by the Chicago Board of Censors," *Exhibitors Herald*, January 19, 1918, 31. There were numerous instances of the Chicago censor's cutting images of nude boys and girls in scenes that did not involve erotic mimicry.

59. Other children did mimic eroticized adult stars in the 1930s. In *Ginger*, for example, Jane Withers pulls her hair over her face, adopts a deep voice and Swedish accent, and transforms herself briefly into Greta Garbo, and in *Little Big Shot*, Sybil Jason, too, impersonates Garbo. In both cases, the impersonation is brief and the child does not don adult clothing. Conversely, when Gloria (Sybil Jason) appears in adult clothes in *I Found Stella Parish*, she does so in the context of a childish game of dress-up that requires her male audience to join her in play.

60. Lea Jacobs, *The Wages of Sin: Censorship and the Fallen Woman Film, 1928–1942* (Berkeley, CA: University of California Press, 1995).

61. Pamela Robertson Wojcik, "Shirley Temple as Streetwalker: Urban Space and Childhood in Depression Era Films" (Paper presented at the annual meeting of the Society for Cinema and Media Studies, Chicago, Illinois, March 7, 2013).

CHAPTER 5 — ECONOMIC INNOCENCE

1. Memorandum to Mr. Hart, August 23, 1935, Production Code Files: *George White's Scandals of 1934*, AMPAS.

2. Viviana Zelizer, *Pricing the Priceless Child: The Changing Social Value of Children* (Princeton, NJ: Princeton University Press, 1994). This sacralization extended only to white children, however. This becomes apparent in *Little Miss Marker* during a nightclub performance in which two young black boys, dressed as bellhops, strain to pull a platform carrying two adults and an upright piano. Their labor is incidental to the spectacle and goes without comment within the diegesis.

3. Zelizer, *Pricing the Priceless Child*, 95.

4. At the turn of the century, boys and girls clubs in the US and UK were created around the theme of Arthurian legend with the explicit goal of providing children with the values that would help them to become morally sound adults. The Boy Scouts was inspired, in part, by these clubs, and this organization, too, encouraged boys to read the tales of King Arthur and his knights and to emulate the code of chivalry. Several expurgated editions of

the tales were published specifically for this purpose, including Sidney Lanier's *The Boy's King Arthur*, which Marky receives as a gift in this film. Alan Lupack and Barbara Tepa Lupack, *King Arthur in America* (Cambridge: D. S. Brewer, 1999), 49–73.

5. "Notes of the Stage and Screen," *Pittsburgh Post-Gazette*, May 6, 1934, 49.

6. Zelizer, *Pricing the Priceless Child*, 75.

7. Elbridge T. Gerry, "Children of the Stage," *North American Review*, July 26, 1890, Children on the Stage: Laws, HTC.

8. "Little Sisters Twinkle in Childhood's New Profession," *Ohio State Journal*, September 14, 1915, Thelma and Beulah Burns: Clippings, RLC.

9. "Jackie Coogan to Go On Stage at $2500 a Week," unidentified clipping, Jackie Coogan Scrapbooks, AMPAS.

10. "Fairy Tales Have Been Outdone," *Cleveland News*, March 27, 1921, Jackie Coogan Scrapbooks, AMPAS; Grace Kingsley, "Jackie Midas in Miniature, *Los Angeles Times*, June 4, 1922, Jackie Coogan Scrapbooks, AMPAS; "Jackie's Million," unidentified clipping, Jackie Coogan Scrapbooks, AMPAS.

11. Karl K. Kitchen, "Everything He Touches Turns Into Currency," *Cleveland Plain Dealer*, August 13, 1922, Jackie Coogan Scrapbooks, AMPAS.

12. "Cooganism," *The Saturday Review*, September 27, 1924, 305, Jackie Coogan Scrapbooks, AMPAS.

13. Douglas Churchill, "Life of the Child Star: A Hollywood Fairy Tale," *The New York Times Magazine*, May 22, 1938, Child Stars: Clippings, HTC.

14. With the 1939 Child Actor's Bill, better known as the "Coogan Act," the state of California overturned the longstanding tradition whereby a child's earnings were understood to belong to his or her parents (Zelizer, *Pricing the Priceless Child*, 111). The inadequacy of the law was brought to light in the 1990s, when another child actor, Macauley Culkin, sued his parents for the money he had earned as a child star.

15. "Fairies Still Live in California," *Cleveland Plain Dealer*, October 11, 1918, Gloria Joy: Clippings, RLC.

16. LeRoy's illness prevented him from appearing in the film as planned, and he remained in "retirement" after all. "Paramount worried as much as any parent," (Paramount Press Release, October 1939. Baby LeRoy: Clippings, AMPAS).

17. Unidentified clipping, *Motion Picture*, September 1917, Marie Osborne: Clippings, BRTC.

18. In fact, when Shirley Temple entered her majority, she discovered that, out of the millions of dollars she had earned for the studios and her family, she was entitled to only $89,000, half of which represented the value of an elaborate playhouse that had been built on her parents' property. Shirley Temple Black, *Child Star: An Autobiography* (New York: McGraw-Hill, 1988), 484.

19. Harry Brand, Shirley Temple Biography, Twentieth Century-Fox Publicity Department, March 14, 1938. Shirley Temple: Clippings, AMPAS; "The New Pictures," *Time*, December 31, 1934, 24:27, 16.

20. Kay Osborn, "Who is the Genius Behind Shirley Temple?" Unidentified clipping, Shirley Temple: Clippings, BRTC.

21. "Shirley Off to Boston with 40 Bags," *Boston Globe*, July 29, 1938, Shirley Temple: Clippings, HTC.

22. James Kincaid, *Child-Loving: The Erotic Child and Victorian Literature* (New York: Routledge, 1994).

23. Philip Jenkins, *Moral Panic: Changing Concepts of the Child Molester in Modern America* (New Haven, CT: Yale University Press, 1998).

24. John F. Kasson, *The Little Girl Who Fought the Great Depression: Shirley Temple and 1930s America* (New York: W.W. Norton & Co., 2014), 210–215.

25. W. B. Courtney, "Mothers Little Darlings," *Colliers*, October 12, 1935. Child Stars: Clippings, HTC.

26. Douglas W. Churchill, "Life of the Child Star: A Hollywood Fairy Tale," *The New York Times Magazine*, May 22, 1938, Child Stars, HTC.

27. Ironically, Shirley Temple herself did not make her radio debut until her career was in decline. In 1939, she performed *The Blue Bird* for CBS's *Screen Guild Theatre*, where she was introduced by Darryl Zanuck.

28. Graham Greene, Review of *Wee Willie Winkie*, *Night and Day*, October 29, 1937. Reprinted in David Parkinson, *The Graham Greene Film Reader: Reviews, Essays, Interviews & Film Stories* (New York: Applause Theatre Book Publishers, 1993), 234.

29. Black, *Child Star*, 484.

EPILOGUE

1. Unidentified clipping, Review of *National Velvet*, *Time*, 1944, Elizabeth Taylor scrapbook No. 30, AMPAS.

2. James Agee, Review of *National Velvet*, *The Nation*, December 23, 1944, 781–782.

3. Rachel Devlin, *Relative Intimacy: Fathers, Adolescent Daughters, and Postwar American Culture* (Chapel Hill, NC: University of North Carolina Press, 2005).

4. Review of *Meet Me in St. Louis*, *The New York Times*, November 29, 1944.

5. James Naremore, *The Films of Vincente Minnelli* (New York: Cambridge University Press, 1993). In this sense, O'Brien built on the personae not of Shirley Temple but of Temple's contemporaries: Jane Withers, Mitzi Green, and Edith Fellows, who played delightfully bratty girls during the Depression era.

6. Andrew Sarris, "Freudian Fantasy," *The New York Times*, December 18, 1966, BR 10; Molly Haskell, *From Reverence to Rape: The Treatment of Women in the Movies, Second Edition* (1974; Chicago: University of Chicago Press, 1987), 123

INDEX

ABOUT THE AUTHOR

KRISTEN HATCH is an assistant professor in the Department of Film & Media Studies and the Visual Studies Program at the University of California, Irvine.